STRATEGERY

How George W. Bush Is Defeating Terrorists, Outwitting
Democrats, and Confounding the Mainstream Media

BILL SAMMON

Since 1947
REGNERY
PUBLISHING, INC.
An Eagle Publishing Company • Washington, DC

Library of Congress Cataloging-in-Publication Data

Sammon, Bill.
  Strategery : how George W. Bush is defeating terrorists, outwitting
Democrats, and confounding the mainstream media / Bill Sammon.
    p. cm.
  Includes index.
  ISBN 1-59698-002-8
  1. Bush, George W. (George Walker), 1946—Relations with journalists. 2. Bush, George W.
(George Walker), 1946—Public opinion. 3. Mass media—Political aspects—United States. 4.
Press and politics—United States. 5. Presidents—United States—Election—2004. 6. United
States—Politics and government—2001–7. United States—Foreign relations—2001–8. Bush,
George W. (George Walker), 1946—Military leadership. 9. Iraq War, 2003–10. Public opinion—
United States. I. Title.
  E903.3.S364 2006
  973.931092—dc22

                          2006000168

Published in the United States by
Regnery Publishing, Inc.
One Massachusetts Avenue, NW
Washington, DC 20001

www.regnery.com

Distributed to the trade by
National Book Network
Lanham, MD 20706

Manufactured in the United States of America

10 9 8 7 6 5 4 3 2 1

Books are available in quantity for promotional or premium use. Write to Director of Special
Sales, Regnery Publishing, Inc., One Massachusetts Avenue NW, Washington, DC 20001, for
information on discounts and terms or call (202) 216-0600.

STRATEGERY

"For as long as whole regions of the world simmer in resentment and tyranny—prone to ideologies that feed hatred and excuse murder— violence will gather, and multiply in destructive power, and cross the most defended borders, and raise a mortal threat. There is only one force of history that can break the reign of hatred and resentment, and expose the pretensions of tyrants, and reward the hopes of the decent and tolerant. And that is the force of human freedom."

GEORGE W. BUSH
Second Inaugural Address
January 20, 2005

To Becky

CONTENTS

BLACKBERRY BLUES

I t was difficult to concentrate on the question I wanted to ask President Bush at his post-election press conference because the journalist in front of me kept fidgeting in his seat. The culprit was John Roberts of CBS, the network that had angered Bush during the campaign by using forged documents to criticize his military service. Roberts was now staring at his BlackBerry, one of those handheld electronic devices that allowed users to surf the Internet from virtually any location, including Room 450 of the Eisenhower Executive Office Building, where the press conference was in full swing. Sitting in the second row, Roberts seemed driven to distraction by whatever was on the screen of his "CrackBerry"—which is what the infernal devices were nicknamed by their hopelessly addicted users. I tried to read it over his shoulder, but just then he passed it up to the front row, which was occupied by senior Bush advisers. He handed the device to White House communications director Dan Bartlett just as CNN's John King, who was sitting next to Roberts, handed his own BlackBerry to national security adviser Condoleezza Rice. I watched with fascination as the two aides read the screens and then exchanged grave glances. Something must have happened! My reporter's curiosity went into overdrive, utterly obliterating my ability to concentrate on the question I wanted to ask the president.

Truth be told, I was rather pleased with my question, which dealt with Bush's foreign policy. I was interested in whether his doctrine of preemption had essentially run its course during his first term. After all, with our troops already stretched thin in Iraq and Afghanistan, we didn't exactly have the resources to preemptively invade another country that might misbehave. For all practical purposes, the threat of preemption would be off the table for the second term, forcing Bush to emphasize the other half of his foreign policy—democratization. No longer able to send large numbers of troops into Middle Eastern dictatorships, the president would have to rely on diplomatic and economic means to effect change in the region. I suspected that history would ultimately compartmentalize Bush's foreign policy into preemption during the first term and democratization during the second. And so I crammed all these thoughts into a long-winded question in my reporter's notebook. But instead of mentally rehearsing the question, I was now obsessed with getting my hands on that fiendish CrackBerry.

Just then, Bartlett turned around and handed it back to Roberts. Mercifully, Roberts turned around and handed it to me. On the screen was a "news alert" from the Associated Press: "Palestinian Leader Yasser Arafat has died." I looked at Roberts, who arched his eyebrows in an expression that said "I thought you'd want to know about this." He had already asked the president a question and was not about to get a second bite at the apple. He knew I had not yet asked my question and would likely be called on momentarily. I thanked him and returned his BlackBerry in order to ponder my next move.

Should I ask Bush about this breaking development? After all, Arafat was a major world figure whose death was certainly newsworthy. Unlike President Clinton, who hosted Arafat at the White House more than any other foreign leader, Bush had always refused to meet with the Palestinian strongman, whom he regarded as an obstacle to peace. Perhaps his death would be an opportunity for Bush to move forward on the Middle East peace process.

On the other hand, I had already written out my carefully worded question about preemption and democratization. I was leery of straying from the script, especially without knowing more about the Arafat report. Perhaps I should stick to my original plan and leave the Arafat question for someone else. As I wrestled with this dilemma, I could hear Bush wrapping up his answer to another reporter. "I really didn't come here to hold the office just to say, 'Gosh, it was fun to serve,'" he was saying. "I came here to get some things done. And we are doing it. Big Stretch."

That was me! "Big Stretch" was one of several variations on my presidential nickname, "Superstretch," a reference to my 6'7" stature. Bush was calling on me, even though I hadn't figured out what to ask him. I hadn't even formulated a question about Arafat.

As I stood up and took the microphone, it occurred to me that reporters didn't get many chances to ask the president a question for which he was unprepared. The goal of these press conferences, after all, was to knock Bush off his talking points and get him to actually commit news. And so I made a snap decision right then and there to go for it.

"Thank you, Mr. President," I began. "I know you haven't had a chance to learn this, but it appears that Yasser Arafat has passed away."

"Really?" said Bush, genuinely surprised.

The mood of the press conference suddenly changed. Having spent the first half hour basking in what he called his "post-election euphoria," the president was now hit with an unexpected curveball about the death of a world leader he intensely disliked. A sour expression spread across his face, prompting the press cameras in the back of the room to come clattering to life.

"And I was just wondering if I could get your initial reaction?" I ad-libbed. "And also your thoughts on, perhaps, working with a new generation of Palestinian leadership?"

"I appreciate that," Bush said as I sat back down. "My first reaction is: God bless his soul."

The president stole a glance at Rice, who moved her head from side to side almost imperceptibly, signaling this was not a good question for him to be

answering. Bush got the message and paused for a moment to mull a grace-
ful way to cut this discussion short. He concluded that the safest path was to
revert to a bland recitation of boilerplate policy.

"And my second reaction is," he added, openly stalling, "is that we will continue to work for a free Palestinian state that's at peace with Israel."

Bush fell silent for a moment as his expression turned downright dyspep-
tic. The clattering of the cameras rose until he finally called on another
reporter in an effort to regain safer terrain.

I was left to contemplate the significance of his response. I reasoned that
there had to be some news value in the president blessing the freshly departed
soul of a man he had always considered an obstacle to peace. I imagined a
headline going out over the wires: "Bush blesses Arafat's 'soul.'" Granted, it
wasn't World War III, but it would pass for news in this age of instant information. So I settled back to bask in the admiration of my peers.

But after a few moments, John Roberts turned around again—only this
time with a sheepish expression on his face. Gesturing to his BlackBerry, he
whispered, "Bill, there's another news alert. Looks like he might still be alive
after all."

I could feel the blood rushing to my face. I stared at the BlackBerry and
then Roberts, finally managing a sardonic "Thanks a lot, John." I was mortified that I had just misinformed the president about a major news development on live national television. (Arafat would remain alive for another week!)

After the press conference, I hoped I wasn't the only journalist to have
broadcast the bogus news. Surely the TV networks must have flashed the
erroneous bulletin before I asked my question of Bush. But while driving
dejectedly back to the *Washington Times*, I received a call from *Washington
Post* media critic Howard Kurtz, which was never a good thing. Kurtz
explained that the TV networks had been too busy carrying the presidential
press conference to report the Arafat bulletin. He said the first time that viewers of ABC, CBS, NBC, CNBC, MSNBC, CNN, and the FOX News Channel
heard about Arafat's death was from me.

"Great," I groaned. "So I broke it to the nation, too."

Kurtz, who was preparing a story on my blunder for the next morning's *Post*, had already interviewed CBS's Roberts, who insisted he would have handled the situation much better.

"I probably would have couched it a lot more. I would have said, 'There are reports, and if the reports are true....,'" Roberts clucked. "I wouldn't be stating it as fact."

Meanwhile, Jon Stewart's *Daily Show* on Comedy Central was having a field day putting together a piece for that evening's broadcast that featured me asking my now infamous question not once, but twice.

Unsurprisingly, after arriving at my office, I found myself on the phone with White House press secretary Scott McClellan. I tried to assure him that it had not been my intention to blindside the president with a bogus report.

"Ah, don't be so hard on yourself, Bill," McClellan deadpanned. "After all, you got the information from CBS."

~

Strategery is the third in my series of books chronicling the historic presidency of George W. Bush. The first was *Fighting Back*, which examined the transformation of the presidency by the terrorist attacks of September 11. The second was *Misunderestimated*, which told the story of Bush launching Operation Iraqi Freedom. *Strategery* picks up where *Misunderestimated* left off, which is to say in March 2004. That's when John Kerry emerged from the Democratic primaries to square off against President Bush in the general election campaign. This book chronicles that hard-fought election, as well as the tumultuous fourteen months that followed. Through it all, George W. Bush would consistently—though often without credit—defeat terrorists, outwit Democrats, and confound the mainstream media.

—Bill Sammon
January 2006

CHAPTER ONE

THE PARIAH OF PALISADES

K arl Rove knew it was going to be a bad day when he looked out his living room window and saw an angry mob massing on his front lawn. It was a jarring sight—hundreds of seething protesters pouring out of yellow school buses and swarming across the tiny rectangle of green turf in front of his brick home. Their chants shattered the Sunday afternoon stillness of the upscale Washington neighborhood where Rove lived with his wife, Darby, and fourteen-year-old son, Andrew.

"KARL ROVE AIN'T GOT NO SOUL!" they bellowed. "KARL ROVE AIN'T GOT NO SOUL!"

As Rove watched in astonishment, more school buses arrived and disgorged reinforcements, who jammed his yard and spilled into the street. Soon the entire block was teeming with eight hundred protesters, including several with bullhorns, who took up a new chant:

"ROVE, ROVE, COME ON OUT, SEE WHAT THE DREAM ACT IS ALL ABOUT!"

Rove, the senior White House strategist for President Bush, wasn't exactly sure what the "Dream Act" was all about. But he did know one thing—he had to get rid of these people.

"Get off my property!" he hollered before slamming his front door in their faces.

"Seems like he doesn't want to invite us in for tea," cackled one of the ringleaders, Emira Palacios, drawing hoots of derision from the boisterous crowd.

Exhilarated by the realization that they were getting under Rove's skin, the protesters surged forward. They waved placards that bore the acronym NPA, which stood for National People's Action, a radical group that espoused guerrilla tactics to achieve its left-wing goals. When Rove appeared at one of the windows, a ripple of excitement swept through the demonstrators, who were so adept at protesting that they had brought their own film crew. In fact, they even had their own theme song:

> We come from all across this land
> March on Washington, take a stand
> We won't sit down; we'll stand and fight
> Equality and justice—they are a right!

Rove pressed a cell phone to his ear and gesticulated in the direction of the protesters. He was frantically calling White House deputy chief of staff Joe Hagin to have him send over the Secret Service. He paused just long enough to yell something inaudible at the crowd, which roared back its contempt. Wild-eyed and screaming, the protesters stormed the house and actually began pounding their fists on the windows.

> We won't go away until we're heard
> Every sentence, every word
> "But your tactics just won't work," they say
> As we set up a meeting for next Wednesday!

Rove retreated from sight and reappeared at a window on another side of the house, but the protesters merely ran over and began pounding on that glass as well. They were chasing Rove from room to room in his own home! Again he withdrew and reappeared in a window on a third side of the house. But by now the demonstrators had mastered this game of cat-and-mouse. They tracked Rove down and slammed their fists against the glass, sending up a terrific racket inside the home. Suddenly Rove regretted the decision not to put drapes on the north and south sides of the house, where the windows offered views of a hill and some trees. The protesters were now able to peer inside at Rove and his family like cats tormenting goldfish in a bowl. Several radicals shoved hand-lettered signs up against the windows with baffling messages like "ROVE: DON'T STEAL THE DREAM." Rove's wife and son were deeply shaken by the sights and sounds of the violent mob besieging their home. So was thirteen-year-old Daniel Drew, a neighbor who happened to be visiting Andrew and was now trapped inside the home. The house's position on a steep incline made it useless for Darby and the boys to flee upstairs—moving to the upper floor would not have provided any respite from the throngs just outside the glass.

"It was like animals," Rove told me. "They literally surrounded three sides of the house and were standing there, pounding on our windows."

> Who's on your hit list NPA?
> Who's on your hit list for today?
> Take no prisoner, take no names
> Kick 'em in the ass when they play their games!

A prisoner in his own million-dollar house, Rove could only imagine what the neighbors must be thinking. The conservative ideologue already considered himself something of a pariah in the neighborhood, known as Palisades, which was populated with politically correct people who worked at politically correct places like the World Bank. Now they couldn't even drive down their own street, which was choked with protesters. It was precisely the sort of drama Rove did not need when he was supposed to be masterminding the president's reelection.

Truth be told, Bush was not making Rove's task particularly easy. Any other president would have waited until his second term to invade Iraq. Any other president would have calculated that he could not afford such an enormous expenditure of political capital until after he was safely reelected. Granted, the decision to invade had been made for reasons of national security. But it also had major political ramifications that Bush had recognized in advance. In fact, two months before the invasion, just as Rove was laying out his grand plan to get the president reelected, Bush wrote down his concerns on a piece of paper and went to see his chief strategist.

"You're not the only smart person who's been thinking about this," he told Rove. "It's going to be a close election. And it's going to be a close election because we face tough decisions in the months ahead. And if I have to do what I might have to do, we will not be fighting a campaign in a time of peace and prosperity. If we're forced into action, people will be unsettled by it."

Translation: Rove would have to bust his hump to engineer a second electoral victory for Bush, who was never content to do things the easy way.

"He is not a guy who says, 'Okay, chart my path to election or reelection by helping me understand what's an 80–20 winner for me,'" Rove explained. "That's not his mindset. His mindset is, 'I've got a limited amount of time that I'm going to be here—what are the big things we need to tackle?' He has enough confidence in himself and enough confidence in the American people that if we do the right thing, we'll be able to explain it and prevail."

While aware of the electoral perils, Bush told me in an Oval Office interview that he never actually tried to calculate just how much political capital he would need to spend on Iraq and still have enough left over for reelection. I politely pointed out that if he didn't get reelected, he couldn't very well continue to implement the policies he considered so crucial to protecting national security. Surely he must have considered delaying the invasion of Iraq, if only for this reason.

"No, never." Bush shrugged matter-of-factly. "I don't remember one time saying to myself, or anybody around me: 'Let's don't do this because it might cost me political points.' No."

So Bush went ahead and spent all that political capital during his first term. Not content to crush Afghanistan's Taliban regime after the terrorist attacks of September 11, 2001, the president pressed on to preemptively invade Iraq in March 2003. Now, a year later, the Iraq war had taken a devastating toll on Bush's job approval ratings, which were beginning to slip below 50 percent. That was quite a comedown for a president whose rating in the immediate aftermath of September 11 had been 90 percent, the highest ever recorded since such polls were first taken in 1938. Rove knew that if Bush's numbers slipped another ten points, a second term would be pretty much out of reach. It was now clear that the Iraq war, from a political standpoint, had absolutely no upside. Invading a sovereign nation that had not threatened anyone for years was extremely controversial, even among many Republicans. To make matters worse, U.S. forces never found the weapons of mass destruction that Bush had cited as his primary justification for war in the first place. And now he was asking for four more years.

"I've made some big decisions in my first term," the president explained to me. "And whether people agreed with them or not, I hope that they saw me as a person that was thoughtful and was willing to stand by the decisions."

Mindful that his detractors numbered in the tens of millions, Bush was gambling that at least some of them would give him credit for sticking to his guns.

"The presidential election is an election on leadership," he told me. "Are you capable of making tough decisions, and can you explain them? And can you convince people that you make decisions based upon principle? And that once you make a decision, are you capable of standing strong on that decision?"

Bush's campaign manager, Ken Mehlman, said he admired the president's high-stakes gambit, even if it made reelection more difficult.

"Here is a guy that fundamentally did something that we haven't seen any modern president do," Mehlman told me. "He said, 'I'm willing to sacrifice my presidency for a cause I believe in, which is the removal of Saddam Hussein—a dangerous dictator who's a threat to America.' And I think that that epitomizes who this guy is."

As for the timing of the invasion, Mehlman was convinced it was based less on politics than the president's fear of another catastrophic terrorist attack.

"I think September 11 convinced him of a gathering threat," he told me. "And I think he recognized correctly that you couldn't wait while the threat gathered. And so I don't think he thought about it in political terms."

While the Iraq war had been highly controversial, at least Bush was able to take some comfort in the knowledge that Afghanistan had been different. Virtually all Americans, not to mention the international community, had united behind the swift and certain ouster of the Taliban. After all, the Taliban had sheltered Osama bin Laden, mastermind of the September 11 attacks. So the invasion of Afghanistan was widely viewed as a righteous act of retribution for the murder of some three thousand innocent Americans—an attack so monstrous that it had been utterly unforeseeable.

Or had it been? Throughout March 2004, Bush was savaged by armchair quarterbacks who accused him of having been asleep at the switch in the months leading up to September 11. The primary accuser was Richard Clarke, a disgruntled ex–White House official who had been in charge of counterterrorism at the time of the attacks. A holdover from the Clinton administration, Clarke wrote a self-aggrandizing book that accused Bush of ignoring warnings before the attacks and doing a "terrible job" of fighting terrorism afterward. Seeking to maximize book sales, Clarke timed the publication to coincide with his testimony before the 9-11 Commission, a congressionally appointed panel investigating U.S. preparedness. With exquisite marketing acumen, Clarke staged a dramatic rollout of his book on the venerated CBS News show *60 Minutes* three days before his March 24 testimony. It was an exceedingly friendly interview, since CBS News was owned by Viacom, the same company that owned Clarke's publisher, Simon & Schuster. The fawning story set the tone for an onslaught of adulatory coverage by the rest of the mainstream media. Day after day, the press lionized Clarke while accusing Bush of having bungled September 11.

Rove could scarcely believe it. Bush's response to September 11 had been the high point of his presidency, the defining moment when he rallied the nation to a great and noble cause—the defeat of global terrorism. "I can hear you!" he cried through a bullhorn in the smoldering rubble of the World Trade Center. That moment electrified the nation and forged a lasting bond between the president and millions of Americans. And yet now Bush's handling of September 11 was actually being used *against* him.

Incredibly, the problem was not limited to Richard Clarke and the 9-11 Commission. That same month, Bush was widely accused of "exploiting tragedy" by including brief images of the World Trade Center in his reelection campaign's first batch of television ads, which began airing March 3. The International Association of Fire Fighters (IAFF), whose members had cheered Bush when he stood among them in the rubble, now hammered him for using footage of firemen carrying the flag-draped remains of a victim from Ground Zero. Like most unions, the IAFF was backing Bush's Democratic opponent, Senator John Kerry of Massachusetts. But the press did not dwell on this ulterior political motive, preferring instead to simply report that firefighters were outraged by the Bush ads. In reality, many rank-and-file firemen remained loyal to the president, just like many of the families of victims at Ground Zero. But the press sought out only those firemen and families who supported Kerry, misrepresenting their partisan sniping as the genuine outrage of all who had lost loved ones. Bush tried to not let it get under his skin.

"Part of the campaign is to be able to show people that you've got the capacity to take the pressure," he told me. "In that this was my second presidential campaign, I was aware of what was coming, in terms of all the pressure, debates, noise."

Speaking of noise, Rove could barely hear himself think, what with all the protesters pounding on the windows along the north, south, and east sides of his house. He was relieved that they had not reached the west side, which

faced his backyard and was surrounded by a tall fence. But as he peered out
the west windows, he caught sight of a protester scaling the fence! The man
was awkwardly grasping a placard while trying to hoist himself to the top.
Rove sprinted into his backyard and reached the fence just as the man was
about to topple over.

"Get the hell out of my yard!" Rove yelled.

The startled protester fell backward into a neighbor's yard.

"I felt like I was at the Alamo, pushing people back over the fence," Rove
told me.

The brazenness of these protesters was nothing short of shocking. Rove normally welcomed robust political debate, especially during the long hours he
toiled at the White House each week. But to have his home invaded on a Sunday afternoon by a rampaging mob of thugs was an extraordinary outrage.

The protesters were also amazingly ignorant. They screamed that Bush was
anti-immigrant (the Dream Act was a legislative proposal to grant amnesty
to illegal aliens). But in fact, Bush was pro-immigrant and had been pilloried
by his fellow Republicans for a guest-worker program that most conservatives regarded as amnesty for lawbreakers. Rove, as the president's chief strategist, had personally borne the brunt of his fellow conservatives' ire over the
immigration issue. The demonstrators had no inkling that one of the people
they had trapped inside Rove's house, Daniel Drew, had been born in India.
The boy was an immigrant, as was his mother, Shakun, who was an immigration attorney.

Rove saw satellite trucks arriving to capture the drama for the evening
news. They trained their cameras on the besieged home, obliterating the last
shred of anonymity in Rove's personal life. Now all the world would see that
the man derided by liberals as "Bush's brain" lived in a tidy but surprisingly
unassuming brick home with a flat roof, capstones over the windows, and a
natural gas lamp flickering out front. The neighbors would undoubtedly be
mortified by the coverage. Rove wouldn't be surprised if they circulated a
petition asking him to relocate. Indeed, after having had the temerity to move

into this peaceful enclave in the first place, the pariah of Palisades was now turning the entire neighborhood into a three-ring circus.

"It was unbelievable," said Shakun Drew, who lived directly across the street. "I mean, there were swarms of people—*hundreds* of people—outside my house. I was coming home from the gym and it was hard to maneuver my car into the driveway."

Drew, a diehard Democrat, picked up a pamphlet that had been dropped by the protesters. When she discovered the reason for their demonstration, she felt compelled to upbraid her fellow liberals.

"Karl is the last person whose house you should be picketing!" she scolded them. "You have no idea how hard this man is working for immigrant benefits. He's an ally of those who want immigration reform."

But the protesters kept right on terrorizing Drew's son and the Rove family. In fact, they didn't even pipe down when uniformed agents of the Secret Service arrived and made their way through the throng to consult with Rove at the front door. As soon as the protesters caught a glimpse of their victim in the doorway, they broke into an ironic rendition of "America the Beautiful."

Unamused, Rove went back inside his house, leaving the authorities to disperse the crowd. But these protesters were in no mood to be hustled away without some measure of satisfaction from Rove himself. They continued taunting him, in English and Spanish, to "come on out." For the next half hour, Rove stared out the windows and marveled at the contempt on their faces. They showed an expression he had first glimpsed nineteen months earlier, during a violent anti-Bush demonstration in Portland, Oregon. Protesters there had charged the presidential motorcade, pounded on the hood of Bush's limousine, and bounced a rock off the windshield of the car that carried Rove. In retrospect, that melee had signaled the rise of the Bush haters, a political phenomenon characterized by a virulent strain of acid partisanship that sometimes bordered on violence. A year and a half later, the phenomenon had spread from the radical protest community of the West Coast to the sleepy

D.C. neighborhood of Karl Rove. Bush hatred had gone mainstream, just in time for the general election campaign.

All of which threatened to redound to the benefit of John Kerry, who had emerged as the presumptive Democratic nominee on Super Tuesday, March 2. That evening, Bush telephoned the Massachusetts senator to welcome him to the general election. A few days later, a Gallup poll showed Kerry leading Bush by a six-point margin. The incumbent had clearly been damaged by months of high-profile Democratic primaries in which ten rivals seemed to agree on only one thing—that Bush was an abysmal president.

Democrats weren't the only ones giving Bush headaches. Arizona senator John McCain, who had been vanquished by Bush in the Republican primaries of 2000, was now being urged to avenge that defeat by becoming Kerry's running mate. Democrats and journalists openly fantasized about a bipartisan Kerry-McCain "dream team" that would "unite the nation" and oust the polarizing president. McCain was practically begged to betray his own party during a March 10 appearance on ABC's *Good Morning America*.

"A lot of Democrats say a dream ticket would be if John Kerry would reach across the aisle, take you as a vice presidential candidate," host Charles Gibson told McCain. "Are you going to say no?"

"Charlie, it's impossible to imagine the Democratic Party seeking a pro-life, free-trading, non-protectionist deficit hawk," McCain demurred.

"But let me, let *me* imagine it," Gibson pleaded. "If he asked you, if he came across the aisle and asked you, would you even entertain the idea, or will you rule it out?"

"John Kerry is a very close friend of mine. We've been friends for years," McCain replied. "Obviously, I would entertain it."

McCain had skillfully opened the door just a crack, knowing the mainstream media would rush in with a flurry of speculative stories about a "unity" ticket. Oh, he went through the motions of throwing cold water on the speculation, but the damage had been done. According to the new conventional wisdom, Bush could no longer count on the support of even his fellow Republicans.

Rove stepped into his dining room, where less than an hour earlier he had discussed McCain and other reelection problems with a handful of trusted operatives from the White House, the Republican National Committee, and the Bush campaign—several of whom were now trapped in the house along with him. For the last six months, these heavy hitters had been quietly gathering each weekend to plot strategy over breakfast. They called themselves the Breakfast Club after a movie of the same name about a group of high schoolers stuck in weekend detention. Rove would fry up great slabs of bacon, venison sausage, and what he called "eggies," which he sizzled in a swirl of cream, butter, and bacon fat. The stuff was so laden with cholesterol that it should have been served with a rib-spreader. And yet it was the very fuel of the presidential reelection strategy.

It was here, in this unassuming dining room, over steaming plates of eggies, that Rove and the other strategists boldly hatched their plot to counter Kerry. They planned a ninety-day blitz to portray him in the worst possible light with ads, speeches, and hard-hitting presidential surrogates. The idea was to burst Kerry's bubble after the euphoria of Super Tuesday and then race to define him negatively in the minds of voters, most of whom had yet to form an opinion of the up-and-coming Democrat. Rove knew he had to make the negatives stick by the onset of summer, when vacation season got under way and most Americans would put presidential politics out of their minds until after Labor Day. He also knew that Kerry was broke after spending his war chest fending off fellow Democrats in the primaries. Bush, by contrast, had no Republican primary challengers and was therefore sitting on a whopping $100 million.

But Democrats were prepared for this imbalance. Mindful that the McCain-Feingold campaign finance law of 2002 banned unlimited donations to political parties, Democrats instead poured millions into outside advocacy groups. These groups, known as "527s" for their tax code designation, were openly flouting the law, which imposed strict donation limits on organizations whose "major purpose" was to influence a federal election. Clearly, the election of John Kerry was not just the "major purpose" of these 527s—it was their *only* purpose. Republicans cried foul, but the Federal Election Commission seemed in no hurry to resolve the dispute. So the 527s raked in millions, allowing Democrats to out-raise Republicans as the general election got under way.

With the opposition raising more money and doing better in the polls, Rove's only hope was to focus on issues that might sway voters toward Bush. As far as Rove was concerned, the most promising three issues were terrorism, taxes, and gay marriage. The idea was to portray Kerry as soft on terrorism, eager to raise taxes, and insufficiently opposed to gay marriage. But getting the public to buy into these characterizations would be tricky, especially regarding the political hot potato of gay marriage.

Kerry insisted that he opposed gay marriage. But unlike Bush, he also opposed a constitutional amendment defining marriage as between a man and a woman. That was the definition of the 1996 Defense of Marriage Act passed by Congress and signed by President Clinton. Kerry had been one of only fourteen senators voting against the act. In March 2004, the *Washington Post* ran an article headlined "Kerry Backs Benefits for Legally Married Gays." The piece quoted an enthusiastic gay marriage advocate saying, "It's the first time in history that a presidential candidate has ever supported full and equal protection for same-sex couples." Clearly, Kerry did not oppose gay marriage as strongly as the president did. But Rove knew how important it was that Bush not give any appearance of bashing gays or playing politics with the Constitution. He could not even afford to discuss the subject publicly very often, for fear of appearing insensitive.

But the issue was very much on the radar screens of grass-roots conservatives, who became alarmed in February when the Massachusetts Supreme Court ordered the state's legislature to legalize gay marriage. Eight days later, in open defiance of California state law, San Francisco mayor Gavin Newsom began issuing gay marriage licenses. Thousands of homosexual men and women flocked to the city hall and were "married" in rapturous ceremonies as news cameras rolled. Horrified conservatives responded by gathering signatures that would put the question of gay marriage on the November ballot in eleven states, including crucial swing states like Ohio. Rove knew these measures would draw conservatives to the polls even if Bush didn't spend a lot of time openly railing against gay marriage.

This "stealth" strategy had the added benefit of giving the president more time to talk about tax cuts and their stimulative effect on the economy. He had pushed through several major tax cuts during his first term and was campaigning to make those cuts permanent. Kerry, by contrast, wanted to raise taxes, a point driven home by a Bush campaign ad in March.

"Kerry voted to increase taxes on Social Security benefits," the TV spot noted. "And he voted against giving small businesses tax credits to buy health care for employees. Kerry even supported raising taxes on gasoline fifty cents a gallon."

The line about gasoline taxes was a preemptive strike aimed at deflecting blame for skyrocketing fuel prices. Although the economy had been growing steadily for more than two years, Bush was viewed as increasingly vulnerable on high gas prices and low job growth. Day after day, he was hammered by Kerry on both points.

But even Kerry understood the central issue of the campaign would be terrorism. And on this subject, the Democrat quickly discovered that his own words could be used against him with brutal effectiveness. In one primary election debate, Kerry complained about an "exaggeration" of the terrorist threat. In another he said the fight against terrorism should be "primarily a law enforcement and intelligence operation" and only "occasionally military." At a fund-raiser he bragged of being privately endorsed by foreign leaders, but then declined requests by Bush to name those leaders. After ten days of stonewalling, Kerry was finally forced to renounce all foreign endorsements, although by then he had publicly received three from unsavory supporters— the Communist dictator of North Korea, the socialist prime minister–elect of Spain, and the anti-Semitic ex-dictator of Malaysia.

Kerry uttered his most memorable gaffe of all on March 16. It happened while the candidate was trying to defend his vote against Bush's request for $87 billion to purchase body armor and other equipment for American troops in Iraq and Afghanistan. "I actually did vote for the $87 billion before

I voted against it," Kerry said. In a single utterance, he managed to encapsulate the entire campaign.

"When they called me and told me he'd said it, I could not believe it—I thought they were joking," Rove told me. "I mean, he gave us the ammunition. But more importantly, he gave us the mindset into how he was willing to conduct his campaign. He basically gave us a road map that allowed us to keep him on the ropes as much as possible. That, to me, was the gift that kept on giving."

Indeed, the Bush campaign quickly incorporated Kerry's blooper into an attack ad. In addition to showing the Democrat as soft on terrorism, it exposed him as the consummate flip-flopper, a perception that Rove and Ken Mehlman gleefully reinforced at every opportunity. In fact, Mehlman believed the line crystallized the stark choice facing voters.

"When John Kerry said 'I voted for the $87 billion before I voted against it,' what he was essentially saying was 'I'm hedging my bets,'" Mehlman told me. "When George Bush said 'I'm willing to risk my presidency on Iraq,' he was essentially saying 'I'm putting it all on the line.'"

Kerry seemed to spend most of his time focusing on a highly unconventional campaign issue—his own service in Vietnam more than a third of a century earlier. Kerry believed that his combat history inoculated him against the common Republican charge that Democrats were weak on national security. He also felt this was one area where his superiority over Bush—who had spent the Vietnam era serving stateside in the National Guard—was beyond question. The mainstream media, which had never gotten over its 1960s fixation with the "quagmire" of Vietnam, was rhapsodic that a bona fide Vietnam war hero had won the Democratic nomination. "When the war in Iraq is debated," ABC news anchor Peter Jennings gleefully announced on March 3, "John Kerry has a combat record—and the president does not." Kerry himself bragged about his Vietnam service so often that it became a target of ridicule. Late-night comic David Letterman, in a bit describing Kerry's typical day, joked that the Democrat mentioned his Vietnam service eleven times while ordering breakfast.

"It reinforced something about him," Mehlman said of Kerry's Vietnam obsession. "From a character perspective, he came across as a guy who is just ambition over everything. By contrast, Bob Dole didn't talk about his service, almost ever. John McCain, when he talks about it, talks about it in a way where it's very clear it affects him very deeply."

Meanwhile, Bush was determined not to make the campaign about the past. He believed that had been his father's mistake in 1992, when the elder President Bush tried to coast to reelection after vanquishing Saddam Hussein in the first Gulf War.

"Any campaign," the son told me, "that says, 'Look at what I did,' is going to fail."

That didn't mean he couldn't talk about his accomplishments. He just had to do it in a way that illustrated to the public how he would act in the future.

"The only reason to look back is to be able to justify what I am going to do," he told me. "You've got to be thinking forward."

Still, Mehlman found it useful to draw some lessons from the previous presidential campaign.

"Let me tell you the best thing that ever happened to us—the recount in 2000," he told me. "It steeled everybody. It put the fear of God in us. One of the things that I firmly believe in life is that success is more dangerous than near failure. Because when you fear failure, you're hungrier, you're tougher, you're smarter, you make more strategic decisions, and you never take a moment for granted."

At this particular moment, what Karl Rove feared most was not John Kerry, but for the safety of his family. He eagerly watched the Secret Service officers begin to move in formation against the protesters.

"They spread out in a line and the next thing you know, the crowd was moving off the lawn and into the street, where they stayed—I was very impressed," Rove told me. "They sat there for a while, but then they said they were not going to leave until I agreed to meet with them."

If Rove had been an abortionist whose home was besieged by pro-lifers, the demonstrators would have been dragged away in handcuffs and prosecuted for racketeering while the press howled about harassment of an innocent physician. But because Rove was the mastermind of President Bush's reelection campaign, he knew the only ones to emerge from this fiasco with sympathetic press coverage would be the lawbreaking protesters.

So Rove grudgingly agreed to a meeting, but only if they promised to get back on their yellow school buses and leave immediately afterward. Ringleader Emira Palacios actually asked to come inside his house, but Rove allowed her no closer than the garage. He opened the door and read her the riot act for presuming that the Bush administration was anti-immigrant.

"Do you know what the president's position is on immigration?" he demanded. "You show up at my house and you don't know what you're talking about."

With withering scorn, he informed Palacios that the protesters had reduced the children in his house to tears.

"I hope you're proud!" he yelled in her face. "Now get out of my house and don't ever come back!"

Palacios opened her mouth to speak, but Rove slammed the door in her face. The meeting, which had lasted precisely two minutes, was officially over.

Now it was Palacios's turn to cry. Trembling from the fury of Rove's blowback, she dutifully instructed her troops to retreat. As they began to board the buses, Palacios paused to complain one last time.

"He is very offended because we dared to come here," she told a *Washington Post* reporter. "We dared to come here because he dared to ignore us. I'm sorry we disturbed his children, but our children are disturbed every day.

"He also said, 'Don't ever dare to come back,'" she recalled. "We will, if he continues to ignore us."

But Rove had no intention of ignoring the bizarre Bush hatred that had nearly crashed through the windows of his own home. Indeed, his job was to counter such vitriolic extremism before Election Day.

As he watched the buses rumble from the shell-shocked Palisades neighborhood, Karl Rove couldn't help but wonder just how nasty this election would become.

CHAPTER TWO

YOU NEVER
ADMIT A MISTAKE

George W. Bush detested prime-time press conferences so thoroughly that he had given only two in the first three years of his presidency. He cringed at the thought of the magnificent East Room being defiled by preening correspondents and their snotty questions. As far as Bush was concerned, the reporters were interested only in making themselves look clever while making him look foolish before a television audience of tens of millions. The president disliked press conferences at any time, in any setting, but he knew he had to preempt accusations that he was hiding from the Fourth Estate. An informal man, Bush preferred to face reporters in the most decrepit chamber in the West Wing, the James S. Brady press briefing room. He also favored sessions in the morning, when he was fresher and TV audiences were smaller. In fact, Bush liked to surprise reporters by giving them only an hour's notice before a mid-morning press conference in the briefing room. That forced journalists to scramble and gave them less time to think up diabolical questions.

So it was with some measure of trepidation that Bush agreed to hold his third prime-time press conference on April 13, 2004. It was, unequivocally, a low point of his presidency. In Iraq, eighty-one American troops had been killed in the previous thirteen days, making April the deadliest month since the invasion. This prompted John Kerry to deride the president's Iraq policy as "one of the greatest failures of diplomacy and failures of judgment that I have seen in all the time that I've been in public life." Meanwhile, the 9-11 Commission was questioning whether the administration had done enough to prevent the terrorist attacks on the Pentagon and the World Trade Center two and a half years earlier.

All this weighed heavily on Bush's mind as he strode down the red-carpeted hallway and ascended the steps to the lectern in the East Room at 8:31 p.m. He was uncharacteristically subdued, even grim, as he began his prepared remarks.

"Good evening. Before I take your questions, let me speak with the American people about the situation in Iraq," he said. "This has been tough weeks in that country."

This has been tough weeks! The famously tongue-tied president was off to an inauspicious start.

"Coalition forces have encountered serious violence," he plowed on. "Remnants of Saddam Hussein's regime, along with Islamic militants, have attacked coalition forces in the city of Fallujah. Terrorists from other countries have infiltrated Iraq to incite and organize attacks. In the south of Iraq, coalition forces face riots and attacks that are being incited by a radical cleric named al-Sadr."

American civilians, Bush added, were also being slaughtered in Iraq. Two weeks earlier, gunmen had ambushed four civilian contractors in Fallujah. Their charred bodies were dragged through the streets and then hung from a bridge before a cheering mob. The horrific images were plastered across newspapers and TV screens, giving Americans the impression that the situation in Iraq was spiraling out of control.

"Our nation honors the memory of those who have been killed, and we pray that their families will find God's comfort in the midst of their grief," Bush said. "We will finish the work of the fallen."

But finishing the work entailed nothing less than creating, out of whole cloth, a democratic government in the very heart of the world's most undemocratic neighborhood—the Middle East. To that end, Bush sketched out a timetable that began with America transferring sovereignty to Iraq by June 30. The next big step would come in January 2005, when Iraq would hold free elections—the first in more than half a century—to choose a transitional assembly. The assembly, in turn, would draft a permanent constitution and present it to voters in October 2005. Finally, Iraqis would elect a permanent government on December 15, 2005.

"Now is the time, and Iraq is the place, in which the enemies of the civilized world are testing the will of the civilized world," Bush warned. "We must not waver."

It was not an easy sell. Americans were horrified by setbacks in not just Iraq, but also in the broader War on Terror. In Pakistan, for example, Islamic radicals had slit the throat of *Wall Street Journal* reporter Daniel Pearl after forcing him to acknowledge on videotape that he was Jewish. Bush tried to explain that such atrocities—now occurring in a variety of nations—were part of the same global struggle that encompassed the Iraq war.

"The terrorist who takes hostages or plants a roadside bomb near Baghdad is serving the same ideology of murder that kills innocent people on trains in Madrid, and murders children on buses in Jerusalem, and blows up a nightclub in Bali, and cuts the throat of a young reporter for being a Jew."

Bush then further broadened the explanation to include events reaching back to the Reagan administration.

"We've seen the same ideology of murder in the killing of 241 Marines in Beirut, the first attack on the World Trade Center, in the destruction of two embassies in Africa, in the attack on the USS *Cole*, and in the merciless horror inflicted upon thousands of innocent men and women and children on September 11."

Warming to his theme, the president argued that while previous administrations misdiagnosed terrorism as a criminal offense, his own administration rightly treated it as war.

"Over the last several decades, we've seen that any concession or retreat on our part will only embolden this enemy and invite more bloodshed," he said. "And the enemy has seen, over the last thirty-one months, that we will no longer live in denial or seek to appease them. For the first time, the civilized world has provided a concerted response to the ideology of terror—a series of powerful, effective blows."

These included the overthrow of both the Taliban regime in Afghanistan and Saddam Hussein in Iraq. Meanwhile, Pakistan had cracked down on terrorism and Libya had voluntarily surrendered its weapons of mass destruction programs. After all these successes, Bush wanted to make it clear that this was no time to backslide.

"The consequences of failure in Iraq would be unthinkable," he said. "Every friend of America and Iraq would be betrayed to prison and murder as a new tyranny arose. Every enemy of America and the world would celebrate, proclaiming our weakness and decadence, and using that victory to recruit a new generation of killers.

"We will succeed in Iraq," he concluded. "We're carrying out a decision that has already been made and will not change: Iraq will be a free, independent country, and America and the Middle East will be safer because of it. Our coalition has the means and the will to prevail. We serve the cause of liberty, and that is—always and everywhere—a cause worth serving."

Bush then began to entertain questions from reporters, starting with Terry Hunt of the Associated Press.

"Some people are comparing Iraq to Vietnam and talking about a quagmire," Hunt began.

Bingo! The reporter had managed to work both "Vietnam" and "quagmire" into the very first question. This was all too familiar to Bush, who had watched with dismay as the press labeled the war against Afghanistan a Vietnam quagmire exactly one week after the first shot was fired, and kept it up until the war was won—a mere month later. The press then slapped the Vietnam quagmire label on the war in Iraq—two weeks *before* it even began.

Again, the media was proven wrong when Baghdad fell just three weeks after the start of Operation Iraqi Freedom.

"How do you answer the Vietnam comparison?" Hunt demanded.

"I think the analogy is false. I also happen to think that analogy sends the wrong message to our troops, and sends the wrong message to the enemy."

Hunt cited public opinion surveys that showed declining support for U.S. involvement in Iraq. Bush said he was not about to alter his foreign policy in response to fluctuations in the polls.

"I just don't make decisions that way," he explained. "I fully understand the consequences of what we're doing. We're *changing the world*. And the world will be better off and America will be more secure as a result of the actions we're taking."

Still, Bush tempered his change-the-world idealism with a somber reality check.

"There's no question it's been a tough, tough series of weeks for the American people," he said. "It's been really tough for the families. I understand that. It's been tough on this administration. But we're doing the right thing. Look, this is hard work. It's hard to advance freedom in a country that has been strangled by tyranny. And yet we must stay the course, because the end result is in our nation's interest."

Unimpressed, Terry Moran of ABC lectured the president about taking the nation to war on "a series of false premises." He ridiculed the idea that Iraq had weapons of mass destruction and that "U.S. troops would be greeted as liberators with sweets and flowers."

"How do you explain to Americans how you got that so wrong?" Moran hectored.

Bush patiently explained the imperative of ousting Saddam. "The lesson of September 11 is: when this nation sees a threat, a gathering threat, we've got to deal with it. Saddam Hussein was a threat. He was a threat because he had used weapons of mass destruction on his own people. He was a threat because he coddled terrorists. He was a threat because he funded suiciders. He was a threat to the region. He was a threat to the United States."

Bush also rejected Moran's insinuation that ordinary Iraqis were angry at America for liberating their nation.

"They're really pleased we got rid of Saddam Hussein. And you can understand why. This is a guy who was a torturer, a killer, a maimer. There's mass graves. I mean, he was a horrible individual that really shocked the country in many ways."

The next question came from Elisabeth Bumiller of the *New York Times*, who demanded, "Two and a half years later, do you feel any sense of personal responsibility for September 11?"

Bush appeared momentarily stunned by the implication that he was responsible for the incineration of three thousand innocent Americans.

"Your question," stammered the president. "Do I feel—"

"Do you feel a sense of personal responsibility for September 11?" Bumiller helpfully repeated.

"There are some things I wish we'd have done when I look back," Bush acknowledged. "I mean, hindsight is easy. It's easy for a president to stand up and say: now that I know what happened, it would have been nice if there were certain things in place—for example, a Homeland Security Department."

The president said it also would have been nice to have the Patriot Act in place before September 11, because the legislation knocked down a wall that had prevented the FBI and CIA from sharing information.

"And the other thing I look back on and realize is that we weren't on a war footing," he observed. "The country was not on a war footing, and yet the enemy was at war with us. It didn't take me long to put us on a war footing. And we've been on one ever since."

Bush then turned to one of his least favorite reporters, NBC's David Gregory, who had once publicly angered the president by speaking French at a press conference in Paris. Bush knew Gregory preferred to be called "David" and corrected anyone who addressed him as "Dave." Unable to resist a play-ful tweak, Bush now called on "Dave."

Gregory asked the president to list "any errors in judgment" that he had made in the war against terrorism. "One of the biggest criticisms of you is that whether it's WMD in Iraq, postwar planning in Iraq, or even the ques-tion of whether this administration did enough to ward off September 11, *you never admit a mistake.*" Gregory fairly spat out this last phrase, making clear the opinion was his own.

"As I mentioned, the country wasn't on a war footing," the president replied. "And yet we're at war. And that's just a reality, *Dave.*"

The president continued: "The truth of the matter is, most in the country never felt that we'd be vulnerable to an attack such as the one that Osama bin Laden unleashed on us. We knew he had designs on us, we knew he hated us. But nobody—in our government, at least, and I don't think the prior government—could envision flying airplanes into buildings on such a mas-sive scale."

As for his failure to find weapons of mass destruction, Bush was unapolo-getic.

"Of course I want to know why we haven't found a weapon yet," he said. "But I still know Saddam Hussein was a threat, and the world is better off without Saddam Hussein."

By now it was clear that these reporters were just as interested in rehash-ing September 11—an event that had transpired thirty-one months earlier—as they were in hammering Bush about the bloody struggle in Iraq, which was still unfolding. Ed Chen of the *Los Angeles Times* stuck with the September 11 theme by suggesting Bush had been warned of the terrorist attacks weeks in advance. As evidence, Chen cited the President's Daily Brief (PDB) of August 6, 2001, which contained a two-page section called "Bin Laden Deter-mined to Strike in U.S." Although the brief contained mostly old news and said nothing about jetliners crashing into buildings, critics pounced on it as proof that Bush had been asleep at the switch.

"Had there been a threat that required action by anybody in the government, I would have dealt with it," the president told Chen. "You can rest assured that the people of this government would have responded, and responded in a forceful way."

Bush was not surprised by the question. The White House had declassified the PDB and made it available to the 9-11 Commission just three days earlier. And the president was used to Monday-morning quarterbacks. But he wasn't accustomed to reporters insinuating that he was personally responsible for the September 11 attacks. Bumiller's question still stuck in Bush's craw as he finished answering Chen. So he decided to revisit the topic.

"I mean, one of the things about Elisabeth's question was—I step back and I've asked myself a lot—is there anything we could have done to stop the attacks? And the answer is that had I had any inkling whatsoever that the people were going to fly airplanes into buildings, *we would have moved heaven and earth* to save the country—just like we're working hard to prevent a further attack."

John Roberts of CBS decided to combine the two themes of presidential negligence and an inability to admit mistakes into a single loaded question.

"Two weeks ago, a former counterterrorism official at the NSC, Richard Clarke, offered an unequivocal apology to the American people for failing them prior to September 11," Roberts began. "Do you believe the American people deserve a similar apology from you, and would you be prepared to give them one?"

"Look, I can understand why people in my administration anguished over the fact that people lost their life. I feel the same way. I mean, I'm sick when I think about the death that took place on that day," Bush said.

"I've met with a lot of family members and I do the best I can to console them about the loss of their loved one," he added. "I oftentimes think about what I could have done differently. I can assure the American people that had we had any inkling that this was going to happen, we would have done everything in our power to stop the attack."

It was not like Bush to second-guess himself, so he decided to end this line of discussion with a dose of his patented straight talk.

"Here's what I feel," he announced. "The person responsible for the attacks was Osama bin Laden. That's who's responsible for killing Americans. And that's why we will stay on the offense until we bring people to justice."

Now that Bush had regained his old confidence, he began tackling questions with shorter, snappier retorts. When CNN's John King asked whether "your coalition is window dressing," consisting largely of "hired guns," the president was ready.

"I don't think people ought to demean the contributions of our friends in Iraq," he said. "People are sacrificing their lives in Iraq from different countries. We ought to honor that, and we ought to welcome that. I'm proud of the coalition that is there."

Bush then pivoted to the long-term impact of his decision to invade Iraq, although he was careful to ascribe that impact to the troops, not himself.

"The legacy that our troops are going to leave behind is a legacy of lasting importance, as far as I'm concerned. It's a legacy that really is based upon our deep belief that people want to be free and that free societies are peaceful societies," he said. "I believe that freedom is the deepest need of every human soul, and, if given a chance, the Iraqi people will be not only self-governing, but a stable and free society."

Eager to bring the president back down to earth, Mike Allen of the *Washington Post* broached a less lofty topic.

"Mr. President, why are you and the vice president insisting on appearing together before the 9-11 Commission?" he said.

The commission had requested separate interviews, presumably to see whether Bush and Cheney could keep their stories straight. But the White House had insisted on a joint interview, prompting the press to howl that the dim-witted Bush could not survive the commissioners' questioning without help from his trusty second in command.

"Because the 9-11 Commission wants to ask us questions, that's why," the president said. "And I look forward to meeting with them and answering their questions."

"I was asking why you're appearing together, rather than separately, which was their request," Allen persisted.

But Bush wasn't budging. "Because it's a good chance for both of us to answer questions that the 9-11 Commission is looking forward to asking us," he repeated. "And I'm looking forward to answering them."

Now it was my turn to ask a question. "Mr. President, you have been accused of letting the September 11 threat mature too far, but not letting the Iraq threat mature far enough," I began. "In the wake of these two conflicts, what is the appropriate threat level to justify action in perhaps other situations going forward?"

"I guess there have been some that said, 'Well, we should have taken preemptive action in Afghanistan,' and then turned around and said, 'We shouldn't have taken preemptive action in Iraq,'" Bush mused before giving yet another reason why the September 11 attacks could not have been prevented.

"Frankly, the world would have been astounded had the United States acted unilaterally in trying to deal with al Qaeda in that part of the world," he said. "It would have been awfully hard to do."

To bolster his argument, Bush got down to specifics. "We hadn't got our relationship right with Pakistan yet. The Caucus area would have been very difficult from which to base. It just seemed an impractical strategy at the time, and frankly, I didn't contemplate it."

Only after the terrorist attacks of September 11 did the destruction of al Qaeda become Bush's top priority, followed by action in both Afghanistan and Iraq, and a strategy of promoting reform across the Middle East.

"We've had some success, Bill, as a result of the decision I took," he said. "Take Libya, for example."

Indeed, Libyan leader Moammar Gadhafi had watched in alarm as the U.S. readied for war against Iraq. When the opening salvo was finally fired, he approached American and British intelligence agencies to confess that he had been concealing his own WMD programs. Nine months later, when Saddam Hussein was unceremoniously dragged out of a spider hole in Iraq, a chastened Gadhafi announced to the world that he would relinquish his weapons programs.

That revelation, in turn, led to the exposure of Libya's supplier of nuclear technology, Pakistani scientist A. Q. Khan, whose customers also included Iran and North Korea, both charter members of Bush's "axis of evil."

"This was a shadowy network of folks that were willing to sell state secrets to the highest bidder," Bush told me. "It was a dangerous network that we unraveled. And the world is better for it."

He added, "So what I'm telling you is that sometimes we use military as a last resort, but other times we use our influence, diplomatic pressure, and our alliances, to unravel, uncover, expose people who want to do harm against the civilized world."

Having given me the longest answer of the evening, Bush then called on *USA Today* reporter Judy Keen, who asked the best question.

"You've made it very clear tonight that you're committed to continuing the mission in Iraq. Yet, as Terry pointed out, increasing numbers of Americans have qualms about it," she said. "And this is an election year. Will it have been worth it, even if you lose your job because of it?"

"I don't plan on losing my job," he fired back. "I plan on telling the American people that I've got a plan to win the War on Terror. And I believe they'll stay with me. They understand the stakes."

Bush went on to say that he was eager to join the fray as the campaign unfolded.

"I look forward to making my case. The American people may decide to change—that's democracy. I don't think so. I don't think so."

Still, the president hastened to acknowledge that his path to victory would be sorely complicated by the ongoing struggle in Iraq.

"Look, nobody likes to see dead people on their television screens—I don't," he said. "It's a tough time for the American people to see that. It's gut-wrenching."

But he added that he would "never allow our youngsters to die in vain. And I made that pledge to their parents. Withdrawing from the battlefield of Iraq would be just that. And it's not going to happen under my watch."

Bush probably should have ended the press conference right then and there. But he decided to continue indulging reporters, who by now were positively obsessed with forcing the president to admit mistakes.

"You've looked back before September 11 for what mistakes might have been made," said John Dickerson of *Time*. "After September 11, what would your biggest mistake be, would you say, and what lessons have you learned from it?"

"Hmm," Bush began. "I wish you would have given me this written question ahead of time, so I could plan for it."

A smattering of polite laughter.

"Aaahh," exhaled the president, now openly stalling for time. He scowled and shook his head from side to side. His expression said "what a boneheaded question." But his mouth said nothing for a full five seconds.

"John, I'm sure historians will look back and say, gosh, he could have done it better this way, or that way," Bush finally managed. "Uhhh."

Another six seconds ticked by in silence. Bush stared at the top of the lectern and pulled a face. At a total loss for words, he puffed up his cheeks in exasperation. The void was filled by the sound of clicking cameras. The photographers, always eager to capture any expression of presidential discomfort, were voraciously snapping away.

"You know, I just, uh," the president stammered as several more seconds rolled by. He was in a freefall. "I'm sure something will pop into my head here in the midst of this press conference, with all the pressure of trying to come up with an answer, but it hasn't yet."

Awkward silence. The attempt to relieve the tension with humor had failed. In the end, the president resorted to apologizing for his failure to answer the question.

"I hope I—I don't want to sound like I've made no mistakes," he said. "I'm confident I have. I just haven't—you just put me under the spot here, and maybe I'm not as quick on my feet as I should be in coming up with one."

That was the understatement of the evening. But the press wasn't finished with its quest for a presidential apology. The final demand came from Don Gonyea of National Public Radio, who had never before questioned Bush.

"With public support for your policies in Iraq falling off the way they have—quite significantly over the past couple of months—I guess I'd like to know if you feel in any way that you've failed as a communicator on this topic?"

"Gosh, I don't know," Bush said. "I mean—"

"Well, you deliver a lot of speeches and a lot of them contain similar phrases, and they vary very little from one to the next," Donyea continued. "And they often include a pretty upbeat assessment of how things are going— with the exception of tonight's pretty somber assessment."

"It is a pretty somber assessment today, Don, yes," Bush said.

"I guess I just wonder if you feel that you have failed in any way?" said Gonyea, finally meandering back to his point. "You don't have many of these press conferences, where you engage in this kind of exchange. Have you failed in any way to really make the case to the American public?"

"I guess if you put it into a political context, that's the kind of thing the voters will decide next November—that's what elections are about," Bush said. "They'll take a look at me and my opponent and say: 'Let's see, which one of them can better win the War on Terror? Who best can see to it that Iraq emerges as a free society?'"

The old confidence was returning again, just in the nick of time.

"I feel strongly about what we're doing," he asserted. "I feel strongly that the course this administration has taken will make America more secure and the world more free, and, therefore, the world more peaceful. It's a conviction that's deep in my soul. And I will say it as best as I possibly can to the American people."

In the end, the president predicted the campaign would come down to a series of crucial questions.

"What is a proper use of American power? Do we have an obligation to lead? Or should we shirk responsibility? That's how I view this debate. And I look forward to making it, Don. I'll do it the best I possibly can. I'll give it the best shot. I'll speak as plainly as I can. One thing is for certain, though, about me—and the world has learned this," he concluded. "When I say something, I mean it."

With that, he turned and walked away, having been reminded all over again why he hated these prime-time press conferences.

CHAPTER THREE

"Quite a Whirlwind"

Mary Mapes was triumphant. Two months of dogged reporting had finally paid off. Tonight, on a *60 Minutes* segment narrated by Dan Rather, she would break the blockbuster story that, with any luck, would bring the Bush administration to its knees. In mere moments, viewers would be shown repulsive photographs of American soldiers gleefully humiliating naked Iraqis at Abu Ghraib, a U.S.-run prison near Baghdad. Mapes, the star producer for CBS News, could barely contain her excitement.

She first got wind of the story back on January 16, when the Pentagon issued an antiseptic press release that cryptically announced, "An investigation has been initiated into reported incidents of detainee abuse." This vague disclosure was ignored by most journalists, although Mapes was intrigued. Ten days later, her interest increased exponentially when CNN reported that the probe might entail photos of "detainees with some of their clothing removed." It dawned on Mapes that the story wasn't getting much coverage precisely because it was not accompanied by the photos in question. She understood that Abu Ghraib was the sort of story that required *pictures* to provoke the outrage of the American public. And so, from her home base in Dallas, Mapes resolved to find those photos at any cost. She began pursuing leads that took her, as she put it, "halfway around the world and back." At one point she trekked all the way to Kuwait, only to come up empty-handed.

The search intensified in March, when U.S. forces in Baghdad announced that six soldiers had been charged in the prison abuse probe. But even that story ended up going nowhere because, again, there were no photos to illustrate it. Mapes instructed her associate producer, retired Marine officer Roger Charles, to capitalize on his military contacts. So Charles posted a notice on a muckraking website, Soldiers for the Truth, seeking information on the photos. The move paid off on March 23, when Charles received a fateful e-mail from a man named Bill Lawson. The former Air Force master sergeant explained that one of the six soldiers charged with abuse at Abu Ghraib was none other than his nephew, Staff Sergeant Ivan "Chip" Frederick II of Virginia.

"Roger called Lawson back so fast his fingers nearly burst into flames," Mapes recalled in her memoir, *Truth and Duty*.

Charles listened patiently as Lawson complained that his nephew had merely been following orders at the prison and now was being turned into a scapegoat. Charles was careful to establish a rapport with Lawson by playing up the fact that both men had spent their careers in the military. Then he asked the all-important question: were there photos of the abuse? Lawson answered yes and said the pictures were being used as evidence against his nephew.

"Chip says that he is in only one of the pictures," Lawson told Charles. "I just hope he's not smiling."

But Charles was already smiling at the bombshell he had just uncovered.

"Roger was exultant when he called me," Mapes wrote in her memoir. "We had found our opening into the story."

Within a matter of days, she secured not just the photos, but the promise of an interview with Frederick. Foolishly, the young soldier calculated that by telling his story to the press, he would inoculate himself against punishment by the military. Mapes took advantage of Frederick's naïveté, suggesting he talk by phone with legendary anchorman Dan Rather.

The broadcast was scheduled for April 14, but the Pentagon begged CBS to delay the story, arguing that it would inflame an already volatile situation in Iraq. Insurgents were killing half a dozen U.S. troops every day and had seized a number of civilian hostages. The Pentagon warned that those hostages might be killed if CBS broadcast photos of U.S. troops merrily abusing Iraqi prisoners. So the segment was rescheduled for April 21, but then General Richard Myers, chairman of the Joint Chiefs of Staff, personally telephoned Rather to ask for another delay. The anchorman relented, but by then other news organizations were starting to get wind of the story. Left-wing polemicist Seymour Hersh secured his own batch of photos and was planning a big splash in the *New Yorker*. Mapes decided her story could wait no longer. It would be broadcast on April 28, regardless of further objections by the Pentagon.

So now, at long last, the moment of truth had arrived. That famous *60 Minutes* stopwatch filled the television screen, accompanied by the familiar *tick tick tick tick tick*. Dan Rather began to read Mapes's script, which opened with a brief overview of the case against the U.S. troops, followed by an ominous disclaimer.

"Tonight, you will hear from one of those soldiers, and for the first time, you'll see some of the pictures that led to the Army investigation," Rather intoned. "We want to warn you the pictures are difficult to look at."

Indeed, the next thing viewers saw was a photo of a man who appeared to be wearing a Ku Klux Klan outfit, only the robe and pointed hood were black instead of white. The man was standing on a small box, with his arms outstretched at his sides and wires dangling from his hands. His face was hidden by the hood. One corner of the photo was emblazoned with the CBS logo, intended to remind the world that this was a network exclusive.

"Americans did this to an Iraqi prisoner," Rather said in a tone calculated to convey maximum shock and outrage. "The man was told to stand on a box with his head covered, with wires attached to his hands. He was told that if he fell off the box, he would be electrocuted."

Rather did not mention that the threat was a ruse by the Americans, who were trying to intimidate the prisoner, not electrocute him. The anchorman then conflated the GIs' misconduct to the murderous practices of Saddam Hussein's torturous regime.

"Abu Ghraib under Saddam Hussein was infamous," Rather said. "For decades, many who were taken here never came out. And those prisoners who did make it out told nightmarish tales of torture beyond imagining and executions without reason."

Viewers now heard the voice of CIA operative Robert Baer.

"I visited Abu Ghraib a couple days after it was liberated. It was the most awful sight I've ever seen," Baer said. "There were bodies that were eaten by dogs, torture, you know, electrodes coming out of walls."

Baer was followed by a former Marine, Lieutenant Colonel Bill Cowan, who equated the atrocities of Saddam's regime to the misbehavior of a few U.S. soldiers.

"We went into Iraq to stop things like this from happening and, indeed, here they are happening under our tutelage," he said.

Actually, Americans were not allowing dogs to eat prisoners at Abu Ghraib or even remotely approaching the murderous excesses of the former Ba'athist regime. But the CBS story pressed on, with more photos of U.S. troops humiliating naked Iraqi prisoners. The network had retouched the photos to blur the prisoners' genitals.

"It was American soldiers serving as military police at Abu Ghraib who took these pictures," the anchorman lamented. "The pictures show Americans, men and women, in military uniforms, posing with naked Iraqi prisoners. There are shots of the prisoners stacked in a pyramid, one with a slur written on his skin in English. In some, the male prisoners are positioned to simulate sex with each other. And in most of the pictures, the Americans are laughing, posing, pointing, or giving the camera a thumbs-up."

Rather then catalogued Frederick's abuse of the prisoners.

"He is charged with maltreatment," the anchorman said. "For posing for a photograph sitting on top of a detainee."

As more sickening images filled the screen, the litany continued: "He is charged with assault for allegedly striking detainees, and ordering detainees to strike each other."

Rather then asked the soldier, by telephone, what happened at the prison.

"We had no support, no training whatsoever," Frederick complained. "And I kept asking my chain of command for certain things, like rules and regulations, and it just—it just wasn't happening."

Rather made a perfunctory show of "protecting" his source, but every time he went through the motions of hinting that Frederick might be a scapegoat, he ended up actually helping the prosecution's case. He even quoted a self-incriminating letter the sergeant had sent home.

"Military intelligence has encouraged and told us, 'Great job,'" confided Frederick. "They usually don't allow others to watch them interrogate, but since they like the way I run the prison, they've made an exception. We help getting them to talk with the way we handle them. We've had a very high rate with our style of getting them to break. They usually end up breaking within hours."

Having now alerted military prosecutors to the ill-advised boasts of Chip "I-Run-the-Prison" Frederick, Rather gave the hapless soldier more rope with which to hang himself. He asked whether Frederick had seen any prisoners beaten.

"We had to use force sometimes to get the inmates to cooperate," Frederick modestly allowed. "They didn't want to listen, so sometimes you would just give them a little nudge or something."

Frederick managed to refrain from winking when he explained the "nudge." Nonetheless, the soldier's conviction was assured. Rather moved on to Cowan, who warned of an anti-American backlash.

"We will be paid back for this," he predicted. "These people at some point will be let out. Their families are going to know, their friends are going to know."

Anticipating complaints from viewers, Rather launched a preemptive strike. He looked into the camera and directly addressed "that person who's sitting in their living room saying, 'I wish they wouldn't do this. It's under-mining our troops, and they shouldn't do it.'"

The camera then cut to Cowan, who warned, "If we don't tell this story, these kinds of things will continue, and we'll end up getting paid back a hundred or a thousand times over."

The piece ended with Rather asking Army brigadier general Mark Kimmitt, deputy director of coalition operations in Iraq, to make sense of "these terrible facts."

"This is reprehensible, but this is not representative of the 150,000 soldiers that are over here," Kimmit assured viewers. "Don't judge your Army based on the actions of a few."

Tick tick tick tick tick.

Alas, Mapes and the rest of the media had no intention of treating Abu Ghraib as the anomaly it was. To the contrary, they seized on the prisoner abuse story as emblematic of everything that was wrong with Bush's Iraq policy.

"It would become a kind of symbol," gushed *60 Minutes* executive producer Jeff Fager to Knight Ridder.

"Abu Ghraib would be a black eye for a military program in the middle of a war," Mapes bragged. "Not only would it hurt this country's image in the Arab world, it also hurt the military's image in this country at a delicate time."

She added self-righteously, "Neither Dan nor I wanted to criticize our soldiers unnecessarily. But there are rules in war."

There were no rules, however, in the mainstream media, which embarked on a hysterical feeding frenzy that was out of all proportion to the misdeeds of a handful of prison guards. As with most feeding frenzies aimed at harming Republican presidents, this one entailed dusting off the tired old media templates of Vietnam and Watergate.

"It's gonna be like My Lai!" crowed Seymour Hersh as he joined Mapes on the Charlie Rose television show.

Hersh had broken the story of the My Lai massacre nearly thirty-five years earlier. But it was a stretch to say that Abu Ghraib was My Lai. At My Lai, U.S.

troops had slaughtered hundreds of Vietnamese civilians, including women and children. By contrast, the troops at Abu Ghraib were not accused of killing anyone. And while their abuse of Iraqi men was deplorable, those men were prisoners of war, not innocent civilians. Nonetheless, Hersh and the rest of the liberal press, always eager for a Vietnam redux, raced to equate Abu Ghraib with My Lai.

"After the story about the American massacre, I think Richard Nixon could no longer appeal to middle America—it was over," Hersh gloated. "This story has the same potential to destroy the ability of our president to rally the American people behind the war."

CNN agreed wholeheartedly. Reporter Bruce Morton predicted that the Abu Ghraib photos "will make it easier for foreigners to hate America. But they will also make us take a hard look at ourselves. We like to think that we're the good guys. But we're not. Not always. We learned this lesson last in Vietnam, in a village called My Lai."

He added, hopefully, "What My Lai really did was make us all think twice about the war."

Over at the *New York Times*, columnist Frank Rich leapt at the chance to tar Bush with the brush of a war that had ended a generation earlier.

"It was in November 1969 that a little-known reporter, Seymour Hersh, broke the story of the 1968 massacre at My Lai, the horrific scoop that has now found its match thirty-five years later in Mr. Hersh's *New Yorker* revelation of a fifty-three-page Army report detailing numerous instances of 'sadistic, blatant, and wanton criminal abuses' at Abu Ghraib. No doubt some future edition of the Pentagon Papers will explain just why we restored Saddam Hussein's hellhole to its original use, torture rooms included."

Echoed fellow *Times* columnist Paul Krugman: "Seymour Hersh is exposing My Lai all over again."

The Vietnam comparisons were not limited to the newspaper's opinion columnists. White House correspondent David Sanger wondered in the paper's ostensibly objective news pages whether the photo of the hooded prisoner "will become the symbolic image of the American occupation—the way the photograph of a naked Vietnamese girl running from an American attack helped turn opinion against American action in Southeast Asia."

In addition to these knee-jerk comparisons to Vietnam, journalists also resurrected the Watergate story template, which had long ago been fashioned into an all-purpose bludgeon for use against Republican presidents.

"What did administration officials know and when did they know it?" demanded Katie Couric on NBC's *Today Show*.

The battle cry was also taken up by Democrats who sensed an opportunity to get rid of Defense Secretary Donald Rumsfeld.

"What did Secretary Rumsfeld and others in the Pentagon know, when did they know it, and what did they do about it?" railed Senator Joseph Biden of Delaware. "If the answers are unsatisfactory, resignations should be sought."

John Kerry went a step further by openly demanding that Bush fire Rumsfeld. The fiercely loyal commander in chief refused to budge, although he privately admonished Rumsfeld for not warning him of the debacle.

"The first time I saw or heard about pictures was on TV," the president muttered after learning Army investigators had possessed the photos for months.

As the scandal raged on, Rumsfeld drafted a letter of resignation and walked it into the Oval Office.

"He hand-delivered it to me," Bush told me. "He just said, 'Read this.'"

But Rumsfeld departed the White House before the president had a chance to read the letter. When the two men later discussed the matter, Bush was not ready to let his defense secretary go.

"I said, 'Thank you, I'll let you know what my thinking is,'" Bush told me. "You know, I thought about it, obviously."

But the more he thought about it, the more he realized he needed Rumsfeld to stick around.

"I didn't say anything, initially, and the reason why is because I thought he was doing a good job," Bush told me. "We're in the middle of a war and I felt that he was doing a fine job of managing this particular battle in the War on Terror."

Still, Rumsfeld wanted the president to know his offer to resign was not an empty gesture. So he drafted a second letter and submitted it to Bush, who remained unreceptive to the idea. After all, in addition to fighting the War on Terror, Rumsfeld was also juggling several enormously important Pentagon initiatives, including the consolidation of U.S. military bases and the drawdown of forces stationed overseas.

"We are transforming our military," Bush told me. "He was doing some very difficult things in the Pentagon and I thought he was doing them very well. And so that's why it was a non-starter."

"I spoke to him afterwards," he added. "I said, 'Look, I want you to stay.'"

The settling of Rumsfeld's job status, however, didn't make the photos any easier to look at.

"I was repulsed by them; I was offended," Bush told me. "I reacted like most Americans reacted, you know: this is not America. This was an intolerable practice by a few people, did not represent the military, nor did it represent the way the American people think," he added. "I was not going to allow the action of those folks to stain the honor of the rest of the troops, because I know how great they are."

So the president embarked on a two-track strategy. He would condemn the abuse of prisoners by a handful of bad apples, while defending the vast majority of U.S. troops. He didn't have to wait long for an opportunity to employ this strategy.

"What is your reaction to photos of U.S. soldiers abusing Iraqi prisoners?" a reporter asked Bush in the Rose Garden on April 30. "How are you going to win their hearts and minds with these sort of tactics?"

"I shared a deep disgust that those prisoners were treated the way they were treated," Bush replied. "But I also want to remind people that those few people who did that do not reflect the nature of the men and women we've sent overseas."

The press was quick to remind the president that the men and women he had sent overseas were continuing to die at an alarming rate. In the two and a half weeks since the East Room press conference, casualties had only mounted.

One reporter asked, "Mr. President, 134 soldiers have died in Iraq this month, more than any other month. A year after you declared an end to major combat, are things getting worse in Iraq rather than better?"

On and on it went. That evening, ABC News devoted its entire *Nightline* show to anchorman Ted Koppel reading the names of 721 service members who had been killed in Iraq since the start of the war. The stunt had been inspired, naturally, by a June 1969 issue of *Life* magazine headlined "The Faces of the American Dead in Vietnam." The eleven-page spread, which featured hundreds of photos of GIs who had been killed in Southeast Asia, helped turn American opinion against the war. ABC was trying to do the same with the Iraq war, according to Sinclair Broadcasting, which owned eight ABC affiliates. Sinclair refused to broadcast the stunt because it "appears to be motivated by a political agenda designed to undermine the efforts of the United States in Iraq."

The broadcast was also criticized by *FOX News Sunday* anchor Chris Wallace, who spent fifteen years at ABC News, where he often filled in for Koppel as host of *Nightline*.

"We thought the ABC News program *Nightline* made a mistake," Wallace told FOX viewers, "listing all the brave men and women who died in Iraq but without providing the context of what they died for."

To remedy that deficiency, Wallace put together a seven-minute tribute titled "What We've Accomplished." It was designed to place the Iraq war in perspective by stepping back and surveying the breathtaking progress that U.S. forces had accomplished in little more than a year.

"First, ending the brutal regime of Saddam Hussein—ending the systematic torture and murder of hundreds of thousands of Iraqis," Wallace began in the gerundial syntax peculiar to TV newspeople. "Since Saddam was overthrown, investigators have found dozens of mass graves, in which more than 300,000 Iraqis were buried.

"Ending the theft of billions of dollars from the Iraqi people. Since 1991, Saddam built forty-eight palaces, at a time when his regime said it did not have the resources to build housing. And an investigation has found Saddam stole more than $11 billion from the UN's Oil-for-Food Program.

"Ending the threat that weapons of mass destruction will be developed and used. Since the invasion, U.S. inspectors have not found WMD. But during its time in power, Saddam's regime manufactured chemical and biological weapons and, at one point, actively pursued nuclear weapons."

Wallace went on to chronicle enormous improvements in the quality of life for ordinary Iraqis. Thanks to the hard work of U.S. troops, Iraqis were benefiting from huge advances in education, health care, and infrastructure. The availability of electricity, sewage facilities, and clean drinking water was spreading dramatically. The economy was also improving, thanks to the introduction of a stable currency and an increase in oil production. As for technology, the newly freed Iraqis were buying computers, TV satellite dishes, and cell phones in droves.

Even more important, human rights had improved immeasurably.

"Since the end of Saddam, a fully functioning legal and judicial system has been developed," Wallace noted. "More than six hundred judges are working in courtrooms across the country. Iraqis charged with crimes now have rights that would have been laughed at under the old regime: the right to remain silent when they're arrested; the right to a fair, speedy, and open trial; the right to a defense lawyer at all stages of the process.

"Iraqis now enjoy freedom of speech. Street protests against the U.S. occupation are now routine in Baghdad, something that in the past would have earned these demonstrators imprisonment or death. There is also something approaching freedom of the press. Under Saddam, all newspapers were controlled by the government."

Viewers were then shown a clip of an Iraqi woman who had been a reporter for twenty-seven years.

"Before, we write as they tell us to write," she said. "Now, we write what we believe."

Unfortunately, the rest of the Arab press was still taking its marching orders from Middle Eastern dictators who had no intention of acknowledging U.S. accomplishments in Iraq. To the contrary, the Arab press—like its American counterpart—had one all-consuming obsession at this moment—Abu

Ghraib. Arab audiences seized on the photos as revealing America's true feelings about Muslims. Desperate to contain the damage to America's international image, National Security Adviser Condoleezza Rice decided to appeal directly to the "Arab street."

"It's important for us to go on al Arabiya and to talk directly to your viewers and your listeners," she told a reporter from the Arab network on May 4. "We are deeply sorry for what has happened to these people."

Bush himself granted an interview to the network the next morning.

"How do you think this will be perceived in the Middle East?" the reporter asked.

"Terrible. I think people in the Middle East who want to dislike America will use this as an excuse to remind people about their dislike," Bush acknowledged. "I want to tell the people of the Middle East that the practices that took place in that prison are abhorrent and they don't represent America. They represent the actions of a few people."

That same morning, he gave an interview to another Arab television network, Alhurra, to emphasize the transparency of the U.S. probe.

"We're an open society. We're a society that is willing to investigate, fully investigate in this case, what took place in that prison," he said. "That stands in stark contrast to life under Saddam Hussein. His trained torturers were never brought to justice under his regime. There were no investigations about mistreatment of people."

The American press, which rarely landed interviews with Bush, seemed peeved by the president's sudden outreach to Arab networks. Within hours, American reporters were lashing out at White House press secretary Scott McClellan.

"How does the president feel about the fact that he has to sit down in interviews and sort of make the case, the moral distinction, between the United States and Saddam Hussein?" one journalist demanded of McClellan.

Other reporters saw an opening in the long-running quest to force Bush to apologize. They pointed out that the president had not explicitly told his Arab interviewers that he was sorry.

"Why was that?" asked Mark Smith of Associated Press Radio.

"Well, we've already said that we're sorry," McClellan noted. "The president is sorry for what occurred and the pain that it has caused."

"He didn't think that was necessary to say in his own voice, with his own words?" Smith persisted.

"He was addressing the questions that were asked," McClellan shrugged.

This elicited incredulity from CBS radio reporter Peter Maer.

"Did you mean to say that the president didn't apologize," Maer asked, "because no one brought it up in either interview?"

"Well, we've already said that we are deeply sorry for what occurred," McClellan said. "The White House has already said that on behalf of the president."

"It's, with all due respect, a little bit different than you or Condoleezza Rice," Maer countered. "If the Arab world had heard the president personally apologize, it would have gone a long way."

"Well, I just told you, the president is deeply sorry for what occurred, and the pain that it has caused," McClellan said.

"Why didn't he say so himself?" Maer persisted.

"The president is deeply sorry for it," McClellan repeated. "And he was pleased to sit down and do these interviews and address the questions that were asked of him."

"Why didn't he say so himself?" Maer repeated.

"I'm saying it for him right now, Peter, and Condi Rice said it yesterday," the beleaguered spokesman replied. "Go back to the interview. The president made it very clear that what occurred was wrong."

"There's a distinction, Scott," a female journalist interjected.

A second woman, April Ryan of Urban Radio Networks, added, "Shouldn't an apology be at the president's forethought, not you saying it?"

McClellan ignored Ryan, but the demands for a presidential apology only mounted. Reporters concluded that Bush needed to be brought down another peg or two before he would capitulate to their demands. So the *Washington Post*, which had been chronicling the scandal with particular glee, threw gasoline on the fire the next morning by publishing a brand-new batch of Abu Ghraib photos. The top of the newspaper's front page featured a snapshot of an Army private named Lynndie England holding the end of a leash tied around the neck of a naked Iraqi man lying on the floor. The image was every bit as repulsive as the infamous photo of the hooded prisoner on the box.

"These pictures shred the last good reason to feel righteous about having gone to war," wrote Nancy Gibbs in *Time* magazine.

Newsweek's Fareed Zakaria, a regular panelist on ABC's *This Week* with former Clinton aide George Stephanopoulos, went even further. "Whether he wins or loses in November, George W. Bush's legacy is now clear: the creation of a poisonous atmosphere of anti-Americanism around the globe. I'm sure he takes full responsibility."

Karl Rove recognized that Abu Ghraib, in addition to being a disgrace, was a certifiable political disaster for the president's fledgling campaign against John Kerry.

"Yeah, it damaged us," Rove confided to me. "It clearly energized the anti-war elements, who said America's now been damaged in the eyes of the world. It emboldened the Michael Moores and the Howard Deans of the world. It put us on the defensive and it occupied space."

Bush campaign manager Ken Mehlman agreed.

"That was an unpleasant period of the campaign," he told me. "But I did not wake up at night saying, 'Oh God, we're gonna lose because of Abu Ghraib.' You can't worry about it, so you figure out the most intelligent way to deal with it. I don't know if it's a blessing or a weakness, and I don't know where I get it from, but I am very good at not worrying about things I can't control. That's just not who I am. I worried a lot about things I could control."

By May 7, Bush knew he was licked. He appeared in the Rose Garden with King Abdullah of Jordan and announced that he had personally apologized to the monarch, who was held out as a representative of the Arab world.

"I told him I was sorry for the humiliation suffered by the Iraqi prisoners, and the humiliation suffered by their families," the president said. "I assured him Americans like me didn't appreciate what we saw, that it made us sick to our stomachs."

In that moment, Mary Mapes's triumph was complete. George W. Bush, the president with a stubborn aversion to apologies, had just announced on live television that he was indeed sorry for the Abu Ghraib prisoner abuse scandal. The victory made it somewhat easier for Mapes to ignore her critics, including her own father, who accused her of liberal bias.

"I'm really ashamed of what my daughter has become—she's a typical liberal," seventy-six-year-old Don Mapes told KVI radio in Seattle. "She went into journalism with an axe to grind, and that was to promote radical feminism."

In the Rose Garden, Bush went on to say he was sorry one last time. Only now he carefully turned the word against those who had overreacted to the photos.

"I was equally sorry that people who have been seeing those pictures didn't understand the true nature and heart of America," the president said. "I also made it clear to His Majesty that the troops we have in Iraq, who are there for security and peace and freedom, are the finest of the fine, fantastic United States citizens, who represent the very best qualities of America: courage, love of freedom, compassion, and decency."

This unabashed endorsement of the American military was not seconded by Democratic senator Edward Kennedy, who rose to the floor of the U.S. Senate on May 10 and thundered, "We now learn that Saddam's torture chambers reopened under new management—U.S. management!"

The other Democratic senator from Massachusetts piled on the next day.

"What has happened is not just something that a few privates or corporals or sergeants engaged in," Kerry told a gathering of campaign donors. "This is something that comes out of an attitude about the rights of prisoners of war. It's an attitude that comes out of America's overall arrogance in its policy that is alienating countries all around the world."

The terrorists in Iraq couldn't have agreed more. That same day, they released a videotape titled "Sheikh Abu Musab al-Zarqawi Slaughters an

American Infidel with His Own Hands." The grainy tape showed al-Zarqawi, a senior al Qaeda leader who ran the Iraq insurgency on behalf of Osama bin Laden, denouncing U.S. troops for their "satanic degradation" of prisoners at Abu Ghraib. Standing with four other armed, hooded men, al-Zarqawi railed against the "shameful photos" that Mapes had succeeded in disseminating throughout the world. He pulled out a large knife as an American captive was shoved to the floor. Nicholas Berg, a twenty-six-year-old contractor from West Chester, Pennsylvania, who had gone to Iraq seeking work, now screamed for his very life. But al-Zarqawi proceeded to personally saw off Berg's head, which was then held up for the camera as four other terrorists shouted "Allah is great!" Sure enough, just as the Pentagon had warned, broadcast of the Abu Ghraib photos led to the execution of a civilian hostage.

Amazingly, this did not shame the American Left into ratcheting down its hysterical ranting over Abu Ghraib. Untroubled by their own role in stoking anti-Americanism, Democrats and journalists continued to blithely equate the amateurish antics of a handful of GIs with the murderous atrocities of al-Zarqawi and Saddam. It didn't seem to bother liberals that the epicenter of Saddam's blood-soaked reign of terror was the same prison they were now turning into a symbol of American disgrace.

Yes, GIs had pretended to wire up a prisoner for electrocution at Abu Ghraib. But Saddam's henchmen had actually carried out such gruesome electrocutions there. Yes, GIs had put a dog leash on a prisoner and snapped a photo. But Saddam's henchmen had actually turned attack dogs loose on innocent Iraqis and rolled videotape as the victims were killed and eaten by the ravenous animals. Yes, GIs had stripped prisoners naked and forced them to simulate sex acts. But Saddam's henchmen had actually forced prisoners to watch as they raped and murdered their wives and daughters. Yes, GIs had sat on top of prisoners and forced them to build human pyramids. But Saddam's henchmen had savagely beaten, whipped, and dismembered countless innocents.

In fact, while the Left was rubbing America's nose in the Abu Ghraib photos, it was ignoring a far more compelling story out of the same prison that would have illustrated the compassion and generosity of the American spirit. Seven Iraqi men whose right hands had been brutally hacked off by Saddam's butchers in Abu Ghraib were flown to Houston and fitted with prosthetic hands. The operations were performed just as Mapes was securing the photos of GIs at Abu Ghraib. In fact, while Mapes was reveling in those repugnant photos and their potential to harm the president, an American filmmaker named Don North was making a documentary about American citizens opening their hearts and wallets to help the seven amputees. Several of the victims insisted that North's film incorporate video footage, shot by Saddam's thugs, of the men's wrists being crudely severed.

That footage, which illustrated the true evil of Abu Ghraib, was widely available to the American press. But journalists refused to broadcast it. They were too consumed with their orgiastic flagellation of U.S. troops and the commander in chief. Night after night, the Abu Ghraib prisoner abuse scandal led all the major television news broadcasts. Day after day, it was splashed across the front pages of America's most influential newspapers. The *Washington Post* was positively giddy over the debacle, giving it front-page treatment every day for weeks on end.

"It's turned into quite a whirlwind," Mapes exulted to the *Dallas Morning News*. "I've never had a story that reverberated like this."

She said she was particularly "fascinated" by the role that technology had played in exposing the scandal.

"The latest in digital equipment was used at Abu Ghraib to record old-fashioned cruelty," she marveled in her memoir. "Digital cameras, computers, the Internet, and other new technology have altered any country's ability to keep dirty little secrets."

The American public, while repulsed by the behavior of the GIs, was even more repulsed by the excessive press coverage, not to mention the obvious bias. In case there was any doubt about the ideology of journalists wallowing in the scandal, the Pew Research Center released a poll on May 23 that showed self-identified liberals in the national press outnumbering conservatives by a staggering ratio of five to one. That same day, CBS News completed a poll that

showed Americans, by a whopping ten to one margin, felt the press was spending "too much" time on the Abu Ghraib scandal. Yet when it came time for
Dan Rather to report on his own poll, he refused to mention this important
finding. Instead, he zeroed in on another statistic.

"With the election just over five months away, President Bush is trying to
stop his major slide in the polls before it's too late," Rather trumpeted at the
top of the CBS *Evening News* on May 24. "A CBS News poll out tonight finds
his job approval rating at an all-time low of 41 percent. And Democratic chal-
lenger John Kerry has now opened an eight-point lead among registered voters. One big reason for the Bush slide: a growing perception that Iraq is out of
control and headed in the wrong direction with faulty planning and strategy."

As if that "perception" had nothing to do with the media's slanted coverage of events. Undaunted, Bush welcomed the seven Iraqi amputees and their
American benefactors into the Oval Office the next day for an emotional
meeting. He would later tell *Paris Match* magazine that the event was "a great
moment in my presidency."

"These were merchants in Baghdad," he explained. "And the currency in
Iraq had begun to devalue, and Saddam Hussein needed a scapegoat. And so
he chose these merchants, who he claimed were manipulating the currency,
and he had their hands cut off for doing so. And then they had an X carved
in their foreheads.

"An American filmmaker made a documentary of this, reminding people
of the brutality of Saddam Hussein, how he just would whimsically torture or
maim people. And a guy in Houston, a man in Houston who works in the television business, has a foundation, saw the documentary, put the money up
and flew these seven men to give them new hands—the latest technologies.

"And they came to the Oval Office to see me. It was an incredibly touch-
ing moment. They were so grateful to the United States and the free world
for liberating their country from Saddam Hussein, and incredibly grateful to
the generosity of these individual Americans who decided to do something
about their plight."

At the end of the meeting, the White House press corps was ushered into the Oval Office. A clearly moved Bush reached over and grasped the prosthetic hand of one of the amputees.

"I'm honored to shake the hand of a brave Iraqi citizen who had his hand cut off by Saddam Hussein. I'm with six other Iraqi citizens, as well, who suffered the same fate. They are examples of the brutality of the tyrant.

"These men had hands restored because of the generosity and love of an American citizen," he added. "And I am so proud to welcome them to the Oval Office."

Bush then invited questions from the press corps. But none of the reporters displayed the slightest interest in the incredible story of these brave Iraqis and compassionate Americans assembled right in front of them in the Oval Office. Instead, the very first reporter asked Bush yet another question about "the prisoner abuse scandal."

No wonder Mary Mapes was triumphant.

CHAPTER FOUR

PELOTON ONE

P resident Bush catapulted over the handlebars of his mountain bike, somersaulting high into the air before landing flat on his back in the Texas dirt. In the next instant, the bicycle came crashing down on top of him, having completed its own somersault after his right foot got caught in the pedal strap. The leader of the free world lay motionless on the side of a steep, rocky hill, not far from a precipitous drop-off. His $3,100 carbon-fiber bike—now missing a reflector that had snapped off in the crash—was splayed across his sweat-soaked body. Blood oozed from a cut on his knee, as if to mock the fifty-eight-year-old for thinking he could protect his knees— which had been battered by decades of high-impact running—by taking up the sport of mountain biking.

Well, at least there were no news cameras to capture this moment of max-imum presidential ignominy. As Bush was painfully aware, virtually the entire media universe was 1,600 miles away, breathlessly covering the opening day of the Democratic National Convention in Boston. That made it pointless for the president to continue stumping for reelection, so he had retreated to his beloved Prairie Chapel Ranch to wait out the Democratic extravaganza, which would last four days and culminate with John Kerry formally accepting his party's nomination.

Bush decided to spend July 26, the first day of the convention, mountain biking across his sprawling property in Crawford, Texas. He had taken up the sport five months earlier, after being forced to abandon his true passion, running. Oh, how he used to relish getting up early and sprinting across his ranch just as dawn was breaking. Or sometimes he would perversely wait until midday, when the summer sun was at its cruelest, before setting out across the dusty flatlands at top speed. He would haul ass for three miles, often finishing in under twenty-one minutes, which was an astonishing physical feat for a man in his late fifties, especially when the temperature was well over one hundred degrees. Joined by a bevy of Secret Service agents and the ubiquitous military aide who carried the nuclear "football" containing the codes Bush would need to launch a nuclear attack, the president called his little entourage the "100 Degree Club." More than one Secret Service agent in the prime of youth collapsed while trying to keep up with the much older president. Bush once invited a young, physically fit reporter, Scott Lindlaw of the Associated Press, to accompany him on a friendly run across Prairie Chapel Ranch. But Lindlaw fell so far behind that he was eventually passed even by the Secret Service golf carts that trailed Bush at a respectful distance. After sucking in the dust from these vehicles as they disappeared over the horizon, Lindlaw found himself utterly alone on a trail that wound through a patch of woods. At length he came to a fork in the trail and, seeing no sign of the running party down either tine, realized he was hopelessly lost on the president's property. News of the reporter's bewilderment had tickled Bush, a fiercely competitive man who routinely subjected himself to adversarial public questioning by Lindlaw and his ilk. But the president also felt a little sorry for the high-spirited reporter, so he decided to let Lindlaw redeem himself by tagging along on today's bike ride. And now the moment of redemption was at hand. Bush was flat on his back and Lindlaw was safely perched on his bike.

Truth be told, the president was still a beginner at mountain biking. By contrast, he had spent a third of a century running. The daily punishment had gradually taken its toll on his right knee, as doctors discovered when they took X-rays and magnetic resonance images in December 2003. They offered to surgically repair the damaged cartilage and eventually install an artificial knee. But Bush was not about to be taken out of commission for God knows how long by an operation that might leave him gimping through his entire reelection campaign—the precise period when he should be projecting an image of vigor and stamina. Besides, the surgery would require him to be heavily anesthetized, raising the possibility of temporarily transferring power to the vice president under the Twenty-fifth Amendment. The press would have a field day with that one. Bush could only imagine the snarky insinuations about him finally making it official by ceding authority to Cheney. So he resolved to find other ways to exercise. He tried one of those elliptical training machines that felt like a cross between running and bicycling. Although it gave him a low-impact workout, it deprived him of the sheer joy he had derived from exercising in the great outdoors. He also tried swimming, since he had a pool right outside the Oval Office and another one outside his ranch house. The latter he had dubbed the "Whine Pool" in honor of his twin daughters, Barbara and Jenna, who had whined that they urgently needed the pool, only to lose interest once it had been built. Alas, even the president lost interest in the pool when he realized he could not enjoy the expansiveness of his property from the confines of a rectangular pit of water.

And so in February 2004, Bush switched to biking, which allowed him to enjoy his sprawling ranch without further damaging his knees. But instead of buying a road bike that was meant for traveling on paved surfaces, Bush opted for a mountain bike with knobby tires that was designed for more rugged terrain. A Washington bike shop put together a high-end model known as a Trek Fuel 98 that boasted a handmade frame and a suspension system that absorbed the shocks of rough trails. Bush soon discovered that the only thing more exhilarating than plunging down a rocky ravine at thirty-five miles per hour was huffing and puffing his way up an equally steep incline on the other end at nine miles per hour. He rode with reckless abandon for ninety minutes at a stretch, which brought his heart rate up to more than 170 beats per minute. With these health benefits, however, came the constant danger of injury. Although Bush wore a helmet and mouth guard, he soon discovered that mountain biking was far more hazardous than running, swimming, or using an elliptical machine.

On May 22, for example, when Bush was in the sixteenth mile of a seventeen-mile ride, his tires slipped out from under him as he descended a steep slope of loose soil. He pitched headfirst into the dirt, scraping his chin, nose, upper lip, right hand, and, of course, both knees. The wounds were cleaned by White House physician Richard Tubb, who suggested the president be driven back to his house in a four-wheeled vehicle. But Bush refused, reasoning that such spills were part and parcel of the sport of mountain biking. Cuts, bruises, abrasions, and the occasional broken bone were badges of honor among the daredevils who pushed themselves and their bikes to the limits on terrain most people would find unsuitable even for hiking. Indeed, that same week, one of Bush's Secret Service agents broke three ribs and a collarbone during a bike ride with the president. It was the sort of spectacular wipeout that these mountain bikers would probably recall with relish in the years ahead. So no, Bush was not about to ride home in the back of a golf cart. He climbed back on his mountain bike and pedaled the final mile.

Besides, such minor injuries to the president's body paled in comparison to the political slings and arrows he was absorbing on an almost daily basis. Republican senator John McCain was being his usual unhelpful self, openly chiding the Bush campaign for trying to portray Kerry as weak on defense. The Democrat had a long history of voting against defense expenditures, which the president figured was fair game for a flurry of attack ads. But McCain disapproved.

"No, I do not believe that he is, quote, weak on defense," the Republican said of Kerry on NBC's *Today Show*. "I don't agree with him on some issues, clearly. But I decry this negativism that's going on—on both sides."

Undaunted, Vice President Cheney continued to hammer Kerry for numerous votes against military expenditures.

"The senator from Massachusetts has given us ample doubts about his judgment and the attitude he brings to bear on vital issues of national security," Cheney said in a speech.

Again, McCain rose to Kerry's defense. When asked on CBS's *Early Show* whether Kerry's election would compromise national security, McCain replied, "I don't think that. I think that John Kerry is a good and decent man. I think he has served his country."

McCain, who had mused back in March that he would "entertain" the possibility of becoming Kerry's running mate, had spent the ensuing four months being openly courted by Democrats and journalists alike. Although the spectacle was a distraction to Bush, it also didn't say much for the depth of the Democrats' bench.

"Democrats are so eager to regain the White House in November that they are willing to overlook members of their own party, and to accept a candidate who disagrees with one of the core tenets of their platform, the right to an abortion," the *New York Times* reported on its front page on May 15.

"Senator McCain would not have to leave his party," former Democratic senator Bob Kerrey of Nebraska told the paper. "He could remain a Republican, would be given some authority over selection of cabinet people. The only thing he would have to do is say, 'I'm not going to appoint any judges who would overturn *Roe v. Wade.*'"

McCain kept insisting he had no interest in the job, but that didn't stop the media from salivating. Two days later, he was practically begged to reconsider on *Meet the Press*.

"Senator McCain, as an American, you can stay a Republican—you can be a loyal Republican," pleaded NBC's Tim Russert, who previously worked for two New York Democrats, Governor Mario Cuomo and Senator Daniel Patrick Moynihan. "It would be a fusion or a unity ticket. Would you contemplate it in any way, shape, or form? Would you take Senator Kerry's phone call if you knew he was calling about it?"

The following week, Dan Rather got into the act.

"Belief appears to be growing that the Democratic dream team—and President Bush's nightmare—would be Kerry and Republican senator John McCain," Rather said with glee. "Look at this: the latest CBS News poll indicates Kerry with an eight-point lead over President Bush. With McCain on a Kerry ticket, the lead grows to fourteen."

This tantalizing possibility was not lost on Kerry, who met repeatedly with McCain to find out if he was interested in the vice presidential spot. Kerry even tried to sweeten the pot by promising McCain plenty of sway over defense issues. The courtship dragged on for months, but in the end, McCain begged off, forcing Kerry to resort to his second choice—a Democrat.

On July 6, Kerry tapped North Carolina senator John Edwards to be his running mate. Jay Leno of NBC's *Tonight Show* cracked, "John Kerry said 'I can't tell you how proud I am to have John Edwards on my team, especially after John McCain turned me down.'"

The press, however, downplayed the fact that Edwards was the second choice and focused instead on his upbeat persona and flashy smile. Journalists fawningly repeated Kerry's boast that he and Edwards had "better hair" than the Republican ticket. Meanwhile, the press barely mentioned Edwards's voting record in the Senate, which was ranked the fourth most liberal by the nonpartisan *National Journal* magazine (Kerry's was first). Such adulation was quite a contrast from four years earlier, when journalists had railed against Bush for selecting Cheney, whom they branded a rigid conservative with a jarringly right-wing voting record.

The day after the Edwards selection, Bush was asked to weigh in.

"He's being described today as charming, engaging, a nimble campaigner, a populist, and even sexy," a reporter gushed. "How does he stack up against Dick Cheney?"

"Dick Cheney can be president," Bush snapped before turning to another journalist. "Next."

It didn't take long for the Kerry-Edwards team to stumble. On July 8, the Democrats appeared at a fund-raiser at Radio City Music Hall in midtown

Manhattan, giving their stamp of approval to celebrities who savaged Bush with vulgar and vitriolic diatribes.

Singer John Mellencamp called the president a "cheap thug that sacrifices young lives" and "made this world unsafe."

Actor and comic Chevy Chase declared that Bush had invaded Iraq "just so he could be called a wartime president."

"The president's a liar," he said, drawing whoops and cheers from the glitterati. "I don't trust him, I don't like him, and I think he's venal. I'm frightened by Bush, if you want to know the truth," he added. "This guy's as bright as an egg timer."

Actress Meryl Streep managed to simultaneously denigrate the president's Christianity as well as U.S. soldiers who had launched the opening salvo in Operation Iraqi Freedom.

"I wondered to myself during 'Shock and Awe,' I wondered which of the megaton bombs Jesus, our president's personal savior, would have personally dropped on the sleeping families of Baghdad?"

Actress Jessica Lange called the Bush administration "a self-serving regime of deceit, hypocrisy, and belligerence." This was in keeping with her 2002 criticism of Bush to an audience in Spain. "I despise him," she spat. "I despise his administration and everything they stand for." She added, "It is an embarrassing time to be an American. It really is. It's humiliating."

All the while, comic Whoopi Goldberg roamed the stage, swilling wine from a bottle and making vulgar double entendres about female genitalia and the president's last name.

At the end of what Kerry called this "extraordinary evening," he and Edwards took the stage to thank the audience for contributing $7.5 million and to praise the celebrities for bashing Bush.

"Every performer tonight, in their own way—either verbally, through their music, through their lyrics—have conveyed to you the heart and soul of our country," Kerry said.

The mainstream media, which was present, virtually ignored Kerry's overt endorsement of the hatefest. In fact, the story might never have come to the public's attention if not for reporter Deborah Orrin, who described the spectacle in an article published by the *New York Post*. The Bush campaign pounced.

"Do most Americans in their hearts, think that calling the president a 'thug' and a 'killer' represents the 'heart and soul' of our nation?" wrote Bush campaign manager Ken Mehlman in an open letter to Kerry campaign manager Mary Beth Cahill. "We don't think so."

Bush quickly incorporated the episode into his campaign speech in order to highlight the values gulf between Kerry and himself.

"The other day my opponent said that a bunch of entertainers from Hollywood conveyed the heart and soul of America," Bush told a rally in Waukesha, Wisconsin.

"Booo!" cried the audience.

"No, I believe the heart and soul of America is found in places in Wisconsin, in places just like Waukesha," he added, drawing applause. "Our nation is strong because of the values we try to live by: courage, compassion, reverence, and integrity."

Such quaint presidential pronouncements were largely ignored by the press, which was busy promoting yet another anti-Bush screed from Hollywood—*Fahrenheit 9/11*. This propaganda film by certified Bush-hater Michael Moore actually portrayed Iraq under Saddam as an idyllic paradise, epitomized by scenes of children blissfully flying kites and a happy couple exchanging wedding vows. Moore then cut to shots of U.S. bombs exploding in Baghdad, creating the false impression that GIs were targeting civilians and not military installations. These and other egregious misrepresentations were explained away by the mainstream media as courageous expressions of free speech. In fact, the press lavished so much favorable publicity on *Fahrenheit 9/11* that it made more money than any other documentary in history. Unimpressed, Republicans coined a new word to describe the film—"crockumentary."

Besides, conservatives had their own film to rally around—*The Passion of the Christ*. Directed and produced by Mel Gibson, the film portrayed the suffering and crucifixion of Jesus with graphic realism. Liberals tried to discredit the film by suggesting it was anti-Semitic, but audiences flocked to theaters, making *Passion* more than three times as successful as *Fahrenheit*. Churches organized outings for large segments of their congregations, collecting the e-mail addresses of all parishioners who saw the film. Evangelical groups gathered these addresses by the millions, creating a database with significant political potential. The database was utilized by groups like "Redeem the Vote," the Christian answer to MTV's secular "Rock the Vote." The group persuaded actor Jim Caviezel, who portrayed Jesus in *The Passion of the Christ*, to record a webcast aimed at preventing a rerun of 2000, when four million evangelicals opted not to vote in the presidential election. While Caviezel did not explicitly endorse the president, he implicitly reminded Christians that Bush shared their opposition to abortion, judicial activism, and homosexual marriage.

"In this election year, Americans are faced with some of the most important issues in the history of our country," he said. "In order to preserve the God-given freedoms we each hold dear, it's important that we let our voices be heard."

Indeed, all through the long, hot summer of 2004, the culture wars raged on across the red and blue states, often downplayed by the candidates, who focused more on issues of national and economic security. The threat of state judiciaries imposing gay marriage alarmed social conservatives, as did a federal court ban on the Pledge of Allegiance in public schools because it contained the phrase "under God." Although the ruling was reversed by the U.S. Supreme Court on June 14, the threat of judicial activism disturbed red-state Republicans. At the same time, several Catholic bishops announced that they would refuse to give Communion to John Kerry, a Catholic, because he supported abortion, including partial-birth abortion. Most Americans, including Democrats, opposed partial-birth abortion, placing Kerry once again on the wrong side of the cultural divide.

But such thoughts were little comfort to Bush as he lay flat on his back in the Texas dirt. And to think he had come to the ranch to relax and forget about the rigors of the campaign trail. So far, about the only relaxation he had managed to squeeze into his schedule consisted of finishing two books he had been reading—a military history called *Washington's Crossing* and an intellectual thriller titled *The Rule of Four*. In addition, Bush had watched some television coverage of Lance Armstrong winning his sixth consecutive Tour de France. The president was friendly with Armstrong, despite his fellow Texan's opposition to the Iraq war. Bush admired the way Armstrong, a thirty-two-year-old cancer survivor, utterly dominated his younger competitors in winning the Tour an unprecedented six times in a row. The president also liked how the scrum of bicyclists hurtling along country roads was called the *peloton*, French for a tightly bunched group of athletes. He had begun using the term "Peloton One" to describe the little knot of mountain bikers who trekked across Prairie Chapel Ranch. He figured it was a natural extension of Air Force One and Marine One, his other primary modes of transportation. Ironically, while Bush was taking delight in tossing around French words, Kerry was taking heat from conservatives for parroting France's complaints about the war in Iraq.

Aside from cheering on Armstrong and finishing his books, Bush was spending most of his time in Crawford the same way he spent it back in Washington—entirely consumed with presidential duties. All morning, for example, he had met with advisers to discuss how to implement the recommendations of the 9-11 Commission. He then did some brainstorming about his newest batch of campaign ads with Mark McKinnon, the Bush team's advertising guru. Later in the day, National Security Adviser Condoleezza Rice would be arriving for her own batch of meetings with the president. It was a small miracle that he had time for the bike ride, a blessed ninety-minute reprieve.

The ride had started uneventfully. When Lindlaw showed up at the appointed time, Bush was fiddling with a fishing rod that he often used in the man-made lake just outside his house. He set aside the rod, straddled his mountain bike, and began leading Peloton One to the farthest corners of his ranch. There was only one rule on this journey—do not pass the president. Bush wanted to be in the point position as he indulged in one of his favorite pastimes—showing off his ruggedly beautiful property. He led the group past a modest stone-and-glass office building that was under construction, nearly completed. He mentioned that he planned to practice his second inaugural address in the 2,500-square-foot structure, but then corrected this Freudian slip by saying he would actually be practicing the acceptance speech he planned to deliver at the Republican National Convention in five weeks. At one point he traversed a fifty-acre swath of freshly turned earth, explaining that it was where First Lady Laura Bush was cultivating blue-stemmed flowers for wider distribution throughout the property. At another point, he dodged dung on a trail that cut through a meadow of supremely unimpressed cows.

Soon Bush was biking with reckless abandon, attacking hills with a vengeance and grunting audibly as he scaled steep inclines. The Secret Service agents puffed along behind him, their pistols clearly visible beneath their shirts. Lindlaw kept trying to ask Bush political questions, but the president kept deflecting them, reminding him that this was supposed to be a nonpolitical outing. Perhaps to silence the reporter, Bush announced that they were about to encounter a sharp left turn and then a steep drop-off.

"I'm gonna show you a hill that would choke a mule," he boasted with a grin.

With that, he plunged down an incline of loose rocks that proved treacherous under the bike's knobby tires. Bush pumped the brakes, but was unable to control his front tire as it lurched into a nosedive. That's when he started to sail over the handlebars. He managed to quickly free one of his feet from the pedal straps, but the other was hopelessly entangled. In the next moment the rear tire was rocketing skyward and the president was flat on his back, visibly shaken.

Bush wondered how this would be portrayed in the press. Reporters had had a field day back in 2002, when he had choked on a pretzel and passed out while watching a football game alone in the White House residence. On the way to the floor, his face had smacked into a coffee table, causing his eyeglasses to cut into his skin. Afterward, during a flight aboard Air Force One, he had sent a bag of pretzels back to the press cabin, with a note admonishing, "Chew slowly." Then, in 2003, the president awkwardly fell from a Segway motorized scooter at his parents' home in Kennebunkport, Maine. Bush had been horsing around with a tennis racket and trying to ride the scooter at the same time. Photos of the falling president appeared on the Internet almost instantaneously, prompting alarm among Secret Service officials that someone had breached the perimeter of the waterfront compound, known as Walker's Point. But it turned out that the press photographers were simply using extremely powerful lenses from a great distance. They had been watching Bush the whole time, waiting for just such a moment. Why hadn't any photographers been on hand when Kerry took a tumble while snowboarding down a mountain in Idaho back in February? When a reporter asked Kerry about falling down, he blamed it on his Secret Service agent, with whom he had collided. "I don't fall down," Kerry snapped. "The son of a bitch knocked me over!" Bush knew that if he ever cursed out his own Secret Service agent, a man who had pledged to take a bullet for him, the press would go apoplectic. Yet Kerry's mean-spirited comment had been buried by the mainstream media. It was almost as if the press were rooting for Kerry to win.

In fact, *Newsweek* assistant managing editor Evan Thomas, a card-carrying member of the mainstream media, came right out and admitted as much.

"Let's talk a little media bias here," he said on the TV show *Inside Washington* on July 10. "The media, I think, wants Kerry to win. And I think they're going to portray Kerry and Edwards—I'm talking about the establishment media, not FOX, but—they're going to portray Kerry and Edwards as being young and dynamic and optimistic and all. There's going to be this glow about them."

He added matter-of-factly, "That's going to be worth maybe fifteen points."

Certainly Thomas was doing his part. That very week, he penned a fawning article about Kerry picking Edwards. "In politics, self-made men seem to fall into two categories: sunny and dark," he wrote in *Newsweek*. "Dick Cheney projects the bleakness of a Wyoming winter, while John Edwards always appears to be strolling in the Carolina sunshine."

Such puff pieces were not the only manifestation of the media's bias. News organizations also reflexively defended the Kerry campaign whenever it stepped into trouble, even going so far as to suggest, without a shred of proof, that those troubles had been mysteriously orchestrated by Bush officials and their dirty tricks.

On July 19, a story broke that should have caused a major scandal for Kerry. Sandy Berger, a senior adviser to Kerry and candidate for secretary of state if the Democrat won, admitted through his lawyer that he had illegally removed highly classified documents about terrorism from the National Archives in Washington. The FBI was conducting a criminal investigation and had already searched the home and office of Berger, who had served as national security adviser under Bill Clinton. It turned out that Clinton had dispatched Berger to the Archives in fall 2003 to review potentially troublesome documents that might come up when the 9-11 Commission questioned Clinton administration officials. Berger walked into a high-security document viewing room and stuffed classified papers into his briefcase and the pockets of his pants and jacket. The theft was noticed by Archives employees, who set up a sting operation for Berger's next visit. They put special marks on documents that he perused and, sure enough, some of those documents turned up missing when Berger departed. The papers were drafts of a critique of the Clinton administration's handling of terrorist threats during celebrations marking the turn of the millennium. The critique had been written by former White House counterterrorism chief Richard Clarke, now famous for skewering Bush in a book and in testimony before the 9-11 Commission. Clarke had penned a "tough review" of the Clinton administration's shortcomings in dealing with the terrorist threat, Clarke's lawyer told the *Washington Post*.

The story had all the makings of a major scandal. A former president's top national security aide purloined classified documents that might prove embarrassing in the hands of the 9-11 Commission. The purloiner was now an adviser to a presidential candidate, thereby raising the natural question of whether he was illegally passing secrets to the campaign. To top it all, the stolen critique was penned by the same man now being celebrated by the Left for slamming Bush's handling of September 11. The juxtaposition fairly dripped with hypocrisy. Any self-respecting investigative reporter would have been in high dudgeon. To be sure, if Condoleezza Rice had been caught stuffing her blouse and skirt with classified documents critical of her own administration's handling of terrorism, there would be demands for investigations on the scale of Watergate. Democrats and the press would be howling, "What did Bush know and when did he know it?" Some would even be calling for impeachment.

But because the probe was targeting a Democrat, the press was much more forgiving. Reporters accepted Berger's preposterous explanation at face value.

"I inadvertently took a few documents from the archives," he shrugged. "I deeply regret the sloppiness involved."

The next day, he added, "I made an honest mistake."

Naturally, this explanation was heartily endorsed by Clinton, the man who had sent Berger to the Archives in the first place. Clinton defended Berger while in Denver to sign copies of his autobiography, *My Life*, for which he was paid over $10 million, the largest advance ever for a nonfiction book.

"I believe his explanation," chuckled Clinton, who dismissed the flap as a "non-story." "We were all laughing about it on the way over here. People who don't know Sandy might find it hard to believe, but all of us who have been in his office have found him buried beneath papers."

The former president also insinuated that Bush officials had cynically leaked news of the investigation to distract attention from the findings of the 9-11 Commission, which were due a couple of days later.

"I wish I knew who leaked it," Clinton hinted. "It's interesting timing."

The press adopted the same defense strategy, portraying Berger as a lovable, absentminded slob, the target of Republican dirty tricks.

"In the Clinton White House," *Washington Post* reporter Susan Schmidt wrote in a front-page story on July 21, "he was known as someone who would constantly lose track of papers or appointments without subordinates to keep him organized and on schedule."

Schmidt went on to quote a former Clinton administration colleague as saying, "For those who know and love him, it's easy to see how this could happen."

Time magazine writer Joe Klein endearingly labeled Berger the "absentminded professor." "The notion that he would do something mortally sinful is about as likely as Brent Scowcroft or George Shultz or name your foreign policy priesthood member," Klein said on CNN's *Paula Zahn NOW*. "This is a very solid, decent guy. I'd be shocked if there was something really terrible that he did here."

Over at the *New York Times*, White House correspondent David Sanger used sarcasm to diminish the seriousness of the crime, writing archly, "Republican leaders have suggested a nefarious plot."

Nefarious or not, Kerry was sufficiently alarmed by the disclosure to fire Berger from his campaign, although he let the adviser publicly assert that he was voluntarily resigning. This only made the media more determined to defend Berger.

Dan Rather came right out and blamed Republicans, without a scintilla of proof, for disclosing the story. "This was triggered by a carefully orchestrated leak about Berger, and the timing of it appears to be no coincidence," he said on CBS's *Evening News*.

On ABC's *Good Morning America*, the bias was breathtaking. Host Charles Gibson solicited ostensibly objective analysis from George Stephanopoulos, host of ABC's *This Week*. Gibson didn't bother informing viewers that Stephanopoulos, a self-described liberal Democrat, used to work with Berger in the White House under Clinton.

"Is the timing of this leak suspicious?" Gibson asked.

"Every single Democrat I talked to raised this issue," Stephanopoulos said. "They say 'Come on, six days before the Democratic Convention, two days before the 9-11 Commission report, seven months after the investigation begins, we're only finding out about it now?' And some are even suggesting that maybe Attorney General John Ashcroft was behind it."

Again, no evidence connected Ashcroft or anyone else in the Bush administration to any disclosure of information about the Berger probe. Yet somehow, in the upside-down world of Washington, Bush ended up as the bad guy in the Berger burglary. Ironically, the president told me he never viewed the episode as a political issue in the campaign, although he confided that he was "surprised" by the serious breach of security.

None of these thoughts were far from Bush's mind as he lay motionless in the Texas dirt, still pinned by his own mountain bike. He knew, deep down in his bones, that Evan Thomas of *Newsweek* had spoken the truth. The press was openly pulling for Kerry-Edwards to beat Bush-Cheney. From the moment Kerry had chosen Edwards nearly three weeks ago, the Democratic ticket had been ahead in the polls. Kerry's lead would probably increase only further in the coming days, thanks to the "bounce" that most challengers enjoyed in the wake of their nominating convention. If that happened, Bush might as well stay flat on his back.

Just then, Lindlaw appeared over the president. He reached down and hoisted the Trek 98 off Bush's chest. A medic approached, but the president waved him off. He was shaken up, but insisted he could complete the ride. He stood up and straightened the bike's handlebars, which the crash had knocked out of alignment with the front wheel. He decided to leave the broken reflector where it lay as a cautionary marker for future journeys. Slinging one leg over the bike frame, Bush began rolling again, only this time more tentatively. He kept bouncing one foot off the ground to steady the bike as he completed the steep descent. But soon he was pedaling again for all he was worth, his back still covered with Texas dirt.

"We've got thrills, spills—you name it," he said to Lindlaw.

At this point the reporter could not resist needling Bush by describing a bike that was more than twice as expensive as the president's Trek 98. It was a custom-made Serotta Ottrott road bicycle that cost $8,000. With great relish, Lindlaw explained that this magnificent vehicle was owned by none other than John Kerry. Bush kept right on pedaling as he deadpanned his monosyllabic response.

"Who?"

CHAPTER FIVE

"More Balloons!"

W hile President Bush was flat on his back in Texas, John Kerry was down on all fours in Florida. Unlike Bush, however, Kerry was being photographed. And he just so happened to be wearing a baby blue "bunny suit"—complete with matching hood—that made him look, well, ridiculous. Grinning from a small opening in the hood that exposed his face, Kerry was crawling out of a circular hatch in the space shuttle *Discovery* during a tour of NASA's Kennedy Space Center in Cape Canaveral, Florida. Like all visitors to this sensitive piece of equipment, Kerry had donned the protective "bunny suit" to prevent him from contaminating any surfaces inside the spacecraft. The pajama-like outfit utterly enveloped the candidate's body below the neck. The hood covered his entire head, neck, chin, and cheeks, leaving just enough of an opening for Kerry's eyes, nose, and toothsome smile. Adding to the surrealism of the photo was a long, flexible air duct—a wider version of the sort found on clothes dryers—that seemed to trail Kerry out of the hatch. Those who saw the image were reminded of the old political maxim that warns candidates against being photographed in funny hats or unusual costumes. There were instant comparisons to another Massachusetts Democrat who dealt his presidential campaign a severe blow by striking an equally unfortunate pose—Michael Dukakis, who donned an ill-fitting helmet for his infamous tank ride in 1988. Now the press was wondering if Kerry had made the same blunder.

The *New York Times* said the photo "made him look like the sperm played by Woody Allen in *Everything You Always Wanted to Know about Sex but Were Afraid to Ask.*" The *Washington Post* advised: "As a general rule, anyone aspiring to be the commander in chief should always try to avoid looking like a Teletubby." Others said the candidate resembled an Oompa Loompa from the 1971 film *Willy Wonka & the Chocolate Factory*. Still others said he looked more like Ralphie Parker, the nine-year-old forced to don an effeminate bunny costume in the 1983 classic *A Christmas Story*.

The *New York Post* published the photo with the headline "Boston, we have a problem." The *Boston Herald* dubbed Kerry "Bubble Boy." The Bush campaign gleefully e-mailed side-by-side photos of Kerry and Dukakis to every political journalist in the universe. The Kerry campaign responded by firing off photos of Bush picking his nose, leading a cheer at Yale, and wearing ceremonial kimonos with Australian prime minister John Howard. But the focus remained on Kerry in the bunny suit, prompting his campaign to once again fall back on the old GOP-dirty-tricks defense.

"This is a leaked photo," wailed campaign manager Mary Beth Cahill to Brit Hume on FOX News Channel. "There was no press there. There was nothing. All of a sudden these photographs are out."

Hume pointed out that the photo was taken by NASA, which, he noted, is "not a particularly political organization." Indeed, NASA said it checked with the Kerry campaign before releasing the photo to the press. Yet Cahill refused to budge from her conspiracy theory.

"This is a legitimate tour of a NASA facility, and this photograph appeared out of nowhere—we were surprised," she said. "We're not surprised now."

"Do you smell a dirty trick here?" Hume asked.

"Well, what do you think?" Cahill shot back sardonically.

The bunny suit debacle was not the only episode to cast Kerry in a less-than-macho light just before the opening of the Democratic National Convention. On his flight to Florida, Kerry surprised the press by diverting the campaign plane to Boston in order to throw out the first pitch in a Yankees-Red Sox game at Fenway Park. The idea was to display a bit of spontaneity on the eve of the tightly scripted convention. But when Kerry took the field, he was booed by half the fans in his own hometown. The crowd grew even more unruly when Kerry opted not to ascend the pitcher's mound, preferring to throw from the grass in front of the mound to better his chances of getting the ball over the plate. Alas, even from that shortened distance, Kerry's pitch bounced forlornly into the dirt at home plate before ever reaching the catcher.

"I held back," he explained to reporters who asked about his feeble pitch. Blaming the catcher, Kerry added, "He was very nervous. I tried to lob it gently."

ESPN had a field day with Kerry's less-than-stellar pitching performance and was soon comparing it to the president's appearance in Game Three of the 2001 World Series. Just weeks after September 11, Bush showed up at Yankee Stadium wearing a bulletproof vest that restricted his arm movement. He had planned to throw from the grass, but was advised otherwise by shortstop Derek Jeter. "This is New York," the Yankee warned. "If you throw from the base of the mound, they're going to boo you." So Bush ascended the mound and fired a strike. The crowd exploded into chants of "USA! USA! USA!" Kerry, by contrast, was now being mocked for "throwing like a girl," an image that was reinforced hours later by the bunny suit debacle. These were not good omens for a candidate who constantly strove to appear macho by windsurfing, snowboarding, bicycling, and reminding people that he had served in Vietnam.

But at least his wife was showing signs of toughness. At about the same time that Kerry was pitching into the dirt, Teresa Heinz Kerry was telling a journalist at the convention to "shove it." It happened right after the billionaire ketchup heiress gave a high-minded speech calling for a more civil tone in politics.

"We need to turn back some of the creeping, un-Pennsylvanian, and sometimes un-American traits that are coming into some of our politics," she told fellow Pennsylvanians at the statehouse in Boston. "My prayers for you, for me, for the country, for the world, are that we keep this at a high level, with dignity, with respect, and with a great idealism and courage that took our forefathers to build this great nation."

Immediately after the speech, Teresa was approached by a journalist who politely asked her a question.

"You said something about 'un-American' activity," said Colin McNickle, editor of the *Pittsburgh Tribune-Review*'s editorial page. "What did you mean?"

"No, I didn't say that," Teresa replied as cameras recorded the exchange. "I did not say 'activity' or 'un-American.' Those were your words."

She stalked away, only to return moments later in a rage. As McNickle explained in *National Review*, "There was a point—when she came back at me—that I wondered if she would actually hit me. I think every journalist has experienced 'the look.' And she had 'THE LOOK.'"

Jabbing an accusing finger at the journalist, Teresa demanded, "Are you from the *Tribune-Review*?"

"Yes I am," McNickle said.

"Understandable," Teresa fairly spat. "You said something I didn't say—now *shove it!*"

It was a jarringly coarse and mean-spirited outburst from a woman who wanted to become the nation's First Lady, especially right after imploring an audience to keep the political discourse "at a high level, with dignity, with respect." Worse yet, she flatly denied saying "un-American" when in fact she had clearly said it. She refused to retract her false denial.

"Good for you," cheered New York senator Hillary Rodham Clinton. "You go, girl!"

Indeed, the Kerry campaign's spin machine went into overdrive to transform Teresa's boorishness into a virtue. The candidate championed his wife as someone who "speaks her mind." Kerry senior adviser Tad Devine expressed delight that Teresa "tells it like it is," a trait he called "enormously refreshing."

By the time Teresa gave her big speech on the second night of the convention, she had utterly transmogrified her appalling behavior into a noble badge of feminist self-empowerment.

"My name is Teresa Heinz Kerry and by now I hope it will come as no surprise that I have something to say," she declared, drawing rapturous applause in the convention hall. "My right to speak my mind, to have a voice, to be what some have called 'opinionated' is a right I deeply and profoundly cherish. And my only hope is that one day soon, women—who have all earned their right to their opinions—instead of being labeled opinionated, will be called smart and well-informed, just like men."

Born in Mozambique to Portuguese parents, Teresa spoke with an accent unfamiliar to American ears. She pronounced her name tuh-*DEH*-zuh and was fluent in five languages, all of which she showed off in her convention speech, much to the bafflement of American viewers.

"I would like to speak to you from my heart," she began before switching out of English. "*Y a todos los Hispanos y los Latinos* . . ."

Fair enough. President Bush often sprinkled Spanish phrases into his speeches to Hispanic American audiences as a welcoming gesture to the burgeoning minority. Teresa's use of Spanish got a big round of applause at the convention, although non-Spanish speakers had no idea what she had said.

". . . *a tous les Franco-Americain* . . ." she continued. Uh-oh. Sounded like French, which raised a few eyebrows, given France's opposition to Operation Iraqi Freedom. Still, there was polite applause from the party faithful.

". . . *a tutti Italiani* . . ." Good thing she had used the word *Italiani*, which signaled to the audience that she must be speaking Italian. Still, she was switching languages so often that it was hard to keep up. Tepid applause.

". . . *a toda a familia Portugesa e Brazileria* . . ." Hmmm. Must be Portuguese, although the audience seemed unsure. Could she be speaking Brazilian? Did such a language even exist? The applause was now perfunctory.

". . . and to all the continental Africans living in this country . . ." Whew! She was back in English. At least now the nation could understand what she was saying. And yet she kept making unfamiliar references to Africa, throwing around terms like the Higher Education Apartheid Act, the Sharpeville Riots, and Witwatersrand University. That last was where Teresa had gone to college before moving to America and marrying Henry John Heinz III, heir to the vast Heinz ketchup fortune. Her husband later became a Republican senator from Pennsylvania before dying in a plane crash in 1991, leaving his immense wealth to his widow. Four years later, Teresa married Kerry, whom she had met at an Earth Day event. And now she was extolling her husband's environmental credentials.

"With John Kerry as president, global climate change and other threats to the health of our planet will begin to be reversed," she said.

Teresa also suggested that the United States, under George W. Bush, had grown thoughtless, greedy, and immoral. She called for a return to an earlier era, when Americans still had high ideals.

"Americans believed that they could know all there is to know, build all there is to build, break down any barrier, tear down any wall," she rhapsodized. "We sent men to the moon. And when that was not far enough, we sent *Galileo* to Jupiter, we sent *Cassini* to Saturn, and Hubble to touch the very edges of the universe in the very dawn of time."

Post-speech analysis by pundits on FOX News Channel and CNN illustrated the enormous ideological gulf between the two networks. On FOX, commentator Fred Barnes told anchorman Brit Hume that Teresa had bombed.

"This was the first time that the spouse of a nominee—a presidential nominee—was a featured speaker at a convention, and I suspect it will be the last, given her performance," he said. "Brit, you used the word 'unusual.' What a euphemism. It was eccentric, it was bordering on the bizarre, it was different, and it was extremely self-indulgent."

FOX News Sunday host Chris Wallace added, "I have to say, by the end, I half expected her to break out into 'Don't Cry for Me, Argentina.'"

But over at CNN, the speech was a hit.

"I thought it went fantastic, frankly," gushed Nina Easton of the *Boston Globe*. "I thought she came off as the finest European actress, really. I mean, she was likable, she's gorgeous, she was kind of warm and earthy, and for people who don't know her—and this was your first introduction to her—I thought she did spectacular."

Anchorman Aaron Brown was particularly enthralled with Teresa's riff about being opinionated. "Boy, she handled that perfectly," he marveled.

But Brown's effusiveness was no match for the unabashed cheerleading of John Harwood of the *Wall Street Journal*.

"I'll tell you what else, Aaron," he began. "People talk about John Edwards being the sexiest politician in America. I think Teresa Heinz may be the sexiest spouse of a national candidate in my memory. She comes across pretty, strong, soulful—*tender* even, in a way."

Like the other speakers at the convention, Teresa had been ordered by her husband's handlers to refrain from overtly bashing the president. The Kerry campaign feared that runaway Bush hatred among liberal Democrats would turn off moderate swing voters. There was also a feeling that Kerry needed to sell himself instead of just railing against the president all the time. Indeed, many Democrats professed having little enthusiasm for Kerry, whom they regarded as an almost generic candidate who played the role of "anybody but Bush." The last candidate to truly inspire Democrats had been Howard Dean, who imploded in the primaries with his "I Have a Scream" rant. Now many Democrats felt stuck with Kerry, a man who lacked Dean's visceral, if misguided, passion. So the word went out to Democrats at the convention to stop talking down the president and start talking up Kerry.

The Democrats were overcompensating for their long summer of Bush-bashing by unilaterally declaring a cease-fire. Their hesitation at this crucial moment in the campaign was ruthlessly exploited by Republicans, who showed up in Boston to ruin the party by staging a sort of shadow convention. The Bush campaign aggressively booked surrogates on cable news channels for hundreds of individual segments. These networks were happy to inject a little conflict into their coverage of the convention, which reporters were already deriding as a bland, predictable infomercial. The networks were particularly receptive to Republicans during the daytime hours because there wasn't much else to cover until the evening, when the big-name Democrats gave their prime-time speeches. The Bush team's aggressiveness, combined with the Kerry team's self-imposed gag rule, played a significant role in America's view of the Democratic National Convention.

So did the widespread expectation that Kerry, who had been ahead of Bush in the polls ever since choosing John Edwards as his running mate three weeks earlier, would get an additional bounce from the convention itself. Indeed, the Bush campaign's chief strategist, Matthew Dowd, was already citing historical trends that indicated Kerry would get a post-convention bounce that would put him a whopping fifteen points ahead of the president. Sure, Dowd was intentionally inflating expectations so that he could crow when Kerry fell short of the lofty prediction. But if even half of Dowd's prediction came true, Kerry would have a commanding lead of seven or eight points over the president just three months before the election.

Of course, that scenario depended on a successful rollout of Kerry on the fourth and final night of his convention. So Hollywood director Steven Spielberg was enlisted to put together a flattering film of the candidate, complete with inspirational narration by actor Morgan Freeman. Naturally, the nine-minute film, directed by Spielberg protégé James Moll, emphasized Kerry's service in Vietnam. It included footage that Kerry himself had shot on an 8 mm camera he kept with him in Vietnam. There was a staged shot of Kerry striding resolutely through the jungle, as if it would never occur to future viewers to question how such a scene came to be filmed in the first place. Kerry even returned to old battle sites in order to record footage for future campaigns, although he spent decades denying that was the intention.

"It is so innocent," he insisted to Bill Keller of the *New York Times* in 2002. "I have no intention of using it for campaign purposes."

Now that he was indeed using it for campaign purposes, it was hard to believe Kerry's insistence that he had not reenacted anything. Indeed, the *Boston Globe* reported in a fawning 1996 article that Kerry spent his time in Vietnam "so focused on his future ambitions that he would reenact the moment for film. It is as if he had cast himself in the sequel to the experience of his hero, John F. Kennedy, on the *PT-109*."

Since Kerry's footage did not contain scenes of actual battles as they unfolded, Moll decided to do some reenacting of his own. He staged shots of bullets firing into the water, which he interspersed with actual footage of Kerry's Swift Boat. The resulting artifice did the trick, putting the convention crowd in awe of John Kerry, Vietnam Hero. When Kerry finally took the stage, he was ready to clinch the sale.

"I'm John Kerry, and I'm reporting for duty," he began, snapping a well-rehearsed salute to the cameras.

It was Kerry's way of letting the nation know that his nomination acceptance speech would be, more than anything else, about Vietnam. In this, he did not disappoint.

"I am accompanied by an extraordinary band of brothers led by that American hero, a patriot called Max Cleland," he said.

Cleland, who had introduced Kerry for this speech, was a former Democratic senator from Georgia who had lost both legs and part of an arm in Vietnam. Kerry had been utilizing Cleland extensively throughout the campaign, portraying the triple amputee as the victim of GOP attacks on his patriotism in the 2002 election, which Cleland lost. Out for revenge, Cleland now regularly appeared with Kerry and a handful of other Vietnam veterans who supported the Democrat. Kerry had taken to calling them his "band of brothers," the title of a book on World War II by the late Stephen Ambrose, whose career had been tainted by a plagiarism scandal.

"Our band of brothers doesn't march together because of who we are as veterans, but because of what we learned as soldiers," Kerry said. "We fought for this nation because we loved it, and we came back with the deep belief that every day is extra. We may be a little older, we may be a little grayer, but we still know how to fight for our country."

Knowing that he was up against a hawkish, wartime commander in chief, Kerry was eager to demonstrate his own national security credentials and figured Vietnam was his best shot. So he laid it on pretty thick.

"I know what kids go through when they're carrying an M-16 in a dangerous place, and they can't tell friend from foe. I know what they go through when they're out on patrol at night and they don't know what's coming around the next bend. I know what it's like to write letters home telling your family that everything's all right, when you're not sure that that's true. As president, I will wage this war with the lessons I learned in war."

In case anyone missed the point, he added, "I defended this country as a young man, and I will defend it as president."

Kerry then railed against Republicans for "wrapping themselves in the flag," although he did so himself in the very next breath.

"You see that flag up there?" he asked, pointing to an enormous U.S. flag directly above him. "We call her Old Glory, the stars and stripes forever. I fought under that flag, as did so many of those people who were here tonight and all across the country. That flag flew from the gun turret right behind my head and it was shot through and through and tattered, but it never ceased to wave in the wind. It draped the caskets of men that I served with and friends I grew up with."

Warming to his theme, the sixty-year-old candidate suggested that his five months in Vietnam more than thirty-five years ago had been nothing less than the definitive experience of his life, the crucible in which his core values had been forged.

"I learned a lot about these values on that gunboat patrolling the Mekong Delta with Americans—you saw them—who come from places as different as Iowa and Oregon, Arkansas, Florida, California. No one cared where we went to school. No one cared about our race or our backgrounds. We were literally all in the same boat. We looked out, one for the other, and we still do."

In a strictly literal sense, Lieutenant Kerry had indeed been in the same Swift Boat as the nineteen-year-old grunts under his command. But in a socioeconomic sense, he wasn't even in the same ocean. Accordingly, for the purposes of this speech, which would be his formal introduction to millions of American voters, Kerry decided not to mention the elite boarding schools he attended in Switzerland and New England or the summer retreats in France and Cape Cod. Come to think of it, there was no need to mention

Morgan Fairchild or Catherine Oxenberg, the stunning, high-toned actresses he dated between his marriages to rich heiresses. No, the idea was to keep the focus on the regular Joes who had served in Vietnam and were now gutting it out in Iraq.

"For the brave men and women in uniform who risk their lives every day and the families who pray for their return," Kerry said, "I accept your nomination for president of the United States."

Actually, Kerry had flirted with the idea of not accepting the nomination at the convention. That's because he knew he would have to stop spending money from his primary campaign war chest the moment he became the general election nominee. From that point forward, he would be limited by federal law to spending just $75 million before Election Day. Bush had the same limitation but would not be accepting his own party's nomination until a full five weeks later, when the Republicans would gather for their convention in New York City. That meant the president had more than an extra month to spend freely from his primary campaign war chest. Belatedly it had dawned on Kerry that he would have to make his $75 million last ninety-four days, compared to a mere fifty-nine days for Bush. So Kerry publicly floated the notion of somehow deferring acceptance of his nomination for a month or more after the convention. Bush campaign officials had a field day with this trial balloon, which they said merely reinforced Kerry's image as a flip-flopper.

"Only John Kerry could be for a nominating convention, but be against the nomination," cracked Ken Mehlman, the president's campaign manager. "This is just the latest example of John Kerry's belief that the rules are for other people, not for him."

Such withering criticism eventually forced Kerry to abandon the idea, which he decided not to revisit at the convention. But he did feel compelled to respond to Republican accusations that he was indecisive, pessimistic, unpatriotic, and uncomfortable with religion.

"There are those who criticize me for seeing complexities—and I do—because some issues just aren't all that simple," Kerry told the convention.

"And I want to say this to you tonight: I don't wear my religion on my sleeve," he added. "But faith has given me values and hope to live by, from Vietnam to this day."

Having worked in yet another reference to Vietnam, Kerry proceeded to insist he was not the dour hand-wringer portrayed by Republicans all summer.

"They say this is the best economy that we've ever had and they say anyone who thinks otherwise is a pessimist. Well, here is our answer: there is nothing more pessimistic than saying that America can't do better. We can do better, and we will. We're the optimists. For us, this is a country of the future. We're the can-do people."

The leader of the can-do people then took maximum umbrage at the one criticism that stung most deeply.

"And tonight, we have an important message for those who question the patriotism of Americans who offer a better direction for our country," he said. "We are here to affirm that when Americans stand up and speak their minds and say America can do better, that is not a challenge to patriotism. It is the heart and soul of patriotism."

Having defended his patriotism, Kerry went on to accuse the president of forcing families "to take up a collection to buy body armor for a son or daughter in the service." And yet Kerry himself had voted against the president's $87 billion funding package for body armor and other equipment needed by troops in Iraq and Afghanistan.

It was not the only example of hypocrisy in Kerry's speech. He also invoked September 11, despite the fact that Democrats were already warning Bush not to exploit the attacks during his upcoming convention in New York. Indeed, after savaging the president for daring to include fleeting images of September 11 firefighters in early campaign ads, Kerry now invoked those same heroes for his own political ends.

"Remember the hours after September 11 when we came together as one to answer the attack against our homeland?" Kerry asked. "We drew strength when our firefighters ran up stairs and risked their lives so that others might live, when rescuers rushed into smoke and fire at the Pentagon, when the men and women of Flight 93 sacrificed themselves to save our nation's Capitol, when flags were hanging from front porches all across America, and strangers became friends. It was the worst day we have ever seen, but it brought out the best in all of us."

Having devoted the majority of his speech to his five months in Vietnam, Kerry barely mentioned his twenty years in the Senate. He briefly noted that he supported a balanced budget and a Clinton initiative to beef up police departments.

"I ask you to judge me by my record," he nonetheless implored, saving his favorite Senate accomplishment for last. "I reached out across the aisle with John McCain to work to find the truth about our POWs and missing in action and to finally make peace in Vietnam."

Amazingly, Kerry had managed to work yet another reference to Vietnam into the shortest segment of his speech—the part explaining how he had spent two decades in the Senate. He even squeezed in a reference to McCain, a bona fide Vietnam war hero who had been Kerry's first choice for vice president. In fact, there were so many Vietnam references that comic Jay Leno couldn't resist a playful jab.

"I learned an interesting little bit of trivia about John Kerry," he deadpanned. "Did you know he was once a soldier in Vietnam? Has that been mentioned before?"

I made a point of asking the president whether Kerry had blundered by making Vietnam the cornerstone of his entire campaign.

"I don't know if you'd call it 'blunder,'" Bush replied. "It didn't work."

Mercifully, Kerry opted against ending his speech with another Vietnam reference. Instead he rattled off a litany of gauzy platitudes.

"It is time to reach for the next dream. It is time to look to the next horizon. For America, the hope is there. The sun is rising. Our best days are still to come.

"Thank you," he concluded. "Good night. God bless you, and God bless the United States of America."

Kerry stepped away from the lectern, which automatically lowered and disappeared into the floor as the sound system began blaring the U2 song "Beautiful Day." The crowd cheered appreciatively as Kerry waved, snapped another salute, and raised a clenched fist. Recognizing someone in the audience, he bowed slightly and brought his hands together on his chest as if praying. He had been making this curious gesture of supplication—almost like an Asian bow—throughout the campaign.

Kerry kept repeating his repertoire of gestures as he wandered the stage, waiting for the convention's climactic finale—the balloon drop. One hundred thousand red, white, and blue balloons were supposed to cascade down from the rafters as the Democratic candidate waved triumphantly for the ultimate photo op. The idea was to be overwhelmed by the sheer number of balloons, a virtual rainstorm of rubber, until the delegates were hip-deep in the things. But a full ninety seconds after the end of Kerry's speech, not a single balloon had materialized.

"Go balloons! Go balloons! Go balloons! I don't see anything happening!" exclaimed a disembodied voice on CNN. It was convention producer Don Mischer frantically instructing his employees to drop the balloons from the rafters, where they were tethered in great tube-like nets that were supposed to be unfurled by pre-positioned ropes. CNN helpfully displayed Mischer's name on the screen so viewers could tell who was having the meltdown.

"Go balloons! Go balloons! Go balloons! Standby confetti. Keep coming, balloons. More balloons. Bring it—balloons, balloons, balloons! We want balloons, tons of them. Bring them down. Let them all come!"

A handful of balloons began drifting away from the ceiling, but most remained snug in their nets. It was ruining the big photo op, even as Kerry was now joined onstage by Edwards, who hugged his boss and began his own series of distinctive gestures. He would draw his fist close to his shoulder and then violently fling it upward and outward. In the split second it took for his arm to fully extend, Edwards's fist would morph into the classic thumbs-up pose. With an enormous grin on his face, he would then snap out his other arm with equal athleticism to give the crowd a double thumbs-up. If anyone had gotten in the way of those flinging, snapping arms, they would have been knocked out cold. Certainly any balloon would have been bounced a great distance. But the balloons were still tethered to the ceiling. To make matters worse, the confetti began to rain prematurely.

"No confetti! No confetti yet! No confetti!" Mischer hollered on live television as more precious time rolled by. In fact, a whopping three and a half minutes had elapsed since the end of Kerry's speech. The candidates' wives, Teresa and Elizabeth, came onstage for the balloon-less celebration. The delegates should have been bathing in balloons by now. Instead, a few strays descended lazily toward the floor.

"All right, go balloons, go balloons! We need more balloons! All balloons! All balloons! Keep going!"

By now, millions of CNN viewers across the nation and around the world could hear the unmistakable alarm rising in Mischer's voice. It was obvious he did not know his words were being broadcast on live television. More than four minutes had elapsed and the candidates' children were now onstage. This was the moment that Edwards's adorable toddlers should have been gleefully bouncing balloons into the audience.

"Come on, guys, let's move it—*Jesus*! We need more balloons. I want all balloons to go, God *damn* it! Go confetti. Go confetti. More confetti. I want more balloons. What's happening to the balloons? We need more balloons. We need *all* of them coming down. *Go balloons!*"

Mischer was positively beside himself. The balloon drop was considered enormously important in political circles and could even be viewed as a harbinger of a candidate's success. In 1980, President Jimmy Carter finished his convention speech and waited haplessly for a monsoon of balloons, but got only a trickle. It was later deemed an omen of Carter's doomed campaign. And now the same thing was happening here at the FleetCenter in Boston on live television! The stage was now teeming with all sorts of second- and third-tier Democrats, including former Kerry rivals Al Sharpton and Dennis

Kucinich, a couple of real back-benchers. Mischer's frantic commands to the balloon droppers morphed into a hysterical rant that was broadcast, live and unedited, to millions of mortified Americans.

"Balloons?! What's *happening*, balloons?! There's not enough coming down! *All* balloons! What the *hell*?! There's nothing falling! What the *f—k* are you guys doing up there?! We want more balloons coming down!"

Thus ended the Democratic National Convention of 2004.

"More balloons! More balloons! More balloons!"

CHAPTER SIX

"REMINISCENT OF GENGHIS KHAN"

For the first few seconds, the television commercial looked and sounded like yet another testimonial to John Kerry's brave service in Vietnam. It opened with a black-and-white photo of Kerry and nineteen other Swift Boat officers posing together on a military base in South Vietnam, circa 1969. There was inspirational music as the camera slowly closed in on Kerry's smiling face. There was the uplifting voice of Kerry's running mate, John Edwards, whose handsome visage soon filled the screen.

"If you have any questions about what John Kerry is made of," Edwards was saying in his best closing-argument voice, "just spend three minutes with the men who served with him."

But then the inspirational music morphed into something ominous. Edwards's final words, "served with him," trailed off and echoed forebodingly as his visage was replaced on the screen by a single sentence of text: "Here's what those men think about John Kerry."

"I served with John Kerry," said a reasonable-looking man with wire-rimmed glasses and gray hair.

"I served with John Kerry," said a second man in a sober suit and tie. He had the sort of quiet, authoritative voice one hears on commercials for stodgy investment firms.

"John Kerry has not been honest about what happened in Vietnam," said an avuncular third man, identified onscreen with the text: "George Elliott, Lieutenant Commander, Two Bronze Stars."

"He is lying about his record," added the man in the wire-rimmed glasses, now identified as "Al French, Ensign, Two Bronze Stars."

Behind French the camera zoomed in on the old photo of the Swift Boat officers, although instead of focusing on Kerry, the lens pulled in tight on French himself, as a young man sporting black-rimmed glasses and dark hair. Obviously, French had served alongside Kerry in Vietnam. So had many of the other men now speaking in this commercial, judging from additional close-ups of the black-and-white photo. Older, balder, and now wrinkled with age, the men had nonetheless weathered the past thirty-five years fairly well. Each was identified onscreen by name, rank, and number of medals.

"I know John Kerry is lying about his first Purple Heart because I treated him for that injury," said Medical Officer Louis Letson.

"John Kerry lied to get his Bronze Star," added Gunner's Mate Van Odell. "I know. I was there. I saw what happened."

Now the screen behind the speakers was filled with grainy, black-and-white images of Swift Boats plying the murky waters of the Mekong Delta.

"His account of what happened and what actually happened are the difference between night and day," said Lieutenant Jack Chenoweth, winner of the Navy Commendation Medal.

"John Kerry has not been honest," said Rear Admiral Roy Hoffmann, possessor of the Distinguished Service Medal.

"And he lacks the capacity to lead," added Commander Adrian Lonsdale, who had been awarded a Legion of Merit Bronze Star.

The photos of the Swift Boats were now replaced by images of a long-haired Kerry protesting the Vietnam War. There was a shot of Kerry being arrested during an antiwar protest in Massachusetts in 1971. Wearing a black turtleneck and leather jacket, Kerry held his hands behind his head as he was led away by police.

"When the chips were down, you could not count on John Kerry," said Lieutenant Larry Thurlow, a Bronze Star recipient.

"John Kerry is no war hero," said fellow Bronze Star winner Lieutenant Bob Elder with an air of confident authority.

"He betrayed all his shipmates," said Lieutenant Commander Grant Hibbard, who had earned two Bronze Stars. "He lied before the Senate."

The screen behind Hibbard was filled with a 1971 photo of a shaggy-haired Kerry telling the Senate Foreign Relations Committee that his fellow Vietnam veterans had committed war crimes. Kerry's long face was glum, his deep-set eyes ringed by dark circles. He was flanked by a bearded, long-haired man, frozen in mid-clap by the camera.

"John Kerry betrayed the men and women he served with in Vietnam," said Lieutenant Shelton White, recipient of two Bronze Stars.

More protest photos. There was one of Kerry among men with beards, long hair, and floppy hats. There was another that showed hippies dressed sloppily in Army fatigues and brandishing rifles, evidently demonstrating against the war. They had painted their faces white, which gave them a ghostly appearance. A third photo showed Kerry in the foreground of a massive protest.

"He dishonored his country," said Gunner's Mate Joe Ponder, a Purple Heart winner, matter-of-factly. "He most certainly did."

Lieutenant Bob Hildreth, owner of a Bronze Star and Purple Heart, brought the message full circle by intoning, "I served with John Kerry."

The footage of Hildreth dissolved into a full-screen close-up of Kerry during his 1971 Senate testimony. His hair came down well over his ears and the fingers of his right hand were curled pensively against his face.

"John Kerry cannot be trusted," Hildreth concluded.

A narrator's grave voice intoned, "Swift Boat Veterans for Truth is responsible for the content of this advertisement."

Most Americans had never heard of the Swift Boat Veterans for Truth when their hard-hitting ad was first broadcast on August 5, 2004. That's because the group had been frozen out of the national conversation by the mainstream media. For three long months, the Swifties, as they called themselves, had been trying to tell their story to the press, which utterly ignored them. The effort began on May 4 with an open letter to Kerry that questioned his fitness to be commander in chief. The letter was signed by nearly two hundred veterans, eighteen of whom—including an admiral—denounced Kerry at a press conference in Washington that same day. The session at the National Press Club lasted an hour and twenty minutes. One after another, the decorated veterans stood up and explained why Kerry did not deserve his medals. They calmly condemned him for branding his fellow Vietnam veterans war criminals. And yet these compelling and extraordinary claims were summarily dismissed by the Fourth Estate, which attended the press conference but refused to actually cover it.

The exasperated Swifties were forced to look for other ways to get their message out. In June, they met with Republican strategist Chris LaCivita to explore the possibility of a TV commercial. But LaCivita, himself a decorated combat veteran, was wary of questioning Kerry's war medals.

"Whoa, slow down, guys," he told the two Vietnam veterans who walked into his office in June and proposed the idea. "Whether he earned his medals or not is irrelevant, 'cause our guy don't got any. That's a contrast I don't necessarily want to start bringing up."

LaCivita explained that any attack on Kerry's Vietnam service would invite unfavorable comparisons to Bush, who, after all, had not gone to Vietnam. But the Swifties would not be dissuaded. One of them, John O'Neill, gave LaCivita the manuscript of a book he had just co-authored. It was titled *Unfit for Command* and was scheduled for publication in August.

That night, overloaded with caffeine and nicotine, LaCivita paced the floor and read the manuscript. A former Marine who received a Purple Heart for a combat wound in the 1991 Gulf War, LaCivita was impressed by the credibility of the story. He was especially struck by the level of detail and sheer volume of corroboration. After several more meetings with the Swifties, he agreed to make the commercial.

And so, on a Saturday in July, some sixty Swift Boat veterans gathered in a Washington advertising studio and spent thirteen hours being filmed in front of an enormous green screen. LaCivita would later superimpose the Vietnam-era photographs on this screen behind the veterans as they spoke. Instead of using a piece of canned theme music, he commissioned an original score for the sixty-second spot. The finished product was nothing short of devastating. LaCivita knew he had produced the most powerful political commercial of the 2004 campaign.

But he also knew that Kerry and Bush, along with special-interest groups on both sides, were on pace to spend a total of $1 billion on their own television ads during the course of the campaign. By contrast, the Swift Boat Veterans for Truth could scrape together only $500,000 for their initial ad buy. They were an advocacy group known as a 527, after the section of federal tax code that made such groups possible. The 527s had sprung up through a loophole in the McCain-Feingold campaign finance law of 2002, a law that John McCain had promised would put an end to the unlimited contributions that had been pouring into presidential politics for years. Democrats had exploited this loophole quickly and aggressively, while Republicans had held back, worried about legalities. As a result, the vast majority of some $60 million in 527 advertising had gone to Democratic groups. The half million raised by the Swifties was a drop in the bucket. It would barely be enough to air their ad in three states—Ohio, Wisconsin, and West Virginia. Unable to afford major media markets like Columbus, Milwaukee, or Wheeling, LaCivita had to settle for smaller markets like Youngstown, Wausa, and Charleston.

The original plan was to spring the ad on July 28, the night before Kerry's acceptance speech at the Democratic National Convention. But at the last minute a check didn't clear and the whole buy had to be postponed for a week. Unable to spoil Kerry's party, LaCivita settled into his Richmond home to watch the candidate's speech on television. He considered it an unpleasant but necessary part of his job. But when he saw all the Vietnam veterans precede Kerry to the stage, his interest perked up. When he saw Vietnam veteran Max Cleland introduce the candidate, his heart beat a little faster. And when he saw Kerry salute the cameras and announce that he was "reporting for duty," LaCivita nearly fell out of his chair.

"Talk about leading with your chin," he exclaimed. "We had no idea that Kerry was going to make his four months in Vietnam the centerpiece of his convention. Oh boy, is this going to be fun."

Suddenly, waiting until after the convention to run the Swift Boat ad seemed like a stroke of genius. It would be infinitely more relevant and powerful in the wake of Kerry's Vietnam overkill. A veteran of brass-knuckled political campaigns, LaCivita knew full well the political firestorm that was about to be unleashed by the mild-mannered Swift Boat veterans.

"They were being ignored," LaCivita said. "This ad is going to force the national media to pay attention to them. And then all hell is gonna break loose."

LaCivita's family members, who had seen the ad before it aired, were worried about the fallout. When Kerry saluted at the convention, LaCivita's wife turned to him and asked, "Do you know what you're getting yourself into?" His parents went a step further, asking their son whether he had changed his home phone number.

But LaCivita was looking forward to the fight. He even sent copies of the ads to TV newsrooms. He knew that free airtime on national news shows would increase the ad's impact exponentially, even if the mainstream media attacked the spot in the process. He also made the ad available to Internet sites like the Drudge Report and HumanEventsOnline, which had a combined audience in the millions. The strategy worked like clockwork, creating a political earthquake that riveted the media's attention. The ad was so devastatingly effective that Kerry didn't dare respond for fear of lending it credibility. So reporters turned to their favorite Republican, Senator John McCain, who gave the story legs by immediately expressing his outrage.

"The ad is dishonest and dishonorable," the former Vietnam prisoner of war told the Associated Press. "John Kerry served honorably in Vietnam."

Alarmed by the ad's political potential, journalists denounced it in the strongest possible terms. Ron Brownstein of the *Los Angeles Times* called it a "snuff film." Mike Barnicle of MSNBC railed, "This isn't an ad, it's political pornography." Craig Crawford of *Congressional Quarterly* added, "It's just another lie."

Author Douglas Brinkley told the liberal *Salon* webzine, "These are malicious fabrications in the heat of the election." But Brinkley had written a fawning book about Kerry's Vietnam service, titled *Tour of Duty*, which was itself published in the heat of the election. In fact, the book's distortions had been the final straw for many Swifties, prompting them to break their long years of silence and finally criticize Kerry.

The Bush team was smart enough to refrain from endorsing the incendiary Swift Boat ad. When reporters demanded specific denunciations of the spot, Bush officials instead called for a moratorium on all ads by 527s, since the vast majority of these largely unregulated groups were Democratic.

"I think all these ads should be taken off the air," shrugged Republican National Committee chairman Ed Gillespie. He was also careful to emphasize that the Bush campaign had "never questioned Senator Kerry's service."

This posture proved enormously frustrating to Kerry because he could not directly blame Bush for the attack on his Vietnam service. So he decided to attack on another front—the president's handling of September 11. On the day the Swift Boat ad was released, Kerry mocked Bush for briefly remaining in a second-grade classroom after being informed of the terrorist attacks. Stunned by the news and wary of deepening the nation's panic, the president chose to remain in the classroom until the children finished their phonics lesson, a story called *My Pet Goat*. He waited exactly five minutes, an interval that liberal filmmaker Michael Moore exaggerated to seven minutes in his Bush-hating film *Fahrenheit 9/11*. Taking his cue from the film, which was still in theaters, Kerry savaged the president's response.

"Had I been reading to children and had my top aide whispered in my ear, 'America is under attack,' I would have told those kids very politely and nicely that the president of the United States had something that he needed to attend to," Kerry huffed, drawing applause from a conference of supposedly objective black journalists in Washington. "And I would have attended to it."

But a month earlier, Kerry admitted he had been so stupefied by the terrorist attacks that he couldn't even "think" for some twenty minutes. On September 11, Kerry was attending a Democratic leadership meeting in the Capitol office of Senate Minority Leader Tom Daschle when the two jetliners slammed into the World Trade Center in New York.

"We watched the second plane come into the building," Kerry recounted on *Larry King Live*. "And we shortly thereafter sat down at the table. And then we just realized nobody could think. And then boom, right behind us, we saw the cloud of explosion at the Pentagon.

"And then word came from the White House they were evacuating, and we were to evacuate," he added. "And so we immediately began the evacuation."

By that time, Bush had been responding to the attacks for more than twenty minutes. Using the Florida school as a makeshift command post, he had telephoned Vice President Dick Cheney, FBI director Robert Mueller, and New York governor George Pataki. Also during those twenty minutes, the president consulted with his top White House aides—chief of staff Andy Card, communications director Dan Bartlett, and press secretary Ari Fleischer. Rejecting a statement they drafted for him, Bush grabbed a pen and scrawled out his own message on three sheets of paper. Then he addressed the nation and headed for Air Force One, all before the attack on the Pentagon, at which time Kerry—by his own admission—was finally snapping out of his reverie.

Bush officials were outraged by Kerry's cheap shot, but didn't have to wait long for an opportunity to get even. During his remarks to the black journalists, Kerry said something that summed up the central difference between himself and Bush on the overarching question of who would do a better job of protecting the nation against terrorism. Amazingly, Kerry told the journalists he would wage a "more sensitive war on terror" than Bush. The gaffe was quickly thrown back in Kerry's face.

"America has been in too many wars for any of our wishes, but not a one of them was won by being sensitive," said Vice President Cheney, drawing howls of laughter from a gathering of soldiers, veterans, police officers, and firemen in Dayton. "President Lincoln and General Grant did not wage sensitive warfare—nor did President Roosevelt, nor Generals Eisenhower and MacArthur. A 'sensitive war' will not destroy the evil men who killed three thousand Americans and who seek the chemical, nuclear, and biological weapons to kill hundreds of thousands more.

"The men who beheaded Daniel Pearl," he added, "will not be impressed by our sensitivity. As our opponents see it, the problem isn't the thugs and murderers that we face, but *our attitude.*

"I listened to what Senator Kerry had to say in Boston, and, with all due respect to the senator, he views the world as if we had never been attacked on September 11," Cheney concluded. "Those who threaten us and kill innocents around the world do not need to be treated more sensitively. They need to be destroyed."

The Dayton Convention Center exploded in applause. The vice president's wife, Lynne Cheney, was cheered just as loudly in Joplin, Missouri, after an audience member asked for her reaction to Kerry's gaffe.

"With all due respect to the senator, it just sounded so foolish," she said. "I can't imagine that al Qaeda will be impressed by sensitivity."

She accused Kerry of espousing the "extreme left" view that Americans are somehow to blame for terrorism.

"'If we'll just adjust our attitude' seems to be the idea," she marveled. "This is the kind of left-wing foolishness that certainly isn't appropriate for someone who would seek to be commander in chief."

The day after Kerry's gaffe, Bush sought to press his advantage by publicly baiting the Democrat about his constantly shifting positions on the Iraq war. Republicans had already spent months excoriating Kerry for having voted to authorize the war, only to later call himself the antiwar candidate. They'd had a field day with his infamous flip-flop on funding for body armor—"I actually did vote for the $87 billion before I voted against it." Well, now Bush wanted to pin Kerry down on whether, in hindsight, he still would have voted for the war, even though the United States had not found the weapons of mass destruction that Bush had cited as justification for the war in the first place. The president himself was unequivocal about his belief that toppling Saddam Hussein had been a just and noble cause, WMD or no WMD.

"Even though we did not find the stockpiles that we thought we would find, we did the right thing," he told picnickers in New Hampshire. "There are some questions that a commander in chief needs to answer with a clear 'yes' or 'no.' My opponent hasn't answered the question of whether, knowing what we know now, he would have supported going into Iraq. That's an important question and the American people deserve a clear 'yes' or 'no' answer. I have given my answer. We did the right thing, and the world is better off for it."

The question was purely rhetorical, of course, since the president figured Kerry would never dignify it with a response. After all, no politician worth his salt would allow himself to be baited into answering an obviously trick question from his opponent. And yet, inexplicably, Kerry rose to the bait. It happened during a photo op at the Grand Canyon, when a reporter asked Kerry to answer the president's question.

"Yes, I would have voted for the authority," Kerry replied. "I believe it was the right authority for a president to have."

The blunder was nothing short of "disastrous," according to *Newsweek*. Reporter Dan Balz of the *Washington Post* wrote, "Kerry and his advisers allowed themselves to be drawn into a new debate about Iraq."

The president, scarcely believing his good fortune, capitalized on Kerry's blunder the next day.

"Almost two years after he voted for the war in Iraq, and almost 220 days after switching positions to declare himself the antiwar candidate, my opponent has found a new nuance," Bush deadpanned to an appreciative audience in Florida. "He now agrees it was the right decision to go into Iraq. After months of questioning my motives and even my credibility, Senator Kerry now agrees with me that even though we have not found the stockpile of weapons we believed were there, knowing everything we know today, he would have voted to go into Iraq and remove Saddam Hussein from power.

"I want to thank Senator Kerry for clearing that up," he allowed, drawing laughter. "But be careful—there's still eighty-four days left in this campaign for him to change his mind."

Meanwhile, the furor kicked up by the Swift Boat ad continued to build until it utterly dominated the presidential campaign. Americans were shocked to learn that Kerry might have exaggerated his Vietnam valor. Nearly 150,000 of them sent in contributions to Swift Boat Veterans for Truth. Once hamstrung by a measly $500,000 advertising budget, the Swifties suddenly found themselves awash in cash. It started coming in at a rate of $20,000 a day. Within the space of two weeks, however, the daily haul had ballooned to more than $250,000. The sheer volume of cash began to register when LaCivita received an excited call from his accountant.

"Chris, I got thirty-seven boxes of unopened mail that's just arrived," she exclaimed. "It's all money! *Unsolicited*!"

No longer limited to tiny media markets, the Swifties aired the commercial in the biggest markets in the all-important battleground states. No longer shunned by the news media, they made 10,000 appearances on television and radio to argue their case for free. What had begun as a small ad buy had grown into a full-fledged, multi-dimensional political campaign unto itself. On August 18, the *Washington Times* threw gasoline on the fire by publishing the first of three front-page excerpts of O'Neill's book, *Unfit for Command*. The next day, CBS released a poll that showed support for Kerry among veterans had plummeted since the Swift Boat ad began airing. The veteran vote had been split, 46–46, between Kerry and Bush after the Democratic convention, when Kerry had emphasized his Vietnam bona fides. But a mere three weeks later, Bush was trouncing Kerry by a staggering eighteen points among veterans.

The freefall was not limited to military voters. A Gallup survey of all registered voters showed that Kerry had become the first candidate since George McGovern in 1972 to get absolutely no bounce out of his convention. In fact, according to Gallup, Kerry actually *lost* a point, while Bush *gained four*! The performance was so dismal that Kerry decided to hire former Clinton press secretary Joe Lockhart, who specialized in political counterattacks. The candidate was also forced to dip into his $75 million war chest—which he had hoped to avoid touching throughout the month of August—to throw together an ad lashing out at the Swifties. By now it was painfully obvious that Kerry's strategy of trying to remain above the fray had been a disaster.

Liberal supporters were furiously pressuring him to personally fight back. Worried Democratic veterans were calling him in droves. And so, on August 19, a full two weeks after the commercial questioning his valor began airing, John Kerry finally fired back at the Swifties.

"They're a front for the Bush campaign, and the fact that the president won't denounce what they're up to tells you everything you need to know," he told a union gathering in Boston. "He wants them to do his dirty work."

It was important for Kerry to blame Bush for the ad, notwithstanding the utter lack of evidence connecting the president to the Swift Boat Veterans for Truth.

"Of course, the president keeps telling people he would never question my service to our country. Instead, he watches as a Republican-funded attack group does just that," Kerry railed. "Well, if he wants to have a debate about our service in Vietnam, here is my answer: bring it on."

This was proof that the Swifties "had a very big impact" on the campaign, according to Mehlman, who praised the outspoken veterans.

"These are people who are incredible," he confided to me later. "You may disagree with what they're saying. But these are heroes. These are people that suffered in prison camps for America. And to respond and say, 'These are bums who don't have a right to speak. But other veterans who agree with us do,' is responding with a hammer and not a scalpel. The Kerry campaign seemed unable to use a scalpel. Instead, they had to use a hammer for everything."

Such praise for the Swifties would have been politically risky for Bush, who had always sought to avoid a debate with Kerry about their service during Vietnam. But the press was determined to debate the president on Kerry's behalf. An NBC reporter came right out and asked Bush if he thought he had "served on the same level of heroism" as his opponent.

"No, I don't," Bush replied. "I think him going to Vietnam was more heroic than my flying fighter jets. He was in harm's way and I wasn't."

Still, the president was unapologetic about his service in the Texas Air National Guard.

"On the other hand, I served my country," he said. "Had my unit been called up, I would have gone."

When another reporter asked whether "Kerry lied about his war record," the president replied, "I think Senator Kerry served admirably. He ought to be proud of his record."

This consistent praise of Kerry's military service stood in stark contrast to the Democrat's personal attacks on Bush's service. The criticism began back in February, when Kerry questioned whether Bush fulfilled his military obligations after transferring from one National Guard unit in Texas to another in Alabama. The White House had cited the president's honorable discharge as proof that he fulfilled his duties. But Kerry remained unconvinced.

"Was he present and active on duty in Alabama at the times he was supposed to be?" Kerry demanded. "Just because you get an honorable discharge does not, in fact, answer that question."

He continued the attack on Bush in April, telling ABC that the Republican Party "can't even answer whether or not he showed up for duty in the National Guard." The next day, Kerry told the *Dayton Daily News* that the president "can't account for his own service in the National Guard." In case anyone missed the point, the Kerry campaign issued a list of nine questions implying that Bush had shirked his duties.

The president never counterattacked, figuring it was useless to go after a decorated Vietnam War veteran. But now the Swift Boat veterans were saying things Bush could not. Their ads were utterly mesmerizing the nation. Incredibly, a spot first launched in only three states had now been seen or heard by 56 percent of all Americans, according to a poll by the University of Pennsylvania. Much to the alarm of the Kerry campaign, the poll also said that 46 percent of "persuadable voters" found the ad believable.

Even World War II hero Bob Dole, who was considered more of a statesman than a partisan bomb-thrower, questioned Kerry's medals.

"What I will always quarrel about are the Purple Hearts," he told CNN. "He got two in one day, I think. And he was out of there in less than four months, because three Purple Hearts and you're out."

Dole himself had received a Bronze Star and two Purple Hearts—one for taking Nazi machine-gun fire in the back and arm while trying to rescue an injured radio operator in Italy. He spent nearly three years in a hospital and his right arm was paralyzed for life. And now he couldn't understand how he had ended up with fewer medals than Kerry.

"Three Purple Hearts and never bled, that I know of—I mean, they're all superficial wounds," he said of Kerry. "And as far as I know, he's never spent one day in the hospital. I don't think he draws any disability pay. He doesn't have any disability—and boasting about three Purple Hearts, when you think of some of the people who really got shot up in Vietnam."

While Kerry was reeling from such criticism, the Swifties launched a second ad that was even was more devastating than the first. That's because the new spot, instead of focusing on the contentious and endlessly arguable question of whether Kerry earned his medals while in Vietnam, tackled the unequivocal facts of Kerry's antiwar testimony after returning to the States. Instead of quoting veterans who served alongside Kerry in South Vietnam, the new ad quoted veterans who had been tortured in North Vietnamese prisons while Kerry was back in the States, branding them war criminals. And instead of relying solely on veterans to cast Kerry in an unfavorable light, the new ad employed the candidate's own words.

And yet it began the same way the old ad had ended—with the black-and-white photo of a glum-faced Kerry testifying before the Senate Foreign Relations Committee in 1971. The same sunken eyes, the same shock of unruly hair, the same fingers curled effetely against the same pale, gloomy face. Only this time, the photo was accompanied by the sound of Kerry's own voice.

"They had personally raped, cut off ears, cut off heads . . ." he was saying. As if to underscore the impact of his words, the text was spelled out across the screen as foreboding music played in the background.

The shot dissolved into the other famous photo of Kerry testifying, the one with the bearded man behind him captured in mid-clap. The thirty-four-year-old image served as a black-and-white backdrop to fresh color video of a Swift Boat vet now speaking in the foreground.

"The accusations that John Kerry made against the veterans who served in Vietnam was just devastating," said Joe Ponder, the gunner's mate and Purple Heart winner who had been featured in the first ad. A big, beefy guy in a suit and tie, Ponder came across as a gentle giant who occasionally struggled with subject-verb agreement. Under his name on the screen were the words, "Wounded Nov. 1968."

"...randomly shot at civilians..." Kerry interjected.

Back to Ponder: "And it hurt me more than any physical wounds I had."

"...cut off limbs, blown up bodies..." Kerry was intoning in the slow, deliberate manner of a prosecutor reciting the grisly details of a particularly harrowing indictment. As the camera closed ever so slowly on the photo of him testifying, other Swift Boat vets appeared in the foreground.

"That was part of the torture, to sign a statement that you had committed war crimes," explained Ken Cordier, identified onscreen as a prisoner of war in Vietnam from December 1966 to March 1973.

"...razed villages in a fashion reminiscent of Genghis Khan..." Kerry continued, oddly pronouncing the *g*'s in Genghis the way one pronounces them in Gigi. His Boston Brahmin accent seemed so affected, so ripe for ridicule, that *Newsweek* would falsely report that the Swifties had employed an actor to read Kerry's words. Yet anyone who had seen the full footage of Kerry's testimony, which was being aired repeatedly on C-SPAN throughout the campaign, was immediately struck by the exaggerated New England elocution, as if the twenty-eight-year-old was trying to show that he had come from an especially cultured and elite family.

"John Kerry gave the enemy—for free—what I and many of my comrades in the North Vietnamese prison camps took torture to avoid saying," said Paul Galanti, a prisoner of war from January 1966 to February 1973. "It demoralized us."

"...crimes committed on a day-to-day basis..." Kerry droned.

Back to Cordier: "He betrayed us in the past, how could we be loyal to him now?"

"...ravaged the countryside of South Vietnam..." Kerry continued.

"He dishonored his country, and more importantly, the people he served with," Galanti concluded. "He just sold them out."

The ad was like a punch in the gut to the Kerry campaign, which responded by again resorting to mockery of Bush for his initial response to the September 11 terrorist attacks. Kerry campaign press secretary Stephanie Cutter even invoked the name of the book that students had been reading with Bush in the Florida classroom.

"John Kerry is not the type of leader who will sit and read *My Pet Goat* to a group of second-graders while America is under attack," she spat.

Kerry filed a complaint with the Federal Elections Commission, saying the Swifties were illegally colluding with the Bushies. But it was hopeless. The Swift Boat controversy was now utterly overshadowing issues that Kerry had hoped to highlight in August—health care and the economy. And he might as well forget about scoring points against Bush over the war in Iraq. It was all Swift Boats, all the time.

"All the guys who were with me on my boat absolutely document what I've said," Kerry said defensively at a town hall meeting in Minnesota on August 26. "You're now hearing about the lie. I am absolutely telling you the God's honest truth with regard to what happened over there."

It was no use. A Gallup poll released later that day showed a stunning drop in the number of people who said Kerry's military service would make them more likely to vote for him. The number had been cut in half in the space of three weeks—from 42 percent to 21 percent—all because of the Swifties. According to RealClearPolitics, a website that averaged the various national polls, the president finally pulled ahead of Kerry in the last days of August, after having trailed the Democrats since the Fourth of July.

"I think the mistake that Kerry made was making the entire essence of his campaign that he served in Vietnam," Mehlman told me. "Ultimately, it wasn't that relevant of an issue."

Besides, by trying to score political points with boasts about his service in Vietnam, Kerry invited criticism about his subsequent protests against the war.

"No one's taking away anything from his service; the question was his judgment when he came back," Mehlman said. "Do people agree with when you came back and you said those things about American troops?"

In the end, when Kerry and the press realized the extent of the damage, they decided to go for revenge, pure and simple. They resolved to punish Bush by going after his military record with the same zeal as the Swifties, who launched their third ad on August 26 and made clear they would continue to speak out right through Election Day.

"Several aides are pushing Kerry to directly challenge Bush's stateside service in the National Guard and force the president to prove he fulfilled his service requirements," the *Washington Post* reported.

Opinion columnists were even more blatant about the vendetta.

"Now that John Kerry's life during his twenties has been put at the heart of this campaign just over two months from Election Day, the media owe the country a comparable review of what Bush was doing at the same time and the same age," demanded liberal columnist E. J. Dionne in the *Washington Post*. "If all the stories about what Kerry did in Vietnam are not balanced by serious scrutiny of Bush in the Vietnam years, the media will be capitulating to a right-wing smear campaign. Surely our nation's editors and producers don't want to send a signal that all you have to do to set the media's agenda is spend a half million bucks on television ads."

Al Hunt, liberal executive editor of the *Wall Street Journal*'s Washington bureau, agreed that the military records of the two candidates should be scrutinized equally. Hunt went so far as to predict on CNN that such a comparison would ultimately doom the president's bid for a second term.

"If this election's going to be fought over what these two sons of privilege did in the late sixties," he warned, "it's going to be a Kerry landslide."

CHAPTER SEVEN

SPITBALLS

The most electrifying speaker at the Republican National Convention of 2004 was a Democrat. In fact, it was the same Democrat who had given the keynote address at the Democratic National Convention of 1992—the one that had nominated Bill Clinton. A dozen years later, Senator Zell Miller of Georgia simply could not bring himself to support fellow Democratic senator John Kerry. So he agreed to come to New York City on September 1 and speak on behalf of President Bush at Madison Square Garden, which was packed to the rafters with Republican delegates. He began by going after his fellow Democrats.

"Today, at the same time young Americans are dying in the sands of Iraq and the mountains of Afghanistan, our nation is being torn apart and made weaker because of the Democrats' manic obsession to bring down our commander in chief," Miller said. "What has happened to the party I've spent my life working in?

"I can remember when Democrats believed that it was the duty of America to fight for freedom over tyranny," he said. "But not today. Motivated more by partisan politics than by national security, today's Democratic leaders see America as an occupier, not a liberator. And nothing makes this Marine madder than someone calling American troops occupiers rather than liberators."

He added, "No one should dare to even think about being the commander in chief of this country if he doesn't believe with all his heart that our soldiers are liberators abroad and defenders of freedom at home. But don't waste your breath telling that to the leaders of my party today. In their warped way of thinking, America is the problem, not the solution. They don't believe there is any real danger in the world except that which America brings upon itself through our clumsy and misguided foreign policy."

Miller knew he would be falsely accused of questioning the patriotism of fellow Democrats, so he decided to preempt that argument.

"It is not their patriotism, it is their judgment that has been so sorely lacking," he said. "They claimed Carter's pacifism would lead to peace. They were wrong. They claimed Reagan's defense buildup would lead to war. They were wrong. And no pair has been more wrong, more loudly, more often than the two senators from Massachusetts, Ted Kennedy and John Kerry. Together, Kennedy and Kerry have opposed the very weapons systems that won the Cold War and that are now winning the War on Terror."

Miller then rattled off a long list of weapons systems that Kerry had opposed during his Senate career.

"This is the man who wants to be the commander in chief of our U.S. armed forces? U.S. forces armed with what? Spitballs?"

Knowing that his status as a member of the Democratic Party gave his arguments against Kerry greater weight, Miller ripped into his colleague with gusto.

"Senator Kerry has made it clear that he would use military force only if approved by the United Nations. Kerry would let Paris decide when America needs defending. I want Bush to decide," he said. "For more than twenty years, on every one of the great issues of freedom and security, John Kerry has been more wrong, more weak, and more wobbly than any other national figure."

Finally, Miller dared to tread where the Bush team dared not—Vietnam.

"As a war protester, Kerry blamed our military," he recalled. "John Kerry wants to re-fight yesterday's war.

"President Bush believes we have to fight today's war and be ready for tomorrow's challenges," he added. "George W. Bush wants to grab terrorists by the throat and not let them go to get a better grip. From John Kerry, they get a yes-no-maybe bowl of mush that can only encourage our enemies and confuse our friends."

Miller concluded with a dire warning. "We've got some hard choosing to do. Right now the world just cannot afford an indecisive America. Faint-hearted self-indulgence will put at risk all we care about in this world.

"In this hour of danger, our president has had the courage to stand up," he concluded. "And this Democrat is proud to stand up with him."

Delegates in the convention hall loved the speech, although the main-stream media was appalled. Chris Matthews of MSNBC's *Hardball* made this abundantly clear when he interviewed Miller via satellite afterward. Matthews was broadcasting live from Herald Square, several blocks from the convention hall.

"You really believe that John Kerry and Ted Kennedy do not believe in defending the country?" Matthews asked his fellow Democrat.

"Well, look at their votes," Miller began.

"I'm just asking you to bottom-line it for me," interjected Matthews, whose trademark was talking over his guests.

"Wait a minute," Miller said. "I said I didn't question their patriotism."

Unconvinced, Matthews plowed on. "Do you believe that they don't believe in defending the country?"

"I question their judgment," Miller managed.

"Do you believe they want to defend the country?" Matthews persisted.

"Look, I applaud what John Kerry did as far as volunteering to go to Viet-nam," Miller allowed. "I applaud what he did when he volunteered for com-bat. I admire that, and I respect that. And I acknowledge that. I have said that many, many times. But I think his record is atrocious."

"Well, let me ask you, when Democrats come out, as they often do, liberal Democrats, and attack conservatives, and say they want to starve little kids, they want to get rid of education, they want to kill the old people…" Matthews began.

"I am not saying that," Miller objected. "Wait a minute."

"…that kind of rhetoric is not educational, is it?"

"Wait a minute," Miller said. "Now, this is your program. And I am a guest on your program."

"Yes, sir," Matthews agreed.

"And so I want to try to be as nice as I possibly can to you. I wish I was over there, where I could get a little closer up into your face."

"Hah!" laughed Matthews.

"But I don't have to stand here and listen to that kind of stuff," Miller said. "I didn't say anything about not feeding poor kids. What are you doing?"

The grin on Matthews's face vanished as it dawned on him that Miller was not kidding after all.

"No, I'm saying that when you said tonight—I just want you to—"

"Well, you are saying a bunch of baloney that didn't have anything to do with what I said up there on the rostrum," Miller said, pointing at the stage behind him.

"Okay," Matthews said. "Do you believe, Senator, truthfully, that John Kerry wants to defend the country with spitballs? Do you believe that?"

Miller was rendered momentarily speechless. He paused for several beats with an incredulous look on his face that said "Can you really be this dumb?" Finally, he resorted to speaking to Matthews as if he were a particularly dense and unruly teenager.

"That was a metaphor, wasn't it?" he said. "Do you know what a metaphor is?"

"Well, what do you mean by that metaphor?" Matthews shot back.

"Wait a minute," Miller said. "He certainly does not want to defend the country with the B-1 bomber or the B-2 bomber or the Harrier jet or the

Apache helicopter or all those other things that I mentioned. And there were even more of them in here. You've got to quit taking these Democratic talking points and using what they are saying to you."

"No, I am using your talking points and asking you if you really believe them," Matthews countered.

"Well, use John Kerry's talking points," Miller said. "He put out this— whenever he was running for the U.S. Senate—about what he wanted to cancel. 'Cancel,' to me, means to do away with."

"Well, what did you mean by the following . . ." said Matthews, undeterred.

"I think we ought to cancel this interview," Miller said with a scowl. But then he chuckled good-naturedly, as if to signify he was willing to give Matthews another chance.

"Well, that would be my loss, Senator," said Matthews, suddenly a gentleman. "Let me ask you about this, because I think you have a view on the role of reporters in the world. You have said and it has often been said so truthfully that 'it is the soldier, not the reporter, who has given us the freedom of the press.' Was there not . . ."

"Do you believe that?" Miller said. "Do you believe it?"

"Well, of course—it's true," Matthews said. "But it's a statement that nobody would have challenged. Why did you make it? It seems like no one would deny what you said. So *what's your point?*"

"Well, it evidently got a rise out of you . . ." Miller said.

"Well, I think it's a shot at—"

"Because you are a reporter—"

"That's right—"

"You didn't have anything to do with freedom of the press," Miller said.

"Well, you could argue it was not nurses who defended the freedom of nursing," Matthews said. "Why did you single out freedom of the press to say it was the soldiers that defended it and not the reporters? We all know that. Why did you say it?"

"Well, because I thought it needed to be said at this particular time, because I wanted to—" Miller began, only to be interrupted again.

"Because you could get an applause line against the media at a conserva-tive convention!" Matthews thundered like a prosecutor.

This prompted cheers from the pro-Kerry crowd at Herald Square. But it elicited groans from an off-camera guest, former Republican congressman J. C. Watts of Oklahoma.

"Aww, Chris," muttered Watts, as if trying to save a colleague from com-pounding a hopelessly embarrassing gaffe. "My God."

"No, I said it because it was..." Miller began, only to stop in mid-sentence. He smiled, dropped his head, and shook it from side to side in the semaphore of bemused exasperation. "You're hopeless," he finally managed, his smile fading.

"Hah!" Matthews barked with an enormous, open-mouthed grin.

"I wish I was over there," Miller said.

"Hah, hah, hah, hah!"

"In fact, I wish that we lived in the—"

"Senator!" Matthews was braying with an expression of pure mirth. "Senator!"

"I wish we lived in the day—"

"Please come over!" Matthews taunted, prompting additional cheers from his live audience.

"I wish we lived in..." Miller tried again. "Chris..."

"We're in a—gotta warn you—we're in a tough part of town over here. But I do recommend you come over, because I like you."

For the second time, Matthews had managed to infuriate his guest and then defuse the anger at the last possible moment. Miller smiled and chuck-led good-naturedly to signify he had forgiven the host again. But then Matthews resumed his badgering questions, only to interrupt every time Miller tried to answer. It was downright obnoxious.

"If you're going to ask a question—" Miller began in exasperation. But he was interrupted yet again by the blond motormouth.

"Well, it's a tough question," Matthews said defensively. "It takes a few words."

This was the last straw for Miller.

"Get out of my face."

"Hah, hah, hah!" Matthews brayed, cutting a glance at the whooping crowd for moral support.

"If you are going to ask me a question, step back and let me answer," Miller said.

"Hah, hah, hah!" the host guffawed. "Hah, hah, hah!"

MSNBC cut to a shot of the crowd behind Matthews, which was jeering at Miller's image on a TV monitor. The unruly liberals pumped their fists in the air and waved placards. Someone hoisted a rainbow-hued banner emblazoned with the word "GAY." Matthews was expertly riling up his fans, which only infuriated Miller more.

"You know, I wish we lived in the day where you could challenge a person to a duel," he said. "Now that would be pretty good."

This remark was too much for NBC reporters Norah O'Donnell and Andrea Mitchell, who let fly with a couple of extended, off-camera horselaughs.

Undaunted, Miller ripped Matthews for having similarly mistreated another guest on a recent episode of *Hardball*. Matthews had savaged conservative columnist Michelle Malkin for daring to cite the book *Unfit for Command* as evidence that some veterans were questioning one of Kerry's Purple Hearts.

"They are legitimate questions about whether or not it was a self-inflicted wound," Malkin had said.

"What do you mean by self-inflicted?" Matthews hyperventilated. "Are you saying he shot himself on purpose? Is that what you're saying?"

He spent the rest of the segment badgering his guest as if she were personally making the allegation. The spectacle had been witnessed by Miller, who now rose to Malkin's defense.

"Don't pull that kind of stuff on me, like you did on that young lady when you had her there, browbeating her to death. I am not her. I am not her."

"She was suggesting that John Kerry purposely shot himself to win a medal," Matthews exaggerated. "And I was trying to correct the record."

"You get in my face, I am going to get back in your face," Miller warned. "The only reason you are doing it is because you are standing way over there in Herald Square."

More laughter from the peanut gallery.

"Senator, Senator, can I speak softly to you?" said Matthews, clinging to the remnants of a smile. "I would really like you to—"

"No, no, because you won't give me a chance to answer. You ask these questions and then you just talk over what I am trying to answer, just like you did that woman the other day."

"Well, Senator," said Matthews, hanging his head sheepishly.

"I don't know why I even came on this program."

"Well, I'm glad you did," said Matthews, now stunned and clearly stalling to regain his composure. "Uh, let me ask you this about, uh, about John Kerry's war record."

"Well, are you going to shut up after you ask me?" Miller demanded. "Or are you going to give me a chance to answer it?"

This time it was Matthews who was rendered speechless. His big grin had been replaced by a wan smile that seemed to acknowledge he had gone too far.

"Yes, sir," he said, utterly deflated. "I am going to give you a chance to answer."

In the end, Matthews was interrupted not by Miller, but by Watts.

"Hey, Senator, this is J. C. Watts."

"Hey, J. C.," Miller said.

"You can put your feet under my dinner table any day of the week," Watts said.

"Thank you," Miller said. "Thank you."

"Well, I guess everybody loves the senator," muttered Matthews, clearly annoyed to see his long harangue peter out into a lovefest.

Matthews was right about everybody loving Miller. Everybody, that is, except the Democrats and mainstream media, which went into overdrive to discredit the senator. Since there was nothing factually inaccurate about

Miller's speech, the Left was reduced to character assassination. Liberals portrayed Miller as a senile old coot who had come unhinged during his speech and subsequent interview with Matthews. One reporter summed up the feelings of the Fourth Estate with three contemptuous words: "Cracker goes crazy." When I relayed this particular insult to Miller during a phone interview as he headed for home, he said he had received a flurry of similar missives. The media's invective was so extreme that he began to worry that perhaps he had hurt the president's campaign. But Bush was already making plans to invite Miller to join him on the campaign trail once the convention was over. The president recognized that Miller had struck a chord that resonated with Middle America. In fact, it was a chord that Bush himself sounded in his acceptance speech the next evening. After all, he knew his strongest argument for reelection was that he would do a better job than Kerry of defending Americans against terrorism.

"I believe the most solemn duty of the American president is to protect the American people," he said. "If America shows uncertainty or weakness in this decade, the world will drift toward tragedy. This will not happen on my watch."

Unlike Kerry, whose criticism of Bush at the Democratic convention had been mostly indirect, the president opted for a frontal assault. When he savaged Kerry for opposing tax cuts and lawsuit reform, the audience booed lustily.

"Wait a minute, wait a minute: to be fair, there are some things my opponent is for," Bush said in mock protest, prompting laughter in the convention hall. "He's proposed more than two trillion dollars in new federal spending so far, and that's a lot, even for a senator from Massachusetts. And to pay for that spending, he's running on a platform of increasing taxes. And that's the kind of promise a politician usually keeps. His policies of tax and spend, of expanding government rather than expanding opportunity, are the policies of the past. We are on the path to the future—and we're not turning back."

"Four more years!" chanted the audience. "Four more years! Four more years!"

Bush then waded into the culture wars, arguing that Kerry was on the wrong side of hot-button issues like abortion, gay marriage, and judicial activism.

"Because a caring society will value its weakest members, we must make a place for the unborn child," he said. "Because the union of a man and woman deserves an honored place in our society, I support the protection of marriage against activist judges. And I will continue to appoint federal judges who know the difference between personal opinion and the strict interpretation of the law." Bush accused Kerry of trying to poach on the president's turf in the culture wars.

"My opponent recently announced that he is the candidate of 'conservative values,' which must have come as a surprise to a lot of his supporters. There's some problems with this claim.

"If you say the heart and soul of America is found in Hollywood, I'm afraid you're not the candidate of conservative values. If you voted against the bipartisan Defense of Marriage Act, which President Clinton signed, you are not the candidate of conservative values. If you gave a speech, as my opponent did, calling the Reagan presidency eight years of 'moral darkness,' then you may be a lot of things, but the candidate of conservative values is not one of them."

Ronald Reagan had died three months earlier, prompting an outpouring of grief and affection from virtually the entire nation. Of the five living presidents who gathered around Reagan's casket in the National Cathedral days later, only one was repeatedly compared to Reagan—George W. Bush. That's because so many momentous events had transpired on Bush's watch, including many of his own making. Looking back over his first term, the president now decided he was entitled to a little bragging at his convention.

"Four years ago, Afghanistan was the home base of al Qaeda, Pakistan was a transit point for terrorist groups, Saudi Arabia was fertile ground for terrorist fund-raising, Libya was secretly pursuing nuclear weapons, Iraq was a gathering threat, and al Qaeda was largely unchallenged as it planned attacks.

"Today, the government of a free Afghanistan is fighting terror, Pakistan is capturing terrorist leaders, Saudi Arabia is making raids and arrests, Libya is dismantling its weapons programs, the army of a free Iraq is fighting for freedom, and more than three-quarters of al Qaeda's key members and associates have been detained or killed. We have led, many have joined, and America and the world are safer."

Although Bush said invading Iraq had been his "toughest" decision, he was unapologetic about the outcome.

"We knew Saddam Hussein's record of aggression and support for terror. We knew his long history of pursuing, even using, weapons of mass destruction. And we know that September 11 requires our country to think differently. We must, and we will, confront threats to America before it is too late. In Saddam Hussein, we saw a threat."

The audience chanted "USA! USA! USA!"

"Members of both political parties, including my opponent and his running mate, saw the threat, and voted to authorize the use of force. We went to the United Nations Security Council, which passed a unanimous resolution demanding the dictator disarm, or face serious consequences. Leaders in the Middle East urged him to comply. After more than a decade of diplomacy, we gave Saddam Hussein another chance, a final chance, to meet his responsibilities to the civilized world. He again refused, and I faced the kind of decision that comes only to the Oval Office—a decision no president would ask for, but must be prepared to make. Do I forget the lessons of September 11 and take the word of a madman, or do I take action to defend our country? Faced with that choice, I will defend America every time."

"USA! USA! USA!"

"Because we acted to defend our country, the murderous regimes of Saddam Hussein and the Taliban are history, more than fifty million people have been liberated, and democracy is coming to the broader Middle East."

Now came the portion of the speech where Bush threw Kerry's assorted gaffes back in his face.

"My opponent and I have different approaches. I proposed, and the Congress overwhelmingly passed, $87 billion in funding needed by our troops doing battle in Afghanistan and Iraq. My opponent and his running mate voted against this money for bullets, and fuel, and vehicles, and body armor."

"Boo!" yelled the audience.

"When asked to explain his vote, the senator said, 'I actually did vote for the $87 billion before I voted against it,'" Bush recalled.

"Flip-flop!" chanted the audience. "Flip-flop! Flip-flop!"

"Then he said he was 'proud' of that vote. Then, when pressed, he said it was a 'complicated' matter. There's nothing complicated about supporting our troops in combat!"

Bush then cited a quotation that I had asked him about eighteen months earlier in an Oval Office interview. As promised, he turned it against Kerry.

"In the midst of war, he has called American allies, quote, a 'coalition of the coerced and the bribed.' That would be nations like Great Britain, Poland, Italy, Japan, the Netherlands, Denmark, El Salvador, Australia, and others—allies that deserve the respect of all Americans, not the scorn of a politician. I respect every soldier, from every country, who serves beside us in the hard work of history. America is grateful, and America will not forget."

The president then laid out, for all to see, his vision of America's role in the world.

"I believe that America is called to lead the cause of freedom in a new century. I believe that millions in the Middle East plead in silence for their liberty. I believe that given the chance, they will embrace the most honorable form of government ever devised by man. I believe all these things because freedom is not America's gift to the world, it is the almighty God's gift to every man and woman in this world."

Bush was clearly mindful of the historic nature of his presidency.

"This moment in the life of our country will be remembered. Generations will know if we kept our faith and kept our word. Generations will know if we seized this moment, and used it to build a future of safety and peace. The freedom of many, and the future security of our nation, now depend on us. And tonight, my fellow Americans, I ask you to stand with me."

"Four more years! Four more years! Four more years!"

"In the last four years, you and I have come to know each other. Even when we don't agree, at least you know what I believe and where I stand.

"You may have noticed I have a few flaws, too. People sometimes have to correct my English. I knew I had a problem when Arnold Schwarzenegger started doing it. Some folks look at me and see a certain swagger, which in Texas is called 'walking.' Now and then I come across as a little too blunt— and for that we can all thank the white-haired lady sitting right up there."

Laughter and rapturous applause as the cameras panned to the president's mother, former First Lady Barbara Bush.

"One thing I have learned about the presidency is that whatever short-comings you have, people are going to notice them. And whatever strengths you have, you're going to need them. These four years have brought moments I could not foresee and will not forget. I've tried to comfort Americans who lost the most on September 11—people who showed me a picture or told me a story, so I would know how much was taken from them. I've learned first-hand that ordering Americans into battle is the hardest decision, even when it is right. I have returned the salute of wounded soldiers, some with a very tough road ahead, who say they were just doing their job. I've held the chil-dren of the fallen, who are told their dad or mom is a hero, but would rather just have their mom or dad. I've met with the wives and husbands who have received a folded flag, and said a final good-bye to a soldier they loved.

"I am awed that so many have used those meetings to say that I'm in their prayers and to offer encouragement to me. Where does strength like that come from? How can people so burdened with sorrow also feel such pride? It is because they know their loved one was last seen doing good. Because they know that liberty was precious to the one they lost. And in those military fam-ilies, I have seen the character of a great nation: decent, idealistic, and strong."

Bush closed by imploring the nation to put this strength and idealism to good use.

"Like generations before us, we have a calling from beyond the stars to stand for freedom. This is the everlasting dream of America—and tonight, in this place, that dream is renewed. Now we go forward—grateful for our freedom, faithful to our cause, and confident in the future of the greatest nation on earth."

The delegates were on their feet, cheering for all they were worth. The sound system blared "Put a Little Love in Your Heart," the old song by Jackie DeShannon. Amid much fanfare, the president was joined onstage by his wife and the Cheneys.

And then, right on cue, the balloons dropped.

CHAPTER EIGHT

"CHANGE THE MOMENTUM OF AN ELECTION"

M ary Mapes was so excited that she called Dan Rather before he finished his broadcast. She left a tantalizing message for him that "something big had come up." Driving east on Interstate 20 toward her home in Dallas, Mapes requested a return call from the anchorman as soon as he finished covering President Bush's acceptance speech at the Republican National Convention.

Not that Rather regarded himself as "covering" anything. It was more like watching helplessly from his anchor chair at Madison Square Garden while the president's speech utterly consumed the one measly hour that CBS was devoting to this final night of the convention. Rather complained bitterly that Republicans had stage-managed the convention so thoroughly that he and his fellow journalists at CBS had been reduced to mere onlookers at a prepackaged sporting event.

"Actually, in sports you can do more," Rather lamented to the *New York Times*. "You can say the fullback missed a block. Here we don't even get to do that."

To make matters worse, the speech ran longer than an hour, which meant that almost immediately after Bush finished speaking at 11:12 p.m. on Thursday, September 2, CBS affiliates cut away to shows like *Entertainment Tonight*. No wonder CBS News and the other broadcast news divisions at ABC and NBC were being trounced in the ratings wars for the first time ever by a lowly cable outlet. FOX News Channel accomplished this seminal feat in television history on Tuesday, August 31, the second night of the Republican convention (the broadcast networks hadn't even bothered to cover the opening speeches on Monday). FOX broadened its lead on Wednesday, actually garnering more viewers than CBS and ABC *combined*. And now, on the convention's fourth and final night, CBS was again crushed by the hated FOX News Channel. What made this particularly painful to Rather was the realization that CBS was available in millions more homes than FOX, yet FOX was drawing more than twice as many viewers. It was nothing short of mortifying.

Swallowing hard, Rather managed to rationalize that the Republican Party would rue the day that FOX had beaten the broadcast networks.

"I tip my cap to FOX," Rather told the *Times*. "I'm sure people in the party are saying that's a great audience and on a channel that's friendly to us. But the wise ones know that this is preaching to the converted. And if they want to reach independent or swing voters, the way to do that is through the over-the-air networks."

Sour grapes aside, Rather was relieved to be departing New York City and heading down to Florida to cover his favorite kind of story—a hurricane. Rather never forgot that it was his coverage of Hurricane Carla back in 1961 that first caught the eye of CBS News executives. They hired the thirty-year-old Texan in 1962 and never stopped sending him to hurricanes. Now, more than four decades later, Hurricane Frances was bearing down on Florida and the seventy-two-year-old anchorman, as usual, was headed into the eye of the storm.

So it was quite late by the time Rather returned Mapes's call. His star producer informed him that she had unearthed another major scoop. After five long years of dogged reporting, she had just obtained what she called the "missing links" in Bush's military service record. According to Mapes, these consisted of previously undisclosed documents that showed, once and for all, that Bush had been a slacker who received special treatment while serving as a fighter pilot in the Texas Air National Guard from May 1968 to October 1973.

"In his military career, Bush was truly born on third base," Mapes had told Rather when she first started researching the story back in 1999. She described Bush's Guard unit as "a safe haven for children of privilege at the height of the Vietnam War."

But Mapes had never been able to prove this theory, which she had held since Bush was governor of Texas and making his first run for the White House. In fact, the deeper she dug, the more her premise collapsed. For example, Mapes interviewed Walter "Buck" Staudt, who insisted that "no influence" had been exerted to get Bush into the 147th Fighter Interceptor Group. "Nobody called me," said Staudt, who had interviewed Bush in May 1968 before he was admitted to the Guard. Mapes also tracked down Major General Bobby Hodges, commander of the unit, who assured her there were "no strings pulled" to get Bush a slot as a pilot. To the contrary, Hodges told Mapes that the unit was "hurting for pilots at that time," due to "big turnover." This absence of a waiting list blew a large hole in Mapes's theory that Bush had used his connections to land a coveted slot in the Guard, displacing less "privileged" applicants who ended up being shipped off to Vietnam. Undaunted, Mapes postulated that Staudt must have deviously set aside slots in order "to take in the children of privilege" while cleverly "maintaining deniability." But she was never able to find any evidence. Although she had Rather go through the motions of interviewing a couple of people, they had no firsthand knowledge of Bush's military service, so the interviews never aired.

In October 2000, Mapes heard a story so implausible that even she didn't bother pursuing it. A retired lieutenant colonel named Bill Burkett claimed to have overheard a telephone conversation about a conspiracy to "scrub" Bush's military records. Incredibly, Burkett said this plot to purge the files of potentially embarrassing documents was then carried out by Bush aide Dan

Bartlett. The skullduggery supposedly took place in 1997 at Camp Mabry in Austin, the headquarters of the Texas Air National Guard. According to Burkett, the files needed to be "scrubbed" before Bush could publish his political autobiography, *A Charge to Keep*, as part of his run for the White House.

"I was on full-time duty at Camp Mabry when Dan Bartlett was cleansing the George W. Bush file," Burkett wrote in a statement that was published on anti-Bush websites three days before the 2000 election. "The archives were closely scrutinized to make sure that the Bush autobiography plans and the record did not directly contradict each other."

When this sensational allegation was picked up the next day by the *Times* of London, Burkett backpedaled by issuing a rambling, thousand-word "clarification."

"Did you allege that the governor's staff doctored the records?" he asked himself rhetorically. "No." Backing off even further, he added, "I was extremely careful not to point an accusing finger."

Having now contradicted himself, Burkett found the mainstream media reluctant to publicize his claims. He made reporters even more skeptical when he reversed himself yet again on March 19, 2003. That's when Burkett published an online screed claiming to have angered Bush when he was governor by "refusing to alter" his "official personnel records." Never mind Burkett's previous yarn about merely being in the right place at the right time when Bush's records happened to undergo a scrubbing. Now he was presenting himself as having been *personally* ordered to carry out the dastardly deed. So much for Burkett being "careful not to point an accusing finger."

Furthermore, Burkett was now saying that his refusal to scrub the files prompted Bush to retaliate. This was supposedly accomplished by sending Burkett on assignment to Panama, where he claimed the membranes covering his brain and spinal cord became inflamed, a condition known as meningococcal encephalitis. When Burkett returned from Panama in 1998, he retired and requested a permanent medical disability. His request was denied by the Texas Air National Guard. Burkett appealed the ruling all the way up to Bush, who upheld the denial. Angry and embittered, Burkett now clearly had an axe to grind. This made reporters even more wary of quoting him.

"He was generally viewed by the press as an anti-Bush zealot. That is how I regarded him, too," Mapes wrote in her memoir. "I thought he was paranoid."

But the media environment changed in February 2004, when Senator John Kerry, a decorated Vietnam veteran, emerged as the Democrat who would square off against Bush in the fall. Sensing a comparison that would work against the president, liberals immediately resurrected the issue of Bush's military record. Left-wing filmmaker Michael Moore actually branded the commander in chief a "deserter."

"George Bush never served in our military in our country," added Democratic National Committee chairman Terry McAuliffe on ABC News on February 1, slurring both the president and the National Guard. "I look forward to that debate with John Kerry, a war hero with a chest full of medals, standing next to George Bush, a man who was AWOL."

Such unproven and incendiary allegations were enough to relieve the mainstream media of its qualms about publicizing Burkett's "scrubbing" conspiracy. Suddenly it was open season on the president's military records. In February alone, some two hundred reporters deluged Burkett with requests for interviews. He obliged one and all, this time going much further with his allegations. Burkett now claimed to have overheard not one, but *two* conversations among Guard officials conspiring to "scrub" the Bush files. Furthermore, Burkett said he *personally witnessed* a general rifling through the files and even *saw some Bush documents in a trash can next to the general*!

These details were dutifully reported by the mainstream media, although the resulting stories made clear that Burkett's claims were inconsistent, to say the least. Still, liberal journalists couldn't resist publicizing them anyway.

Naturally, CBS News got in on the act by dispatching senior White House correspondent John Roberts to interview Burkett. Without provocation, Burkett began ranting that he would not grant an interview unless Roberts obtained permission from author Jim Moore, who had just published an anti-Bush book that quoted Burkett at length. This astonished Roberts because Burkett had already granted interviews to a multitude of media outlets. Nonetheless, Roberts went through the motions of obtaining permission from Moore. Only then did Burkett grant what Roberts called a "meandering" interview about the "scrubbing" of Bush's records. Roberts deemed Burkett so "unreliable" that he instructed a producer to obtain a rebuttal from a Bush official, who dismissed the allegations as "hogwash." Even Mapes acknowledged that Burkett was a controversial source whose story "had not proven out."

Any responsible journalistic organization would think long and hard before airing unproven allegations against a sitting president from a source that its own reporter considered "unreliable." But with virtually every other major news outlet airing Burkett's conspiracy theory, CBS didn't want to be left out of the pack. So on February 12, the "unreliable" Burkett allegations were broadcast on the CBS *Evening News*, anchored by Rather, who also served as the show's managing editor.

Eventually, the feeding frenzy against Bush subsided. By summer, though, when journalists recognized the political toll the Swift Boat Veterans for Truth ads were taking on Kerry, they renewed their efforts to find damaging information about the president's military record. Mapes made no secret of her zeal for such a story.

"I am DEADLY serious about it," she e-mailed a CBS underling that summer. "Do NOT underestimate how much I want this story."

Mapes clearly believed Bush could not hold a candle to Kerry when it came to military service.

"There seemed no question about Kerry's solid military credentials," she wrote in her memoir. By contrast, "Bush didn't keep his promise to his country. He swore he would fly military jets until May 1974 in return for being removed from the danger of being drafted. He didn't even come close, leaving the cockpit more than two years early. He didn't keep his word to the pilots who did fulfill their service, to the commanders who counted on him, or to the military, which spent more than a million dollars teaching him how to fly. He left without giving the National Guard or the country their money's worth. He walked away from his duty."

Hoping to prove this thesis, Mapes sent her superiors at CBS an e-mail assuring them that she was gathering "lots of goodies" about Bush's "refusal of service in Vietnam." She added, "We are in pursuit." The pursuit only intensified when Mapes realized how many other journalists were seeking the same dirt on Bush. She told her bosses on August 3 that reporters from the *New York Times Magazine*, *Harper's*, and *Vanity Fair* were "all chasing the Bush National Guard stuff again." She added, "It is much more intense than it was four years ago and there is a strong general feeling that this time, there is blood in the water."

The blood was being chummed into the water by Burkett, who insinuated on August 25 that he was in possession of previously undisclosed documents about the president's military record.

"George W. Bush, you may be the president. *But I know you lied*," Burkett wrote on an anti-Bush website. "I know from your files that we have now reassembled."

Suitably intrigued, Mapes asked Burkett for these mysteriously reassembled files. But he played hard to get, so Mapes approved a list of enticements that might loosen his grip on the documents. The list was assembled by one of Mapes's underlings, CBS associate producer Michael Smith, whose lust for the documents was so powerful that he referred to them as the "holy grail." Smith even contrived to put Burkett in touch with a book editor for a possible publishing deal.

"Today I am going to send the following hypothetical scenario to a reliable, trustable editor friend of mine," Smith wrote in an e-mail to Mapes on August 31. "What if there was a person who might have some information that could possibly change the momentum of an election, but we needed to get an ASAP book deal to help get us the information?

"What kind of turnaround payment schedules are possible?" he continued. "Can we get a decent sized advance payment and get it turned around quickly?"

Smith, who previously worked as a research assistant to liberal columnist Molly Ivins, emphasized that a book deal could be offered only if Burkett "played ball with the documents."

"If he shows us what we want, then I can call my friend," he concluded, "and start the process."

"That looks good," Mapes replied in an e-mail. "Hypothetically speaking, of course."

The journalists had clearly abandoned their roles as objective chroniclers of the news in order to engage in advocacy journalism, which entailed misusing the media megaphone to achieve a desired political outcome. In this case, the goal, as Smith openly admitted, was to "change the momentum of an election." Since that momentum was currently against Kerry, thanks to the Swift Boat Veterans for Truth, Mapes and Smith obviously hoped the Burkett documents could turn the tide against Bush.

To ensure this result, Mapes threw journalistic ethics out the window. So determined was she to get her hands on anti-Bush documents that she was willing to dangle a book deal in front of Burkett, whom she privately referred to as "our bitter little buddy." To sweeten the pot, Smith suggested additional cash and security for the reluctant source, who fretted about possible retaliation from Bush supporters.

"Just in case Burkett asks—let me make sure I have this right. This is our plan: If he shows us some leg, we are going to talk to him about his options," Smith wrote in another e-mail to Mapes. "If his leg is sexy and useful, then we are going to then do whatever it takes to help him in those areas."

This arrangement was in blatant violation of CBS News' own written standards on journalistic conduct.

Everything we do while covering a story or gathering material for a broadcast must be done within the highest standards of journalistic integrity, the network warned in a handbook issued to all its reporters and producers. *It is vital that CBS News employees remain at "arm's length" from the stories we cover and that we not be perceived in the slightest as participants or interested parties.*

But the trashing of journalistic standards was just getting started. Mapes, after checking with her executive producer, Josh Howard, actually agreed to put Burkett in touch with the Kerry campaign so he could offer advice on how to counter the Swift Boat attacks. Smith called this "forcing" the Kerry campaign to acknowledge Burkett's "wisdom and strategic abilities."

Any cub reporter at a small-town newspaper would instinctively know such a quid pro quo was way over the journalistic line. In case there was any doubt, the point was pounded home in the CBS employee handbook.

The potential for damage to our credibility is perhaps greatest in the area of politics, the handbook warned. *Nothing erodes* [credibility] *faster than viewers or listeners thinking that we have an axe to grind or that we are beholden to anyone or anything other than fairness and the truth.*

Alas, fairness and truth were the first casualties of Mapes's fateful meeting with Burkett at the Pizza House restaurant in Clyde, Texas, on September 2. After three hours of coaxing, Burkett relinquished photocopies of two sheets of paper that he said were taken from the personal file of Lieutenant Colonel Jerry Killian, who had once commanded Bush's squadron. One of the documents was innocuous. But the other, titled "Memorandum for Record," purported to show Killian complaining to himself that Bush "has made no attempt to meet his training certification or flight physical" requirements. According to this document, Killian supposedly ordered "Bush to be suspended from flight status" for failing to undergo the physical. Furthermore, Killian seemed to be casting aspersions on Bush's flying prowess, not to mention his lack of service in Vietnam, by suggesting that he be replaced by "a more seasoned pilot from the list of qualified Vietnam pilots that have rotated."

The memo was dated August 1, 1972, but there was no way to verify that its author was Killian, since he had been dead for twenty years. The document didn't even contain his signature—only his initials. Burkett did not tell Mapes exactly how he had obtained the memo and Mapes did not press him for details on the chain of possession. She was so worried about placating Burkett that she even granted him anonymity.

"These new memos made Bush look like a slacker, not an ace pilot," she wrote in her memoir. "The closest Bush had come to battle during Vietnam was serving in Houston, flying his F-102 on weekends, patrolling the bars, and fighting to get a drink faster than anyone else."

It was after her meeting with Burkett finally ended and Mapes was driving home to Dallas that she finally connected with Rather to crow about her newest scoop. Naturally, she chose not to emphasize Burkett's numerous weaknesses as a source. In fact, Rather recalled that Mapes described Burkett as a "straight-talking West Texan" with a "good reputation in the county where he lives, even among people who do not like him, and they say he is a truth teller." But if Rather believed this characterization, he was being naïve in the extreme. After all, fewer than six months earlier, he had used his very own broadcast, the CBS *Evening News*, for which he served as anchor and managing editor, to air an interview of Burkett by senior White House correspondent John Roberts, who found the source "unreliable." In case Rather hadn't been paying attention to his own broadcast, Burkett's repeated flip-flopping on the "scrubbing" allegation had been abundantly documented in February by the *New York Times*, *USA Today*, the *Washington Post*, the *Los Angeles Times*, the *Boston Globe*, the *Houston Chronicle*, the *Dallas Morning News*, the *Detroit Free Press*, the *Kansas City Star*, the Associated Press, CNN, and MSNBC. Yet somehow Rather was now romanticizing Burkett as a "truth teller." He even resolved to telephone the source and personally thank him for coughing up the documents.

By the time Mapes arrived at her Dallas home, she was having the sort of adrenaline rush experienced by every journalist who is about to break a story of enormous consequence. In the wee hours of the morning, she found herself too "excited, busy, stressed, etc. to sleep," according to an e-mail she sent to colleagues. She wrote breathlessly about her lust for another batch of documents from Burkett, enthusing, "I want it."

But first Mapes had to show Burkett some leg of her own. On September 4, she telephoned the John Kerry campaign to say that "Burkett wanted to talk about the Swift Boat attacks and how the campaign should respond," she wrote in her memoir. She ended up speaking with Joe Lockhart, who had just been brought in to salvage Kerry's campaign in the wake of the Swift Boat debacle. She said she relayed Burkett's argument that "he had some insight into how to handle the Swift Boat veterans' issues." She also explained to Lockhart that if he called Burkett, the disgruntled officer would likely give Mapes additional documents that cast aspersions on the president's military record.

"She basically said there's a guy who is being helpful on the story who wants to talk to you," Lockhart would later tell the Associated Press.

Lockhart, best known as the pugnacious White House press secretary during President Clinton's impeachment, agreed to call Burkett. Mapes helpfully passed along the source's telephone number.

CBS had now crossed several additional journalistic lines. Instead of simply reporting the news, the network was arranging for the Kerry campaign to receive political advice from a Bush detractor. At the same time, CBS had enlisted Kerry's top strategist as an active partner in the newsgathering process. After all, even if no new documents were forthcoming, Lockhart's call to Burkett would surely help the network assuage a temperamental source.

But Burkett's demands did not end with access to the Kerry campaign. He also wanted CBS to hire him as a consultant, pay for his relocation if the political fallout became too intense, and even buy him a pre-paid cell phone. The network bought him the cell phone and made vague assurances in response to his other demands. It was difficult to imagine how the bar of journalistic ethics could be lowered much further.

In the end, this pay-to-play strategy worked. By September 5, Mapes had four more photocopies of one-page documents that Burkett claimed had been taken from Killian's mysterious file on Bush. Again, one was innocuous. A second, dated May 4, 1972, purported to show Killian ordering Bush to take his annual physical exam within ten days. This was not particularly newsworthy in and of itself, although at least this document bore Killian's signature.

The other two sheets of paper, each titled "Memo to File," portrayed Bush as a slacker who was being protected by friends in high places. But neither of these documents bore a signature.

The first, dated May 19, 1972, had Killian summarizing a "phone call from Bush." The two men "discussed options of how Bush can get out of coming to drill from now through November" so the pilot could work "on another campaign for his dad." This was a reference to Winton Blount, a friend of Bush's father, who was running for a U.S. Senate seat in Alabama. Bush had agreed to help with the campaign and, according to the memo, cited this as a reason for his reluctance to take a physical. "He has this campaign to do and other things that will follow and may not have the time. I advised him on our investment in him and his commitment," Killian allegedly wrote. "I told him I had to have written acceptance before he would be transferred, but think he's also talking to someone upstairs."

The second "Memo to File," dated August 13, 1973, was even more damning. It bore the notation "SUBJECT: CYA," which is short for "cover your ass." It portrayed Killian as being pressured by top brass to write a favorable annual rating for an undeserving Lieutenant Bush. "Staudt is pushing to sugar coat it," Killian purportedly wrote to himself. "Staudt has obviously pressured Hodges more about Bush. I'm having trouble running interference and doing my job." The memo cast Killian as reluctant to issue the rating. "Bush wasn't here during rating period," he complained. "I'll backdate but won't rate."

The memo did not explain how Staudt, who had retired from the Guard on March 1, 1972, could possibly exert the slightest influence on active-duty officers nearly eighteen months later. This glaring break in logic did not appear to trouble Burkett, who was more concerned about getting in touch with Team Kerry. The day after relinquishing his documents, he complained to Mapes that the campaign had not called him yet.

"You are right as always on this stuff," she assured him in an e-mail. "I will make some phone calls."

This did not satisfy Burkett, who was growing impatient.

"I need you to pass a message a little earlier than we had expected," he wrote in a cloak-and-dagger e-mail to Mapes. "Have them call and give me a secure number."

Later, Burkett sent her another e-mail emphasizing the need to "expedite" his rendezvous with the Kerry campaign "with a serious call contact today— and as early as possible." He added cryptically, "I hate to do this because it leaves a fingerprint, but if your inside contact won't call me, at least maybe they can give me an e-mail address."

All this nagging finally paid off and Mapes made good on her promise. Lockhart called Burkett later that day and patiently listened to his advice on how the Kerry campaign should respond to the Swift Boat attacks. The unethical relationship between CBS and the Kerry campaign would continue for days, with a Lockhart subordinate even e-mailing Mapes an Associated Press article about freshly discovered Bush military records. The debasement of responsible journalism by CBS News, the "Tiffany Network," was complete.

Mapes and Rather planned to unveil their newly acquired documents on Wednesday, September 8, on CBS's vaunted newsmagazine *60 Minutes*, which Mapes described as "the top franchise of a legendary news division." But first they engaged in a bit of "CYA" themselves by hurriedly rounding up four experts to authenticate the documents. Unfortunately, all four immediately explained that the documents could not be authenticated because they were low-quality photocopies, not pristine originals. To make matters worse, only one of the examiners—Marcel Matley of San Francisco—was given both batches of documents. The other three examiners received only the first batch. Nevertheless, all the examiners agreed to eyeball the papers and provide whatever analysis they could.

Red flags arose almost immediately. At 4:24 p.m. on September 5, Mapes received an e-mail from one of the examiners—Emily Will of Raleigh, North Carolina—who cited a laundry list of concerns. For starters, Will found "problems" with Killian's signature on one of the documents because it differed from signatures found in official Bush records. Will also flatly stated that one of the pages "does NOT look like a military document." In addition, she was struck by the absence of a letterhead on both pages she received.

More important, Will noted that a word on one of the documents "has a superscript th." She was referring to the fact that the "th" in "111th Fighter

Interceptor Squadron" was shrunken and raised to the top of the line—a fancy typographical feature generally not available on typewriters in 1973. It later became a routine function of word processing software for personal computers, but those had not even been invented when the document in question had supposedly been written.

Finally and most significantly, Will warned that both documents had "the general appearance of a proportional spaced and proportional width font." In other words, various letters of the alphabet had differing widths and occupied only as much space on the page as necessary. Again, this was a function associated with modern computers, not thirty-year-old typewriters, which allocated the exact same space on the page to each letter of the alphabet, regardless of its width.

Will reiterated her concerns about typography and signatures in a telephone conversation with Mapes that afternoon. But when she began to raise suspicions about the substance of the documents, Mapes interrupted and told Will that her job was limited to signature and typography analysis. Mapes would handle the substance.

That same day, Mapes spoke with Matley, who said his verification was limited to one signature on one document. He could not authenticate Killian's initials, since he had nothing with which to compare them. And he could not authenticate the typography on any of the documents, since they were all photocopies. Yet this was good enough for Mapes, who began making arrangements for Matley to be flown in from San Francisco for an interview with Rather. Far from expressing alarm at the document examiners' mounting concerns, Mapes sent her bosses an e-mail suggesting that all was well. She attached an Associated Press story alleging that some documents in Bush's military records were missing.

"I have some of these missing documents on my desk," she hyped. "Yikes!"

On the morning of September 6, while waiting for his flight to depart San Francisco, Matley wrote down some notes about the Killian papers, starting with an unequivocal disclaimer.

"Poor copies," Matley wrote. "Could not authenticate documents themselves."

He showed this disclaimer to Mapes when he arrived in New York. According to Matley, he was told by Mapes that CBS was "not interested in all the parameters" of his findings.

Matley was then interviewed by Rather, who concluded the source did not come across well on camera.

"If CBS News had to put an expert out there, he would not be very persuasive," Rather muttered.

So the anchorman interviewed Matley a second time, although this performance wasn't much better than the first. In the end, Rather decided not to use the footage of Matley or even his name in the story.

But instead of relaying these misgivings to CBS News president Andrew Heyward, Rather assured him that he had not "been involved in this much checking on a story since Watergate." During their conversation on September 6, Rather also told Heyward, "This isn't as big as Abu Ghraib, but it's very big, and you should probably look at it before it goes to air."

Suitably warned, Heyward decided to cover his own posterior. The next afternoon, he instructed his top lieutenants—senior vice president Betsy West and executive producer Josh Howard—not to let Rather and Mapes "stampede us in any way." Heyward, who considered the story "a politically sensitive piece," added in an e-mail, "We're going to have to defend every syllable of this one."

Less than twenty-four hours before the scheduled broadcast, Mapes received another call from Will, who practically begged CBS not to air the documents. Her previous concerns about the poor-quality photocopies had grown even stronger. She flatly warned that she could verify neither Killian's signature nor his initials. She reiterated her worries over the superscript "th" and proportionally spaced font. She had even retyped the documents on a computer, using the popular software program Microsoft Word, and found an alarming similarity to the photocopies. Will went on record to CBS that the Killian memos must have been written on a computer and could not have been created on a typewriter more than three decades earlier. She warned Mapes that if CBS insisted on broadcasting the files, "every document expert in the country will be after you with hundreds of questions."

But Mapes blew her off, rationalizing that the examiner had disqualified herself by also raising concerns about the substance of the documents—even to the point of researching Bush's military service on the Internet. Mapes told an underling that Will was more concerned with "the facts about President Bush's National Guard service than on her job," adding, "The facts were none of Will's business."

Shortly after this conversation, however, another document examiner that CBS had hired—Linda James of Plano, Texas—called to raise similar objections. James had found "unexplainable differences in the signatures" and also red-flagged the superscript "th." Exasperated, Mapes responded, "Enough about the [expletive] 'th.'"

But the "th" issue would not go away. Even Roger Charles, the retired Marine colonel who worked for Mapes as an associate producer, called her that evening to add his own concerns about the superscript. The man who had helped Mapes secure the Abu Ghraib photos now cautioned his boss that the format of the documents was at odds with military guidelines.

"Everything but the ceiling tiles" was crashing down around Mapes, according to another associate producer, Yvonne Miller, who worked with her that evening. Miller could see that Mapes was angry and worried about the mounting questions. Miller harbored her own doubts, but decided not to alert senior producers because she figured that would just create controversy and, besides, Mapes had a way of refuting all objections.

Still, Mapes was sufficiently rattled to alert West and Howard that the examiners had "spooked" her. She told them about the superscript issue, although she decided not to mention the signatures or proportional font. West assured Mapes they didn't have to air the story if the documents were not solid. But Mapes quickly shook off the doubts. Late that evening, she e-mailed

Howard that she was "pretty much over that whole little 'th' problem that I had. No one can agree on it because no one knows." She added that if Will "had not brought it up, I wouldn't have obsessed about it. She is also the woman who started arguing with me about when Bush was in Alabama." Mapes concluded, "I think all these people are nuts."

Earlier in the day, White House communications director Dan Bartlett had gotten wind of the story and contacted CBS, since the network had not bothered contacting him for comment. Having been accused by Burkett of personally carrying out the "scrubbing" of Bush's files, Bartlett served as the president's point man on this issue. As such, he made clear to CBS that it would be unfair to give the White House only a few hours to respond to a major investigative piece involving previously undisclosed documents. So CBS read the Killian files to Bartlett over the phone that evening. Bartlett said these documents were "new news" to him and asked CBS to fax them to the White House right away. But CBS refused.

"Reporters never want to get a comment on a big story too soon," Mapes explained in her memoir. "That meant you ran the risk of the White House or whomever the story focused on going public, stealing your thunder, getting out in front of the report."

So Mapes and Rather waited until the next morning, which was the day of the broadcast, to have the documents delivered to the White House. This struck Karl Rove as disturbing evidence that the two journalists were biased.

"From her body language and his body language, their enthusiasm for this story was in large measure fed by the belief that they were playing a constructive and perhaps determinative role in the presidential campaign," he told me. "Look, people get to choose in that line of business what stories they cover and what stories they don't cover. I mean, there were a whole series of stories which the media made a decision it was not going to cover about John Kerry. They made a decision in this instance—I think quite prematurely and quite unfairly—to pursue a story that attacked the president. And I thought it was one of the most incredible examples of how fundamentally unfair the media is. I mean, they send copies of the documents to the White House and expect Dan Bartlett to confirm, in three hours, whether these are genuine documents or not."

Indeed, Bartlett was able to give the papers only a cursory glance before being interviewed by CBS News correspondent John Roberts, who demanded an explanation. Incredibly, Roberts was now brandishing extremely dubious documents from a source he had found to be "unreliable" six months earlier.

"Fifty-five days before an election," Bartlett explained to Roberts, "partisan Democrats are recycling the very same charges we hear every time President Bush runs for election."

Since the memos supposedly were taken from the personal papers of a man who had been dead for twenty years—and not the president's official military files—Bartlett had no way of instantaneously disproving their authenticity. Having laid eyes on them for the very first time just before the interview, the politico could not possibly mount an expert technical challenge to the handwriting or typography.

Yet CBS took this lack of a challenge by Bartlett as nothing less than definitive confirmation of the documents' authenticity. When the interview was over, Roberts telephoned Mapes to explain that Bartlett had not called the documents forgeries. Incredibly, Mapes said that relieved her from using many of the document examiners she had lined up for the story.

At the end of the day, as darkness fell across Washington, Bartlett had the unenviable task of showing the documents to Bush.

"I remember getting off a chopper," the president told me. "And I saw Bartlett standing in the Diplomatic Reception Room. And it was late, and I didn't know why he was there, and I was tired. You get tired in a campaign, you know. And we came walking off the chopper and he got out of sight of the press inside the Diplomatic Reception Room."

As the president walked in, Bartlett handed him a sheet of paper.

"You remember this?" he asked.

"Well, what is it?" Bush shrugged.

"It's a letter from Jerry Killian."

"I don't remember that," said the president, scanning the document. "No, I don't remember that."

Bush paid no attention to the letter's typography. He was too busy studying its content. He tried to imagine his long-dead commander saying such things. But the words on the page simply didn't ring true.

"This just doesn't seem right to me," he murmured. "Something about it that just didn't..."

But Bush didn't have time to anguish over the letter and the rest of the documents Bartlett was waving. He was too busy trying to win the election, which was now only eight weeks away.

"I knew I needed to get some rest for the next day's events," he told me. "I just kind of went on about my business."

Up in New York, Rather was so excited about the White House not denouncing the documents as forgeries that he decided to break the story on the CBS *Evening News*, which aired an hour and a half before *60 Minutes*.

"Good evening," the anchorman intoned at the top of the newscast. "There are new questions tonight about President Bush's service in the Texas Air National Guard in the 1960s and early '70s and about his insistence that he met his military service requirements."

Journalists liked to use the word "insistence" in cases like this because it suggested the target was stubbornly clinging to a lie in the face of massive evidence to the contrary.

"*60 Minutes* has obtained government documents that indicate Mr. Bush may have received preferential treatment in the Guard after not fulfilling his commitments," Rather continued.

The anchorman then launched into an ominous recitation of the Killian papers before adding, "A spokesman for President Bush did not challenge the authenticity of the documents."

Since the entire purpose of the story was to "change the momentum of an election," CBS helpfully provided its own nudge—while maintaining journalistic deniability, of course.

"The Democrats certainly wasted no time jumping all over these new allegations against the president," Rather said in the voice of a detached observer. "They are eager to turn the tables on the issue of Vietnam service and put a little drag on the president's post-convention bounce."

Unlike Kerry, Bush had gained two points during his convention and his opponent had lost two, according to Gallup.

In case anyone doubted which side CBS was on, Rather adopted an even more lopsided tone when introducing the document story on *60 Minutes* later that evening.

"The military records of the two men running for president have become part of the political arsenal in this campaign," he began even-handedly before revealing his bias. "While Senator Kerry has been targeted for what he did in combat in Vietnam, President Bush has been criticized for avoiding Vietnam by landing a much-sought-after spot in the Texas Air National Guard and then apparently failing to meet some of his obligations in the Guard."

Rather again rehashed the Killian documents before adding disingenuously, "We consulted a handwriting analyst and document expert who believes the material is authentic."

This was a reference to Matley, even though he had expressly told CBS that he could not declare the documents "authentic" because they were photocopies, not originals. Furthermore, Matley had limited his analysis to verifying one signature on one document. Two of the documents used in the report did not even contain a signature. A third contained only Killian's initials, which Matley could not verify because he had nothing with which to compare them. As for the typography of the documents, Matley had not vouched for it in the slightest. And yet Rather was citing both "a handwriting analyst and document expert." It was nothing short of a bald-faced lie.

The documents were supposedly buttressed by interviews with former Guard officials—though these officials had no direct knowledge of whether Bush's connections had landed him a spot in the Guard or whether he shirked his duties once there. Incredibly, one of these "sources" was Ben Barnes, vice chairman of the Kerry campaign, who had raised more than $100,000 for the

Democrat. Barnes was now alleging that back in 1968, when he was lieutenant governor of Texas, he put in a good word for Bush, although he had
no way of knowing whether this helped Bush get into the Guard.

"Reflecting back," Barnes told Rather, "it's something I'm not necessarily
proud of."

"Too strong or not to say that you're ashamed of it now?" Rather prodded
helpfully as the segment came to a close.

"Oh, I think that would be somewhat of an appropriate thing," Barnes
allowed. "I'm very, very sorry."

Tick tick tick tick tick went the *60 Minutes* stopwatch, the very symbol of
respectability in the mainstream media.

Moments later, the accolades started pouring in. Mapes's colleagues at *60
Minutes* and the CBS *Evening News* showered her with e-mails lauding her
journalistic prowess.

"Excellent piece," gushed one colleague. "Thanks for including me."

"I continue to be in awe of you," fawned another.

"You are amazing," enthused a third.

"I was just sitting here thinking about how amazing you are," wrote Josh
Howard. "I'm buckled in, ready to see where you'll take us next. Let's go!"

Mapes soaked up the praise of her fellow journalists. Five years of dogged
reporting had finally paid off. The CBS news producer who rocked the Bush
administration with the Abu Ghraib photos back in April had now finally
exposed Bush as a privileged slacker who couldn't hold a candle to Kerry, the
bona fide war hero. Mapes's one-two punch to the president was complete—
and just in time to "change the momentum of an election."

"You continue to astound," lauded yet another colleague.

"I'm in awe of your total command of this project," still another chimed in.

Mapes let the adulation wash over her in great waves. Then she read an
e-mail that, while shorter than the others, seemed to sum up the situation
best of all.

"You are great."

CHAPTER NINE

"WE'RE TOAST"

I t was almost midnight and Harry MacDougald, as usual, was blogging in his bedroom. The forty-six-year-old Atlanta attorney was surfing FreeRepublic.com—his favorite weblog, or "blog"—to commiserate with fellow conservatives about the evening's hot topic: the CBS story about President Bush's military records.

Like most blogs, Free Republic allowed participants to post comments, questions, jokes, and diatribes, often in response to articles in the mainstream media. On this night, a "Freeper" began a new thread of conversation at 11:10 p.m. by posting a freshly written *New York Times* story about the bombshell from Dan Rather.

"The documents," intoned the *Times*, "suggest that Lieutenant Bush did not meet his performance standards and received favorable treatment."

This triggered much grumbling among the Freepers, each of whom used a pen name when posting comments.

"If the *New York Times* would dig into terrorism as deeply as the president's service record, they'd have pinpointed Osama by now," remarked a

Freeper who called himself "68skylark." "And if they found bin Laden, they'd ask him what he thinks about Bush's attendance at Guard drills!"

"Documents from a dead man," harrumphed a Freeper known as "sinkspur." "How convenient."

At 11:17 p.m., a Freeper who went by the name of "Howlin" posted a link to the Killian papers, which CBS News had uploaded to its own website at 9:30 p.m.

"There are the documents," "Howlin" wrote. "Now you see if you think they say what the NYT says they say."

MacDougald, whose Freeper alias was "Buckhead," clicked on the link and began to study the documents that had supposedly come from Killian's personal file more than three decades earlier. The more he looked at them, the more suspicious he became. His skepticism was shared by other Freepers.

"Did you notice that NO ONE was CC'd on those memos?" wrote "Texasforever."

"And what does that mean?" "Howlin" inquired.

"It means he, if he actually wrote them, didn't see fit to send the memos to anyone else," "Texasforever" replied. "So why write them in the first place?"

"I think they were his private papers," "Howlin" offered.

"So why write them?" "Texasforever" shot back. "If he was REALLY trying to CYA then he would have sent his concerns up the chain. Otherwise he would be in deep Sh%T if he had to explain later why he didn't let someone else know about a supposed violation of a direct order. Nope, I don't believe these are legit documents," "Texasforever" concluded. "CBS will not say who they got them from so the originals can be examined."

Less than a minute later, MacDougald finished typing up his own analysis and hit the "send" button on his iMac computer. It was seventeen seconds before midnight.

"Howlin, every single one of these memos to file is in a proportionally spaced font, probably Palatino or Times New Roman," he wrote. "In 1972 people used typewriters for this sort of thing, and typewriters used monospaced fonts.

"The use of proportionally spaced fonts did not come into common use for office memos until the introduction of laser printers, word processing software, and personal computers. They were not widespread until the mid to late 90's. Before then, you needed typesetting equipment, and that wasn't used for personal memos to file. Even the Wang systems that were dominant in the mid 80's used monospaced fonts.

"I am saying these documents are forgeries, run through a copier for 15 generations to make them look old," MacDougald concluded. "This should be pursued aggressively."

"You're absolutely correct," marveled a Freeper named "NYCVirago." "I just looked at the files, and they don't pass the smell test. Most typewritten items from that era would have been in Courier font. And why would these items be copies, anyway, if these memos were for the guy's own personal file? They wouldn't have that run-through-the-copy-machine-a-zillion-times aura to them in that case."

MacDougald quickly grasped the ramifications of his discovery.

"This is going to be hilarious," he predicted at ten minutes past midnight. "Every major news organization is running with this bogus story like it's a new toy on Christmas morning."

Sure enough, the morning newspapers trumpeted Rather's scoop without questioning the authenticity of the documents. Mapes spent the morning reveling in the front-page coverage her scoop had received in the *New York Times*, the *Washington Post*, and *USA Today*.

"I woke up smiling," she wrote in her memoir. "I was exhilarated by another success."

When she arrived at CBS, she treated herself to a victory lap.

"I ran into other producers and correspondents and collected hugs and kisses and congratulations," she boasted. "There were jokes about what we would do as a follow-up. Dan and I had broken the Abu Ghraib prison story in late April. Now this. My team, the people at *60 Minutes*, and Dan all felt like we were on a roll."

But by this time Free Republic, as well as other conservative blogs like Powerline and Little Green Footballs, were amassing an impressive body of evidence that the documents were forgeries—and not even very good ones. The disparate rumblings of "Buckhead" and other bloggers had grown overnight into a mighty roar. By 11 a.m., that roar had reached the ears of Mapes herself.

"Within a few minutes, I was online visiting websites I had never heard of before: Free Republic, Little Green Footballs, Powerline," she wrote in her memoir. "I remembered staring, disheartened and angry, at one posting. '60 Minutes is going down,' the writer crowed. My heart started to pound."

Things quickly went from bad to worse.

"I had a real physical reaction as I read the angry online accounts," she recalled. "It was something between a panic attack, a heart attack, and a nervous breakdown. My palms were sweaty; I gulped and tried to breathe. My chest was pounding like I had become a cartoon character whose heart outline pushes out the front of her shirt with each beat. The little girl in me wanted to crouch and hide behind the door and cry my eyes out. The longtime reporter in me was pissed off."

By afternoon, Mapes managed to harness that anger and swing into damage control mode as even the mainstream media began to question the documents.

"Experts disagree on all kinds of [expletive] about typefaces," she responded to an inquiring reporter in an e-mail at 2:38 p.m. She shrugged off the scientific verification of documents as "sort of a black art."

But the issue would not go away. Just before 3 p.m., it exploded across the Drudge Report, the most influential website in American journalism. While mainstream media reporters liked to look down their noses at cyber-journalist Matt Drudge, they grudgingly acknowledged the considerable impact of his website, which garnered a staggering ten million "hits" by readers every day.

"'60 Minutes' Documents on Bush Might be Fake," blared Drudge, who intentionally posted an upside-down image of the *60 Minutes* stopwatch logo.

"I'm not worried," Rather insisted to Mapes in a phone call. "F.E.A.!"

That was the anchorman's way of defiantly saying, "F— 'em all!"

"It looks like somebody conspired to float false documents," Bush told me. "I just couldn't believe that would be happening [and] it would become the basis of a fairly substantial series of news stories. I guess I was amazed that this would go on."

Soon, however, Bush began to see a silver lining in this cloud of conspiracy.

"A lot of people were angry that this could have happened," he said. "There was a backlash to it."

Indeed, even the mainstream media was outraged. Shortly after the posting on the Drudge Report, which the press used as its unofficial assignment editor, reporters went into another feeding frenzy. Only this time the "blood in the water" that Mapes had once relished was not emanating from Bush. It was hemorrhaging from CBS's own self-inflicted wounds.

The network could have stanched the bleeding by announcing an internal investigation into the debacle and promising to share the results with viewers. But instead, it dug in its heels and lied.

"The documents in the *60 Minutes* report were thoroughly examined and their authenticity vouched for by independent experts," CBS said in a press release that afternoon.

Never mind that all four document examiners consulted by CBS had expressly refused to authenticate the documents because they were photocopies, not originals. Never mind that only one examiner, Marcel Matley, vouched for only one signature on only one document. CBS was now telling the world that multiple "experts" had authenticated, without qualification, the entire batch of documents.

Meanwhile, bloggers had discovered that the Killian documents could be replicated with jaw-dropping precision by simply retyping them in the default settings of the popular Microsoft Word computer program. You could do it on a transparency and overlay it on the Killian documents that had supposedly been produced on a typewriter more than three decades earlier. It was an exact match, right down to the last pixel. Mapes called it a "parlor trick," but acknowledged it was "the most damaging allegation against us." It was especially damaging when she was confronted at CBS headquarters by senior vice president Betsy West, who was brandishing one of the original Killian documents in one hand and a perfect replica in the other.

"Mary, what's going on?" she demanded. "These blogs are saying that the memo can be recreated exactly in Microsoft Word."

Mapes shrugged that she was not an expert on typography. Besides, she already had her hands full. Rather had instructed her to compile a list of talking points to defend the story. The resulting list was rife with prevarications, although one whopper was particularly mendacious.

"The source for the documents was vetted by CBS not just for truthfulness," Mapes wrote, "but for ability to get access to these documents."

Burkett, whose identity was still confidential, was hardly vetted for truthfulness. Everyone at CBS knew he had repeatedly changed his story about Bush's military service. Mapes herself considered him "paranoid" and an "anti-Bush zealot." The network's entire Washington bureau had long regarded Burkett as journalistically radioactive. As for Burkett's "ability to get access to these documents," CBS had never pressed him about how he came to possess them in the first place. Oh, at one point he had mentioned to Mapes that he obtained them from a former chief warrant officer named George Conn, who was now working in Germany. But Burkett warned that Conn would deny being the source of the documents. Mapes placed a couple of perfunctory calls trying to locate Conn, but soon gave up. That was the entire sum and substance of her effort to trace the chain of possession beyond Burkett.

Another talking point was equally misleading. Mapes wrote that the documents had been vouched for by one of the people mentioned in them—Major General Bobby Hodges. According to one of the Killian memos, Hodges was the officer who had been pressured to "sugar coat" an evaluation of Bush. "Hodges supports the documents' authenticity," Mapes wrote. "He agreed they were real." This confirmation had not been cited in the original broadcast, perhaps because Hodges had never even seen the documents. Prior to the original broadcast, Mapes had merely read *portions* of the memos to him over the telephone.

Yet Rather and other CBS officials eagerly disseminated such falsehoods from Mapes's list of talking points to the hordes of reporters now demanding answers from CBS. Few were fooled by the network's frantic dissembling.

"Several document experts contacted by ABC News have raised serious questions about the authenticity of these documents," said White House correspondent Terry Moran on ABC's *World News Tonight* that evening. "They point to the typeface, spacing, and perfectly even imprint of the letters that look more like the creation of a computer than an old-fashioned typewriter.

"And there's this—the little superscript 'th,'" Moran added. "That's something very few typewriters could do in 1972."

Mapes later recalled watching in astonishment as the accusations of forgery "migrated rapidly from Blogger World to big media. It was unbelievable." Gone was the admiration for the Internet she had expressed after breaking the Abu Ghraib story. Back then, she had gushed, "Computers, the Internet, and other new technology have altered any country's ability to keep dirty little secrets." Suddenly, that same technology was exposing Mapes's own dirty little secret— her malicious use of forged documents to discredit the president.

"I was *incredulous* that the mainstream press—a group I'd been a part of for nearly twenty-five years and thought I knew—was falling for the blogs' critiques," she wrote in her memoir. "I was shocked at the ferocity of the attack."

In an effort to counterattack, Mapes searched furiously through the reams of official Bush military records until she found a reference to the 111th Fighter Interceptor Squadron that contained a superscript "th." Unlike the one in the Killian documents, however, this "th" was underlined and did not rise above the top of the line of text. Still, it was good enough for Mapes, who seized on the example as nothing less than complete vindication. Her bosses were less certain.

"I'd leave nothing to chance," CBS News president Andrew Heyward warned senior vice president Betsy West in an e-mail that evening. "Did Mary's expert vet the whole doc or just Killian's signature?"

West replied that, as far as she knew, the "expert(s) examined the whole document." This reference to "expert(s)" was a sure sign that she was beginning to doubt CBS's own press release, which she had helped draft earlier that day, unequivocally citing "experts."

After assuring Heyward that Mapes "remains steadfast," West added, "Privately, of course, we have to stay on top of every allegation in case one of them shakes our confidence in the story."

She didn't have to wait long to have her confidence shaken. That evening, ABC's *Nightline* tracked down Killian's widow and son, both of whom expressed doubt about the authenticity of the documents.

At 4:53 a.m. on Friday, West received an e-mail from *60 Minutes* executive producer Josh Howard, who suggested CBS play the victim card. He even drafted a proposed statement that could be released to the press.

"If indeed one or more of the documents is not authentic, it would mean that CBS News was the victim of an elaborate hoax," Howard wrote in the statement. "Should we find that anyone—the Kerry campaign, the Bush campaign, or anyone else—was responsible for circulating fraudulent documents and orchestrating a hoax, no one would be more anxious to break that story than CBS News. The point would be to shift the conversation from CBS did something wrong, to something wrong was done to us and we're mad as hell."

West replied, "I think we need to defend ourselves with specifics [and] not even concede that we think it could be a hoax."

But the hoax theory was already being floated by ABC's *Good Morning America*.

"Has it come to this?" host Charlie Gibson asked former Clinton aide George Stephanopoulos. "Are we really into dirty tricks, perhaps, of this magnitude?"

"It's certainly possible," replied Stephanopoulos, a self-described liberal Democrat who hosted ABC's *This Week*. "A lot of Democrats suspect this was a set-up, something set up by Republicans."

This exchange provided a glimmer of hope to Heyward, who fired off an e-mail to West at 7:49 a.m.

"Is it possible that it's a clever dirty trick by Rather-haters—a SETUP aimed at CBS?" he asked, citing the Stephanopoulos remarks. "It occurred to me as well, although it seems farfetched."

Heyward was clearly dissatisfied with CBS's weak defense of its story.

"Don't we have to come up with OR SHARE more evidence rather than just 'stand by' our statement?" he asked. "This is a direct attack on our credibility that will stick if we don't come back as hard as possible—not by saying 'we'll investigate all allegations' (which of course we should), but by giving some indication WHY we're so confident.

"Specifically, let's find out much more about Mary's expert(s)," he added, echoing West's vacillation. "How many were there? Why are we keeping their names back? Did any of them raise questions about typography? If not, why not? If so, how were they resolved?"

Heyward, who had been unusually involved in vetting the story before it aired because of its political sensitivity, was now demanding answers to questions he should have raised during the vetting process.

"The critical analysts have no problem going public. Why not the ones who agree with us?" he said. "It makes our position seem cryptic and arbitrary when I don't believe it is. You should talk to Mary more about how she got the documents. At this point, we need to know more than we do."

Still, Heyward made clear that Mapes should not be hung out to dry.

"I think this can all be done without undercutting our own people. Your posture with Mary should be that since we're confident in our reporting, we should be able to prove it," he said. "But it has to be done with specific information, not just stubborn repetition of what we've already said."

Barely more than an hour after warning against "undercutting our own people," Heyward did just that in a conference call with West, Mapes, executive producer Josh Howard, and three people from CBS Communications Group, who had the unenviable job of fielding calls from skeptical reporters. Heyward warned that "if someone f—ed this up, they'll be phoning in from Alcatraz." Then, after a forty-five-minute discussion on damage control, it became clear that the only strategy at CBS's disposal was the one Heyward had cautioned against in the first place—"stubborn repetition of what we've already said."

Accordingly, the network issued another stonewalling statement just before noon. In the process, it managed to lie even more egregiously. One day after Mapes claimed in her talking points that the singular "source" of the documents had been vetted "for truthfulness," CBS now upped the ante by claiming the documents "were provided by unimpeachable sources." As if by magic, "source" had morphed into "sources." And Burkett, whose credibility had always been demonstrably weak, was now "unimpeachable."

Other lies were similarly compounded. One day after issuing a press release falsely claiming the documents had been "vouched for by independent experts," the network now escalated the deception by asserting that the documents were backed by "independent handwriting and forensic document experts." In other words, CBS was now explicitly claiming to have authenticated not just the handwriting, but the documents themselves—even though all four examiners had refused to authenticate *any* of the documents.

"Contrary to some rumors, no internal investigation is underway at CBS News nor is one planned," the release concluded. "We have complete confidence in our reporting and will continue to pursue the story."

Within an hour, it became obvious the press was not buying it. Jim Murphy, executive producer of CBS *Evening News*, heard from a number of reporters who felt the network's defense was incredibly lame. At 1 p.m., Murphy sent his colleagues an e-mail about an unsettling conversation he had just concluded with an editor at *Time* magazine.

"He said he couldn't understand why we haven't issued a more thorough defense," Murphy fretted. "It's making him and his investigative guys think they are missing something."

The e-mail struck a nerve with Gil Schwartz, the head of CBS Communications Group, who had participated in the morning conference call about damage control. Schwartz, too, was fielding a steady stream of adversarial press calls.

"We need two things," Schwartz wrote in an e-mail of his own. "1. We need our expert available NOW to speak to all those who are reporting this story. We need the expert. Now. We need him now.

"2. We need the talking points that can be crafted into a statement of defense and talked about by Dan when he calls people.

"#1 is essential RIGHT NOW. We NEED THAT EXPERT. Without him, we're toast," Schwartz reiterated. "Then we need #2, about six seconds later."

Schwartz had been particularly vexed by questions about the superscript "th," although this did not faze Mapes.

"FOR THE 100TH TIME, THE 'TH' ISSUE IS GONE," she blasted Schwartz in an e-mail. "WE HAVE EXAMPLES FROM THE 'OFFICIAL' WHITE HOUSE DOCS. WE'RE SET."

This did not satisfy Schwartz.

"The problem, Mary, is one of perception," he began patiently enough in another e-mail. "As far as the press is concerned, the 'th' issue is NOT gone. It's very much alive, and they have people crawling all over it. If we wait to address the issue until tonight's news, we will DIE in the press tomorrow. Die. As in . . . dead.

"You tell me. How do I get the message out RIGHT NOW, as in RIGHT THIS VERY MINUTE, that the 'th' thing is no longer an issue?

"They've got a bunch of experts. We have nothing. We need to communicate something in the next hour or so if the story isn't going to thunder away from us on a Friday afternoon. Help me out."

Schwartz finally took matters into his own hands by convincing Heyward to get Rather "on the phone right now." Rather agreed to talk to reporters, using Mapes's talking points from a day earlier.

Meanwhile, Mapes was trying to cobble together a piece for the looming CBS *Evening News* that would buttress the original story. She frantically searched for new experts who would vouch for the documents. Examiners with weak credentials were perfectly acceptable, as long as they agreed the papers were authentic. Examiners who disagreed were rejected out of hand, even if their credentials were strong. Unfortunately for Mapes, most experts—regardless of the strength of their credentials—considered the documents amateurish forgeries.

Mapes decided her only hope was the original group of experts retained by CBS. But two of the four—Emily Will and Linda James—had warned Mapes in advance not to air the documents. A third, James Pierce, could not be reached on deadline.

So Mapes was reduced to calling Matley, the sole examiner cited in the original broadcast. Matley was quick to remind Mapes that he had authenticated only one signature on only one document. In fact, Matley decided it would be prudent to reiterate his reservations in writing, especially now that the whole world was questioning the authenticity of the documents. So he faxed CBS a typed-up version of the handwritten notes that he had shown Mapes before the original broadcast, which began with the disclaimer, "Poor copies: Could not authenticate documents themselves."

Mapes waved off the disclaimer and convinced Matley to be interviewed yet again by Rather. The anchorman had already interviewed Matley twice for the original segment, only to forgo the footage after finding it not "very persuasive." Alas, the third interview was similarly unconvincing, prompting CBS to water down its script for that night's broadcast.

Initially, the script asserted that Matley "still believes the documents are authentic...both the typeface and handwriting." But that was downgraded to "He believes they are real." In truth, Matley hadn't gone even that far.

Rather concluded the interview by suggesting, with a straight face, that CBS had fully anticipated the ferocity of the firestorm unleashed by its original use of the Killian documents.

"Are you surprised the questions came about these?" he asked Matley matter-of-factly. "We're not, but I wonder if you were surprised."

"I knew going in that this was dynamite one way or the other," Matley managed. "It was far more potential damage to me, professionally, than benefit to me. And I knew that.

"And, uh, but we seek the truth," he added. "That's what we do. You know, you're supposed to put yourself out to seek the truth and take what comes from it."

Rather wrapped up the segment by suggesting the controversy had been stirred up by what Hillary Rodham Clinton once called a "vast right-wing conspiracy."

"Today, on the Internet and elsewhere, some people—including many who are partisan political operatives—concentrated not on the key questions and the overall story, but on the documents that were part of the support of the story," he said. "It is the information in the new documents that is most compelling for people most familiar with President Bush's service in the National Guard."

Incredibly, Rather was defending the original broadcast by suggesting that even if the Killian documents were forgeries, their content was somehow real. It was a laughably low journalistic standard that would come to be known as "fake but true." The president was particularly flabbergasted.

"I think most people around the country, including many in the news media, believe that they weren't accurate," he told me.

To counter this perception, Heyward told Mapes late on Friday night to round up as many document experts as possible over the weekend so that CBS could trot them out at a press conference on Monday. But Mapes replied that no experts would verify the documents because they were not originals.

"But *they* have people who are doing that, Mary," Heyward snapped, according to Mapes. "And it's killing us. If the blogs are using people that are lousy analysts to make their case, then let's get some lousy analysts of our own."

So much for the CBS handbook's admonition that *everything we do while covering a story or gathering material for a broadcast must be done within the highest standards of journalistic integrity.* Now the very president of CBS News was calling for "lousy analysts."

Meanwhile, other aspects of the story were beginning to unravel. For example, Major General Bobby Hodges belatedly learned that he was being cited by CBS as having confirmed the authenticity of the documents. Hodges, who had not seen the original broadcast, happened to be in Houston visiting relatives on September 10 and noticed an article on the flap in the *Houston Chronicle*. The newspaper quoted an anonymous CBS official identifying Hodges as the "trump card" in confirming the authenticity of the documents. Hodges was outraged. His anger intensified when one of his relatives showed him copies of the Killian documents that were posted on the Internet. Right away, Hodges could tell they were bogus. For starters, the military jargon and formatting were all wrong. But more important, the information in the memos was just plain false. No one had ever pressured Hodges to "sugar coat" an evaluation of Bush. It was particularly ludicrous to suggest that such pressure came from Staudt, who retired nearly eighteen months before the "sugar coat" memo was supposedly written.

At 9:30 p.m., after driving home from his relatives' house, Hodges telephoned Mapes in New York to inform her that he had now seen the Killian memos and considered them forgeries. He vowed to issue a public statement the next day denying that he had authenticated the documents.

"It was devastating to us," Mapes lamented in her memoir. "He had already spoken with other news outlets, telling them that he believed the documents were forged."

Hodges demanded to know the identity of the CBS official who had fingered him as the "trump card." Mapes said she could not reveal the official's identity and then transferred the call to Rather. So Hodges repeated his complaint about the anonymous CBS official and demanded, "Is that you, Dan?" Rather denied being the source. Of course, he did not mention that he was one of numerous CBS officials who had disseminated Mapes's list of phony talking points, which stated "Hodges supports the documents' authenticity.... He agreed they were real."

Rather did not bother asking Hodges, the network's supposed "trump card," why he thought the documents were forgeries. Instead, he made sure Hodges was hung out to dry the next day on the CBS *Evening News*. Since it was a Saturday, Rather delegated his dirty work to weekend anchor Russ Mitchell.

"Hodges, one of the sources corroborating the CBS News account, now says he believes the documents were not real," Mitchell told viewers. "We believed General Hodges the first time we spoke with him.

"We believe the documents to be genuine," Mitchell added. "The documents were authenticated for CBS News by outside experts."

Thus, the pathological lying continued a full three days after the original broadcast. CBS was still asserting that the documents had been "authenticated," even though all four experts had expressly refused to authenticate them. And the network continued to cite "experts," even though it had relied on only one expert—Matley—to verify only one signature on only one document.

Meanwhile, the *Dallas Morning News* dropped a bombshell that had not been widely known outside of CBS News—namely, that Staudt had retired nearly eighteen months before he supposedly pressured Hodges to "sugar coat" the Bush evaluation. This revelation, according to reporter Pete Slover, "added to mounting questions about the authenticity of documents."

Undaunted by yet another gaping hole in its story, CBS issued more lies.

"From what we've learned, Staudt remained very active after he retired," an anonymous CBS official told the newspaper. "He was a very bullying type, and that could have continued."

But the only things that really continued were the growing firestorm over the authenticity of the documents and CBS's stubborn refusal to come clean. On Monday, September 13, the network was in a full-fledged panic.

"Our entire reputation as a news division now rests on our fielding a couple of experts on our side TODAY. BY PRESS TIME. Tomorrow will be TOO LATE," Schwartz warned Heyward in an e-mail under the subject line "Total Red Alert." "I can't tell you how important this is. There is NO OTHER PRIORITY from a press point of view."

But the vast majority of experts, especially those with extensive typography credentials, had concluded the Killian documents were phonies. CBS was reduced to rounding up a typewriter repairman and a software designer. The network didn't even bother checking their credentials when both agreed to buttress the original story. Rather eagerly cited these "experts" on yet another *Evening News* broadcast.

"CBS used several techniques to make sure these papers should be taken seriously, talking to handwriting and document analysts and other experts who strongly insist that the documents could have been created in the '70s," he assured viewers.

But the next day, two of the experts CBS had originally retained—Will and James—went public with the fact that they had warned the network against using the Killian documents.

"I found five significant differences in the questioned handwriting," Will told ABC's *World News Tonight*. "And I found problems with the printing itself, as to whether it could have been produced by a typewriter."

She also revealed that she had e-mailed CBS a laundry list of concerns about the documents before the original broadcast, only to be summarily blown off.

"I did not feel that they wanted to investigate it very deeply," Will told ABC.

ABC's interview of James was equally devastating to CBS.

"I did not authenticate anything," she said. "And I don't want it to be misunderstood that I did. And that's why I have come forward to talk about it, because I don't want anyone to think that I did authenticate these documents."

Mapes responded to this report by preparing a memo trashing Will and James. She even insinuated that James had become disgruntled because "we were no longer paying her."

The network issued a statement saying "CBS News did not rely on either Emily Will or Linda James for a final assessment of the documents." Of course, the statement neglected to say that the reason CBS did not rely on them was because they contradicted the network's preordained conclusion that the documents were authentic.

That same afternoon, CBS suffered yet another devastating setback. Killian's secretary, the woman who had typed his correspondence when he was in the Guard, came forward to say the documents were fake. The revelation rocked the network, which responded by trashing the secretary, an eighty-six-year-old grandmother named Marion Knox. "As far as we can tell, this individual is not a documents expert," CBS huffed in a statement to the press. Mapes added, "Her memory was very selective." It would have been easier to discredit Knox if she had been a Bush supporter. Unfortunately for the network, she publicly complained that the president had been "selected, not elected" and was "unfit for office." She even remarked that while the documents were forged, their content was accurate.

Then CBS had a brainstorm. Knox could be enlisted to advance the "fake but true" defense of the original story. Heyward huddled with Rather and Mapes and decided to bring Knox to New York for an interview to be aired on *60 Minutes*. Meanwhile, the CBS *Evening News* continued to stonewall. Reporter John Roberts dutifully informed viewers that "CBS News continues to stand by its reporting." CBS News correspondent Wyatt Andrews added, "Some at this network believe the backlash against the *60 Minutes* report is pure politics."

On September 15, one day after CBS issued a statement discrediting Knox, Dan Rather went on the air to hail Knox as "a credible voice" who "wants to set the record straight about the memos."

"I did not type those memos," Knox said.

"You didn't type these memos?" Rather echoed.

"No," she said. "And it's not the form that I would have used. And there are words in there that belong to the Army, not to the Air Guard. We never used those terms."

"You know that you didn't type them?"

"I know that I didn't type them."

"Few, if any, things that I ask you about would be more important than this point," Rather repeated mindlessly. "You say you didn't type these memos—definitely—that you didn't type these memos?"

"Not these particular ones."

"Did you type ones like this?"

"Yes," said Knox, even though she could not recall typing anything of the sort.

"Containing the same or identical information?"

"The same information," Knox said. "Yes."

Rather then proceeded to go through the fake Killian memos, one by one, so that Knox could verify their content.

"And he did write a memo like this?" the anchorman eagerly asked.

"Yes," Knox said.

"So he did write a memo like this?"

"Yeah."

"Not this one, as you can tell, but one like it."

Rather was careful not to inform viewers that Knox was an anti-Bush partisan who considered the president "unfit for office." Instead, he inflated the secretary's authority by declaring, "She spent more than two decades keeping pilots and officers in line."

"I'm gonna say this," Knox allowed. "It seems to me that Bush felt that he was above reproof."

"Did not George W. Bush get into the National Guard on the basis of preferential treatment?" Rather asked without making clear how the secretary could possibly possess such knowledge.

"I'm gonna say that he did," Knox ventured. "I feel that he did, because there were a lot of other boys in there the same way."

Untroubled by this charge of guilt by association, Rather plowed on in his odd staccato.

"Accurate or inaccurate to say that this unit was filled with people who had Republican and Democratic connections, who got in on the basis of preference?"

"At that time, yes," Knox dutifully replied.

Rather then asked the secretary to describe Bush.

"Bush seemed to be having a good time," she said. "It seemed that the other fellows were—I'm gonna say this—sort of resentful of his attitude."

"And what was his attitude?" Rather prodded.

"Well, that he didn't really have to go by the rules."

"He didn't really have to go by the rules?"

"It seemed that way to me."

"Was it common knowledge or not that Lieutenant Bush had not attended some drills?"

"It was sort of gossip around there," said Knox, despite the fact that she had absolutely no knowledge of Bush ever trying to get out of a drill or even failing to show up for one. "They snicker and so forth about what he was getting away with."

"What Lieutenant Bush was getting away with?"

"Yeah."

"There was snickering about that?"

"There was even a resentment," she said. "I think it's plain and simple: Bush didn't think that he had to go by the rules that others did."

Rather wrapped up this segment—built on "gossip," "snickering," and unverifiable charges—by publicly entertaining, for the first time, the possibility that the Killian papers were indeed bogus.

"Are those documents authentic?" he asked, looking directly into the camera. "Or were they forgeries?" He added, "We will keep an open mind."

With that unpleasantness out of the way, he launched into his "fake but true" closing argument.

"Those who have criticized aspects of our story have never criticized the heart of it, the major thrust of our report—that George Bush received preferential treatment to get into the National Guard and, once accepted, failed to satisfy the requirements of his service. If we uncover any information to the contrary, rest assured, we shall report that also."

Tick tick tick tick tick.

In contrast to Rather's public stoicism, CBS News was in the throes of an unmitigated panic behind closed doors. On the afternoon of September 16, Rather, Mapes, and Heyward spent hours on a grim conference call with Burkett, who suddenly changed his story about how he obtained the documents. Admitting that he had lied about getting them from a Guardsman stationed in Germany, George Conn, Burkett now came up with a much more convoluted tale. He said he obtained the documents from a mysterious woman named Lucy Ramirez, who passed them to Burkett through an even more mysterious and unidentified man at a livestock show in Houston. So much for the Tiffany Network's "unimpeachable source." Even Mapes admitted the far-fetched tale "sounded like a marriage of *The Manchurian Candidate* and *Hee Haw.*"

Once again, CBS strained to find a glimmer of hope in this shattering development. After much angst, it was decided that Burkett would become the scapegoat. Never mind that CBS had promised him anonymity from the very beginning. The network wanted to portray itself as the victim of a hoax, so Burkett must be cast as the perpetrator. Rather, Mapes, West, and several other CBS staffers headed to Dallas to interview Burkett on camera. Before the session began, Burkett's lawyer actually told West that CBS should give his client a consulting contract now that he was about to go on the record. West demurred but Burkett agreed to do the interview anyway.

CBS did not wait until the interview aired on September 20 to publicly blame Burkett for the debacle. The network issued a press release outing its own source.

"He provided the now-disputed documents," CBS said, as if the documents had not been disputed within hours of the original broadcast. "He deliberately misled the CBS News producer working on the report." Incredibly, the network was now casting Mapes as a victim.

"Get yourself a lawyer as fast as you can," Rather told Mapes in a phone call. "You need to start protecting yourself. We all do."

Mapes received this stunning advice while in a New York airport.

"I went to the ladies' room at LaGuardia and cried my eyes out," she recalled. "Jesus Christ, I was finished."

The point was underscored by a grim statement issued by Heyward.

"Based on what we now know, CBS News cannot prove that the documents are authentic, which is the only acceptable journalistic standard to justify using them in the report," Heyward admitted. "We should not have used them. That was a mistake, which we deeply regret. Nothing is more important to us than our credibility and keeping faith with the millions of people who count on us for fair, accurate, reliable and independent reporting," said the head of a network news division that had just spent nearly two weeks shamelessly lying to the nation. "We will continue to work tirelessly to be worthy of that trust."

Ten days after CBS publicly scoffed at the notion of an "internal investigation," Heyward glumly announced such a probe would take place after all. The network's humiliation was complete.

"I would do anything to be able to turn back the clock and change the course of these events," Howard anguished in a note he shared at a meeting of *60 Minutes* staffers that afternoon. "Obviously, I can't do that."

On the CBS *Evening News* that night, Rather did his best to blame Burkett for the debacle. "You lied to us," he told the CBS source on camera. Yet the anchorman never admitted that he and the rest of CBS News had repeatedly lied to the nation in a desperate quest to defend the documents.

"We can no longer vouch for their authenticity," Rather told viewers. "I want to say, personally and directly, I'm sorry."

Rather's apology was disingenuous in the extreme. Just before the broadcast, he had argued with his bosses that no apology was necessary. He actually continued to insist that the documents were authentic. But the delusional anchorman was overruled by Heyward, who ordered him to apologize and stop defending the documents. Rather swallowed his pride and issued the apology. But it was every bit as phony as the documents.

Still, the Tiffany Network had not yet reached bottom. Later that evening, Mapes was again confronted by West.

"Mary, *USA Today* has called and asked if you called the Kerry campaign and put them in touch with Bill Burkett in exchange for the documents," West said angrily. "Jesus Christ! What else is going to happen here? This is absolutely unbelievable."

The next morning, the journalistically improper relationship among CBS, Burkett, and the Kerry campaign was splashed across the front page of the nation's largest newspaper.

"He had agreed to turn over the documents to CBS if the network would arrange a conversation with the Kerry campaign," *USA Today* wrote of Burkett. "The network's effort to place Burkett in contact with a top Democratic official raises ethical questions about CBS's handling of material potentially damaging to the Republican president in the midst of an election."

Mortified, CBS had no choice but to air its own version of this story on the September 21 *Evening News*. As if to add insult to injury, Rather was forced to cede the moral high ground to White House communications director Dan Bartlett, the very official whose failure to challenge the documents in the first place been gleefully interpreted by CBS as nothing less than ironclad validation.

"Bartlett accused CBS News and a high-level adviser to the Kerry campaign today of coordinating a personal attack on President Bush over his National Guard record," Rather glumly reported.

The anchorman then showed a clip of Kerry strategist Joe Lockhart recalling how Mapes had asked him to call Burkett.

"She said that he was interested in talking to me and she gave me his number," Lockhart shrugged. "I called him. He gave me some advice on how to respond to the Swift Boat smears against John Kerry."

CBS correspondent Bill Plante then recited a written response by the network.

"It is obviously against CBS News standards to be associated with any political agenda," Plante said with a straight face. "As to what actually happened here, it is one of many issues the independent review will be examining."

Next came a sound bite from the indignant chairman of the Republican National Committee.

"What was the nature of the conversation between various senior campaign advisers for Senator Kerry and the person who apparently provided the documents?" demanded Ed Gillespie. "What were the agreements that they had with one another—CBS, Kerry campaign, and whoever provided the documents?"

This was dutifully followed by another clip of Lockhart.

"The Kerry campaign had nothing to do with these documents," he protested. "There is nothing in this story. And if there was something to this story, they wouldn't be afraid to debate me on that. What this is is a gutless political attack."

Plante, to his credit, appeared unconvinced.

"Innocent or not, a CBS News producer's assistance in connecting a source with the Kerry campaign has at least the appearance of impropriety," he said. "It becomes a political issue in a bitter campaign. Dan."

"Bill Plante, thanks," Rather croaked.

Even Mapes could not deny the impropriety.

"I shouldn't have let Burkett think I might have some kind of sway with the Kerry campaign," she wrote in her memoir. "I should have told Burkett no when he asked me to hand off his phone number."

Rather's fellow journalists at CBS News professed shock at the revelation that their network had been in cahoots with the Kerry campaign. Less than two weeks after Mapes's colleagues had showered her with accolades like "great," "amazing," and "excellent," they now threw around words like "hideous," "outrageous," "unbelievable," and "incredibly stupid." The same sycophants who had professed "awe" at her ability to "astound" were now merely "stunned and horrified."

The Tiffany Network had managed to "change the momentum of an election" all right—just not in the direction it intended. Thanks to CBS, Bush's military record was now considered off-limits as a political issue for the rest of the campaign. No other news organization would dare bring it up because CBS had so thoroughly muddied the waters. Ironically, Mapes and Rather had inoculated Bush against the very charge they had tried to drape around his neck—that he pulled strings to get into the National Guard and then shirked his duties after landing the coveted spot. CBS had single-handedly deprived Kerry of his most potent trump card—a side-by-side comparison of the two candidates' military records.

"Americans are fair people and they viewed this as patently unfair," the president told me. "So in a funny way, I guess it inured to our benefit, when it was all said and done."

Moreover, it gave the Bush campaign a powerful weapon to wield against future stories that had nothing to do with the president's military record.

"It also, frankly, gave us an opportunity, frequently, when things came out in the media that we didn't believe or didn't like, to say, 'It's another CBS story,'" Mehlman told me. "I mean, it gave us a serious response to bad news."

On September 23, Bush stood in the Rose Garden and faced reporters. As usual, he called on those who had their hands up and looked eager to ask questions—journalists from news organizations like the AP, Reuters, NBC, and CNN. But then he did something unusual. He actively sought out a news organization without even knowing whether it was present. His eyes scanned the forest of upraised hands as a mischievous expression played across his face.

"Is anybody here from CBS?"

CHAPTER TEN

TOSSING THE STINK BOMB

M ore than three and a half years into his presidency, George W. Bush had grown accustomed to people deferring to his authority—at least publicly. Even the handful of advisers (like Karl Rove) who sometimes argued forcefully with the president behind closed doors became the very picture of deference when the cameras were turned on. Since Bush enjoyed a fiercely loyal staff and Republican control of both houses of Congress, he didn't have to worry about being called out by members of his own party. Sure, Democrats constantly trashed him behind his back and occasionally challenged him in private meetings. But they were never given a public forum in which they could pointedly rebuke the president to his face. The only people who were afforded such a forum were White House correspondents, who took their best shots at Bush during televised press conferences, like the one back in April when reporter after reporter upbraided the president for refusing to admit mistakes. But even at those sessions, the president was always in command. No one watching on television harbored any illusions about the journalists being somehow equal in status to the commander in chief. Indeed, Bush called on reporters at his own discretion and had no compunction about cutting off a long-winded interrogator. He once publicly chided me in mid-preamble, "Is this a question or a speech?" Such displays of exasperation did not bother most Americans, who, after all, shared the president's disdain for preening reporters.

So when Bush finally took the stage for his first debate with John Kerry on September 30, 2004, he had grown accustomed to being the only alpha male in the room. As the nation's undisputed maximum leader, he found it unnatural and irksome to be placed on a level playing field with a mere senator. For the first time in his presidency, Bush's lectern was not adorned with the official seal of the President of the United States. It was just a plain wooden podium, identical in every way to Kerry's, right down to the three small lights on top—green, yellow, and red—to remind the candidates when to speak and when to be silent. Moreover, when it came to physical stature, Kerry was actually Bush's superior, looming a full four inches over the six-foot-tall president.

Bush was acutely aware that in presidential debates, expectations were every bit as important as actual performance. The expectations game had worked to his advantage back in 2000, when everyone figured Al Gore would annihilate the notoriously inarticulate Bush. But then Bush went out and held his own and—because he exceeded expectations—was declared the winner. Of course, it didn't hurt that Gore had employed all the wrong body language, at one point even bizarrely crowding up to Bush, who shot him a surprised look, followed by a disdainful chuckle that seemed to tell viewers: "Get a load of this moron." There were also Gore's infamous loud sighs that made him look petulant and condescending. *Saturday Night Live* had a field day mocking Gore's debate performance, although the show wasn't exactly kind to Bush, who was portrayed by comic Will Ferrell as an endearing dimwit. During one send-up of the Bush-Gore debates, Ferrell was asked by Chris Parnell, who played the role of moderator Jim Lehrer, "to sum up, in a single word, the best argument for [your] candidacy." Ferrell froze at first, but then his panic gave way to exaggerated cockiness as he said with a smirk, "Strategery." Americans howled with laughter at the malapropism, which Ferrell pronounced *struh-TEE-jer-ee*. Even Bush campaign officials had to admit it sounded like something their boss might say. Far from being offended, they adopted the term as a sort of ironic inside joke. In fact, they laughed all the way to Gore's concession speech. Afterward, Karl Rove began hosting a weekly gathering of top White House strategists in his West Wing office that he wryly called the "Strategery" meeting.

But Bush couldn't play the underdog this time around. He was the sitting president, and his campaign had been tremendously successful at caricaturing Kerry as a craven, flip-flopping opportunist who changed his position almost hourly. In the eyes of many Americans, the Democrat was a walking cartoon. But then the real John Kerry walked onto the stage in Coral Gables, Florida, and Americans saw not a cartoon, but a flesh-and-blood person with poise and grace and serious arguments about important issues. The man appeared downright reasonable and at times even likeable.

"He was just as good," Rove told me, "as we feared."

Instead of droning beyond his allotted time, as the Bush campaign had expected, Kerry kept his answers succinct and within the time limits. A champion debater since high school, he made expert use of his minutes to attack the president, who had no choice but to stand there and take it, at least until it was his turn to speak. Bush could not interrupt Kerry as he could a snotty reporter at a press conference. He could not pull rank on him as he could against an uppity adviser or insolent congressman. He had no option but to simply endure the punishment Kerry was dishing out. Worst of all, he had to remain silent, which was killing him inside.

"This president has made, I regret to say, a colossal error of judgment," Kerry began.

Bush, who never had much of a poker face, looked supremely irritated. He squirmed and fidgeted with his notes while Kerry spoke. As part of the elaborate rules of the debate, the news networks were not supposed to show a candidate reacting to his rival's attacks. But the networks ignored this rule and kept using a split screen to show Bush chafing as Kerry excoriated him.

"What colossal misjudgments, in your opinion, has President Bush made?" the real Jim Lehrer asked helpfully.

"Well," Kerry said with an enormously confident grin. "Where do you want me to begin?"

Bush adjusted the knot of his necktie.

"He rushed the war in Iraq without a plan to win the peace..."

The president nervously itched his face.

"...he misled the American people..."

Puffed out cheeks in exasperation.

"...the president's not getting the job done..."

Shifted weight from one foot to another.

"...it's one thing to be certain, but you can be certain and be wrong..."

Blinked in rapid succession.

"...it's getting worse by the day..."

Shook head from side to side.

"...more soldiers killed in June than before, more in July than June..."

Rubbed eyes.

"...more in August than July, more in September than in August...."

Pursed lips.

"...and now we see beheadings..."

Clenched jaw.

"...and we got weapons of mass destruction crossing the border every single day, and they're blowing people up..."

Grimaced.

"...and we don't have enough troops there..."

Frowned.

"...you don't send troops to war without the body armor that they need..."

Bush was practically jumping out of his skin! The ignominy of having to stand there and take such abuse from the likes of John Kerry, a Massachusetts liberal who actually voted against the $87 billion for body armor, was almost unbearable to this proud Texan. He looked as though his head were about to explode.

When it was finally his turn to speak, Bush made his points just as forcefully as Kerry. He marshaled his arguments, hit his time cues, and even
steered clear of verbal gaffes. In fact, the only real gaffe of the evening came
when Kerry was asked for his opinion on preemptive war.

"If and when you do it, Jim, you have to do it in a way that passes the test,
that passes the global test," he said. "You can prove to the world that you did
it for legitimate reasons."

Bush pounced on this answer, which reinforced the image of Kerry worrying more about French approval than American security.

"I'm not exactly sure what you mean, 'passes the global test,'" he said sardonically. "You take preemptive action if you pass a global test? My attitude
is: You take preemptive action in order to protect the American people. You
act in order to make this country secure."

Kerry compounded his gaffe by complaining that Bush was too skeptical of the United Nations and various international treaties, including the
Kyoto Protocols on global warming. Bush considered the treaty a major
job-killer because it would impose draconian regulations on U.S. firms
while exempting 80 percent of the world, including China and India, from
compliance.

"We've watched this president actually turn away from some of the treaties
that were on the table," Kerry said. "You don't help yourself with other
nations when you turn away from the global warming treaty, for instance, or
when you refuse to deal at length with the United Nations. You have to earn
that respect. And I think we have a lot of earning back to do."

Again, Bush seized on Kerry's answer as an opportunity to paint the
Democrat as overly beholden to foreign approval.

"Let me tell you one thing I didn't sign, and I think it shows the difference of our opinion," he said. "I wouldn't join the International Criminal
Court. It's a body based in The Hague where unaccountable judges and
prosecutors can pull our troops or diplomats up for trial. And I wouldn't
join it. And I understand that in certain capitals around the world that that

wasn't a popular move. But it's the right move not to join a foreign court where our people could be prosecuted.

"My opponent is for joining the International Criminal Court. I just think trying to be popular, kind of, in the global sense, if it's not in our best interest, makes no sense."

In terms of pure debating points, it was the most damaging argument of the night. Bush had intuitively grasped the significance of Kerry's "global test" blunder and promptly used it against him.

"I jumped all over it," the president told me later. "It was kind of like, 'You actually believe that?'"

The attack made an impression on Americans who listened to the debate on radio, as well as those who read the transcript afterward. On television, however, Bush's debating points were overshadowed by his facial expressions.

"I felt I had won the first debate," he told me. "I felt like I did just fine."

He added, "Until the post-debate pictures showed up."

The president was surprised to learn the networks had broken the rules by showing the candidates reacting to each other's comments.

"I felt like there was only going to be one camera, and that would be on the speaker," he told me. "But you've got to understand, that's not an excuse, because there's essentially no rules."

When Bush reviewed footage of his reaction to the "global test" remark, he saw himself become incredulous, not petulant.

"I don't think I was that irritated," he told me, but added, "My facial expressions must have said that."

Indeed, the debating points that Bush scored against Kerry and his "global test" didn't really matter in the mainstream media's all-important post-debate spin. In the end, the press made sure that the only thing anyone remembered about the debate was the look of irritation on the president's face. In no time reporters began short-handing this as Bush's "frown." Just as the Bush-Gore encounter had been reduced to a single piece of body language—"the sigh"—the Bush-Kerry debate would forever be remembered for "the frown." Short-handed even further, Bush was said to have simply "lost" the debate. Amazingly, the president had allowed Kerry to gain the initiative.

"That was a mistake," Ken Mehlman told me. "It was like we had him on his back and we let him up."

Bush was less willing to concede the point.

"That debate was determined by facial expressions, as opposed to content," he told me. "But on the radio, people who listened to it got a different impression."

Bush rejected my theory that he had grown too accustomed to being unchallenged as president.

"Look, a debate is a debate, and it had nothing to do with being the president, and nobody challenging me during four years. Anyway, in the next two debates I was mindful of facial expressions."

Meanwhile, Dick Cheney squared off against John Edwards in the campaign's only vice-presidential debate. Four years earlier, Cheney had actually enjoyed his debate with Senator Joe Lieberman, whom he admired as a worthy opponent. But he felt no such admiration for Edwards, whom he regarded as an unaccomplished opportunist. The Democrat had parlayed his career as a wealthy trial lawyer into a Senate seat, but then decided halfway through his first term that he deserved to be president. Cheney resented the fawning press coverage of Edwards, whom he viewed as utterly lacking in substance when it came to public policy.

At one point during the Cheney-Edwards debate, which was held in Cleveland, moderator Gwen Ifill mentioned that the vice president had recently acknowledged a rare disagreement with Bush. The president wanted a constitutional amendment banning gay marriage; Cheney favored state-by-state regulation of the issue. He didn't go around advertising this view, which had been shaped in part by the fact that one of his daughters, Mary, was a lesbian. An intensely private man, Cheney believed his daughter's sexuality was off-limits as a campaign issue. So he didn't mention it when explaining his position to Ifill. However, when it was Edwards's turn to speak, the Democrat went out of his way to bring up Mary Cheney's sexuality.

"I think the vice president and his wife love their daughter. I think they love her very much," he patronized. "And you can't have anything but respect for the fact that they're willing to talk about the fact that they have a gay daughter."

Well, there it was, right out in the open: "They have a gay daughter." Edwards wasn't exactly outing Mary, whose sexual orientation was generally known inside the Washington beltway. On the other hand, a lot of ordinary Americans had no idea until Edwards decided to announce it to forty-three million viewers on live television. The Democrat's glib presumptuousness bothered Cheney, although he knew that saying so would only draw more unwelcome attention to his daughter. So he let it slide.

"Mr. Vice President, you have ninety seconds," Ifill said.

"Well, Gwen, let me simply thank the senator for the kind words he said about my family and our daughter," Cheney said grimly. "I appreciate that very much."

"That's it?" said Ifill, unaccustomed to politicians leaving precious time on the clock.

"That's it," Cheney said curtly.

"Okay," said Ifill, "then we'll move on to the next question."

Like Cheney, most Americans were willing to give Edwards the benefit of the doubt and not make a big deal of his cheesy remark about the vice president's "gay daughter." But eight days later, Americans were once again reminded of Mary Cheney's lesbianism—this time by Kerry himself. During his third and final debate with Bush, Kerry was asked by moderator Bob Schieffer whether "homosexuality is a choice." Although Schieffer never mentioned Mary Cheney, Kerry made a point of working her into his answer.

"It's not a choice," Kerry replied. "If you were to talk to Dick Cheney's daughter, who is a lesbian, she would tell you that she's being who she was, she's being who she was born as."

The remark stunned the president's aides, who were watching the debate on television in a trailer just outside the hall. Karl Rove turned to National

Security Adviser Condoleezza Rice and domestic policy adviser Margaret Spellings and sputtered, "Did he just say that?"

Rove later told me the sexual reference was no accident.

"I think it was a deliberate decision," he said. "I think Kerry and Edwards sat there and said, 'You know what? If we say "lesbian" or "gay" and the word "Cheney" in the same sentence, it will unglue social conservatives who are supporting Bush-Cheney.'

"I thought it was a very small-minded and almost bigoted mindset of who social conservatives are—as if they would abandon Bush if only Kerry and Edwards said the word 'gay' enough. The Democrats didn't understand that social conservatives are people who are concerned about the thrust of the culture and are not as judgmental and narrow-minded as people assume."

Rove's political instincts were, as usual, correct. Many Americans viewed this second reference to Mary Cheney's lesbianism by the Kerry-Edwards ticket as a gratuitous cheap shot. Kerry campaign manager Mary Beth Cahill declared on FOX News right after the debate that Mary-the-lesbian was "fair game," confirming that the Kerry-Edwards campaign was trying to score political points off the sexuality of the vice president's daughter. Mary's parents were furious.

"I did have a chance to assess John Kerry once more and now the only thing I could conclude: This is not a good man. This is not a good man," Lynne Cheney said minutes after the debate ended. "Of course, I am speaking as a mom, and a pretty indignant mom. This is not a good man. What a cheap and tawdry political trick."

The next day, John Edwards's wife, Elizabeth, upped the ante by telling ABC that Lynne Cheney had "overreacted" because she felt "shame with respect to her daughter's sexual preferences."

"Ooh, I think that's a campaign gaffe we'll be talking about for a long time," said Nicolle Devenish, communications director for the Bush campaign. "I think that just exposed an ugliness on the Democratic ticket."

Unable to keep silent any longer, Dick Cheney fired back at Kerry.

"You saw a man who will say and do anything in order to get elected," he told a Florida audience, which lustily booed the reference to Kerry. "And I am not speaking just as a father here—though I am a pretty angry father—but as a citizen."

Cheney's boss was equally peeved.

"I didn't like it—I thought it was unfair," Bush told me. "It was really not necessary."

It also exposed a lack of political dexterity, according to Ken Mehlman.

"Bringing up the vice president's daughter at the debates was almost a thuggish response," he told me. "It was so clumsy and so heavy-handed. You felt like you were listening to news reports from the East German Ministry. It was just so over the top."

Fewer than twenty-four hours after the debate, Kerry found himself on the wrong end of an intense national backlash. In an attempt to control the damage without actually apologizing, he issued a three-sentence statement insisting he was innocent.

"I love my daughters. They love their daughter," he said, evidently forgetting the Cheneys, like the Kerrys, have two daughters. "I was trying to say something positive about the way strong families deal with this issue."

But the public wasn't buying it. Not even the mainstream media, which was pulling for Kerry, would let him off the hook. CNN's Candy Crowley, in an interview with the increasingly defensive Democrat two days after his lesbian remark, brought it up no fewer than half a dozen times. By now it was clear the gaffe had cost Kerry the third and final debate. After winning the first encounter and tying the much-improved, frown-free Bush in the second, Kerry's self-inflicted loss in the third put him on a downward trajectory only three weeks before the election.

Meanwhile, Bush seemed to be firing on all cylinders as he came down the home stretch.

"I felt relaxed," he told me. "I didn't force myself to be relaxed, but I was relaxed. It was almost as if I was an observer as well as a participant in the campaign."

The president seemed to relish every rally, savor every stump speech, cherish every rope line. He appeared loose and limber, like an athlete stepping into the fray, eager for combat. When I asked him to explain his demeanor, he shrugged.

"Well, last campaign, you know? The last campaign, the last fling of my life," he said wistfully. "Plus, I was energized by enormous crowds. These crowds were big and they were loud and they were very enthusiastic. I mean, there was no question in my mind that coming down the stretch that we were going to win, and the reason why is because I hadn't seen such large crowds that were full of such universally enthusiastic people. These weren't people coming to get a sense of 'who is this guy?' They weren't shoppers. They were absolute advocates ready to then go to work and turn out the vote."

Bush was also jazzed about having his daughters, Barbara and Jenna, accompany him on the campaign trail. Having never participated in their father's previous campaigns, the twins resolved to help out with the last hurrah.

"I used to tease them; it was like the camping trip that I promised them that we were never able to take prior to my political campaigns," the president told me. "And it meant a lot to me to be with them, on the bus trips or, you know, in those rallies.

"I'll never forget one of the first speeches I gave with one of my girls there. And they had no idea what it was like to go into one of these halls with twenty thousand people and to be greeted by—or to see their dad greeted by this just unbelievable energy. And I looked back at little Barbara and she was in tears, which made it a little difficult for me to get started on the speech. But it was really wonderful to have them here.

"It's hard to explain why something like that might have made a difference," he added. "But it did make a difference."

The difference did not go unnoticed by the mainstream media. With Bush hitting his stride down the home stretch, the press decided it was time to toss a "stink bomb"—the sort of high-impact news story that would devastate the president without giving him enough time to defend himself in the closing days of the campaign. Such a strategy had nearly worked four years earlier, when Democrats fed reporters documents that showed Bush had been arrested for driving under the influence of alcohol back in 1976. With that story dominating headlines all weekend before Election Day, Bush's five-point lead over Gore evaporated into a dead heat, resulting in the national nightmare known as the Florida Recount Wars. Bush ended up prevailing by only the narrowest of margins.

Four years later, a new stink bomb was needed, along with a media outlet willing to toss it. CBS News, seeking to avenge its humiliation over the debacle now known as "Memogate," eagerly accepted this duty. With its reputation in tatters, the *60 Minutes* team resolved to redeem itself by blaming Bush for a previously unreported screwup in Iraq. Specifically, CBS planned to accuse the administration of failing to safeguard a cache of weapons that went missing around the time of the U.S. invasion more than eighteen months earlier. The story originated with Mohamed ElBaradei of the International Atomic Energy Agency (IAEA). ElBaradei had opposed the war in Iraq and was miffed that Bush was now opposing his bid for a third term as chairman of the IAEA. ElBaradei had asked the Iraqi interim government for an accounting of missing munitions. The government responded on October 10 with a memo explaining that 380 tons of explosives were missing from a massive arms depot known as Al Qaqaa. It was unclear who had taken the explosives or if the United States military was even remotely culpable for their disappearance. But ElBaradei's memo found its way to CBS News, which planned to sit on the story and then blindside Bush just thirty-six hours before polls opened on Election Day.

Mindful that it was running low on journalistic credibility, CBS invited the *New York Times* to jointly report the story. *Times* executive editor Bill Keller jumped at the opportunity, enthusing that it would be "damaging" to Bush. In fact, Keller liked the story so much that he decided it could not wait for the *60 Minutes* program on Sunday, October 31. He splashed it across the top of page one on Monday, October 25.

"Huge Cache of Explosives Vanished from Site in Iraq," blared the headline, which was misleading in the extreme. The cache amounted to less than one-tenth of 1 percent of the 400,000 tons of munitions the United States had found in Iraq. The country was awash in weapons, which were overflowing from more than 1,000 separate caches. American forces had already destroyed or marked for destruction a thousand times more explosives than what was supposedly missing from Al Qaqaa. Besides, it was extraordinarily hypocritical for the *New York Times*, which for months had been railing against Bush for exaggerating the threat of Iraq's weapons, to suddenly reverse course and sound the weapons alarm eight days before the election. Having created a campaign issue, the newspaper then feigned surprise at this development by publishing a second-day story headlined, "Iraq Explosives Become Issue in Campaign." Naturally, Kerry was quoted denouncing the president's "incredible incompetence" and calling the missing explosives "one of the great blunders of Iraq." The TV news networks, led by CBS, were similarly gleeful in savaging Bush. The story dominated the campaign for days.

"This is a growing scandal and the American people deserve a full and honest explanation of how it happened and what the president is going to do about it," Kerry told supporters in Sioux City on October 27.

"We're seeing this White House dodging and bobbing and weaving," he added, "just as they've done each step of the way in our involvement in Iraq."

Bush told me the weapons stink bomb "was different from the DUI story, which defined me personally—as opposed to my policies. And there's a difference."

Nonetheless, he said, he couldn't let it knock him off stride down the home stretch.

"Look, at that point in time, you've got your eyes focused on the finish line and you try not to let anything distract you or get you off your game," he told me. "I just stayed focused."

Having survived such stories before, Bush remembered the importance of deploying his battle-hardened aides in a counterattack.

"I had plenty of good people back here in Washington dealing with these press matters," he told me.

"I said, 'You deal with it. I'm moving. I'm moving toward the finish line.'"

One of the agencies deployed to punch holes in the story was the Pentagon, which revealed that U.S. forces had removed and destroyed 250 tons of
the explosives from Al Qaqaa as a precaution when the war began. And, contrary to the IAEA's claim that the depot had contained 141 tons of a plastic
explosive known as RDX, the Pentagon said it was only three tons. This new,
exculpatory information was dutifully reported that evening by ABC, NBC,
FOX News, and CNN, but not CBS. Instead, Dan Rather began his newscast
by harping about "those still missing tons of explosives in Iraq." CBS reporter
Jim Axelrod was positively giddy about the damage being done to Bush,
exulting, "The timing of the story couldn't be worse for him."

But Bush was determined to turn Kerry's newfound concern over weapons
in Iraq against him.

"After repeatedly calling Iraq the wrong war, and a diversion, Senator
Kerry this week seemed shocked to learn that Iraq was a dangerous place, full
of dangerous weapons," Bush deadpanned, drawing laughter from an audience in Pennsylvania. "The senator used to know that, even though he seems
to have forgotten it over the course of the campaign. But after all, that's why
we're there. Iraq was a dangerous place run by a dangerous tyrant who had a
lot of weapons."

Ken Mehlman was similarly incredulous at Kerry's about-face on the issue
of weapons.

"I was stunned that he brought it up," the campaign manager told me. "He
was essentially saying it was wrong to remove Saddam Hussein, even though
we've just discovered all these dangerous weapons in the country.

"Politics is like a chess game. If you don't think a few moves ahead, then
you always end up like Homer Simpson, going, 'Doh!'"

Bush also seized on a remark made by Kerry foreign policy adviser Richard
Holbrooke, who had told FOX News a day earlier, "I don't know what hap-
pened. I do know one thing: in most administrations, the buck stops in the
Oval Office."

Bush said, "The senator is making wild charges about missing explosives,
when his top foreign policy adviser admits—quote—'We do not know the

facts.' Think about that. The senator is denigrating the action of our troops and commanders in the field without knowing the facts. Unfortunately, that's part of a pattern of saying almost anything to get elected."

Ironically, Bill Keller had tossed the stink bomb too early, giving Bush enough time to defuse it. The next attempt to derail the campaign came from Osama bin Laden, who released a videotaped message on the Friday afternoon before the election. Bin Laden stopped short of overtly endorsing Kerry, but the terrorist offered a polemic against reelecting Bush.

"People of America, this talk of mine is for you and concerns the ideal way to prevent another Manhattan," he warned on the videotape, which first surfaced on al Jazeera before being broadcast worldwide. "I am amazed at you. Even though we are in the fourth year after the events of September 11, Bush is still engaged in distortion, deception, and hiding from you the real causes. And thus, the reasons are still there for a repeat of what occurred."

In an almost comic understatement, the fugitive terrorist lamented, "We have found it difficult to deal with the Bush administration."

Unfortunately for Kerry, bin Laden then proceeded to parrot the Democrat's litany of complaints against Bush, right down to the Michael Moore–inspired canard about *My Pet Goat.*

"It never occurred to us that the commander in chief of the American armed forces would abandon 50,000 of his citizens in the twin towers to face those great horrors alone, the time when they most needed him," the terrorist taunted. "Occupying himself by talking to the little girl about the goat and its butting was more important than occupying himself with the planes and their butting of the skyscrapers."

Bin Laden also brought up a charge that Kerry had been making every day on the campaign trail—namely, that Bush had unfairly given Iraq reconstruction contracts to Halliburton, the firm once run by Dick Cheney. As if he were reading from a list of Democratic talking points, the terrorist groused about "the size of the contracts acquired by the shady Bush administration-linked mega-corporations like Halliburton." He went on to lament "the policy of the White House that demands the opening of war fronts to keep busy their various corporations—whether they be working in the field of arms or oil or reconstruction."

Warming to his theme, bin Laden rattled off even more Democratic talking points. He called Bush "the liar in the White House." He said the president's expenditures in Afghanistan and Iraq were causing an "astronomical" American deficit. He argued that Americans should never "have allowed the White House to implement its aggressive foreign policies." He called the Patriot Act a "suppression of freedoms." Digging even deeper into the Democratic playbook, he blamed "election fraud" in Florida for the Bush presidency in the first place.

Bin Laden was now on a roll. In yet another echo of Kerry's campaign rhetoric, he argued that Bush should have given weapons inspectors more time in Iraq.

"Americans warned Bush before the war," bin Laden said. "The nations of the world are with you in the inspections, and it is in the interest of America that it not be thrust into an unjustified war with an unknown outcome."

Finally, bin Laden regurgitated the most specious Bush-bashing slogan of them all—that he waged war for oil. Democrats had been throwing around this charge for years, even though Bush had always insisted that Iraqis keep their oil for themselves. In fact, when Congress first put together the $87 billion funding package, several Democrats demanded that reconstruction funds be structured as loans that would be repaid with Iraqi oil revenues. But Bush overrode them, insisting the money be given as an outright grant. Nonetheless, the war-for-oil accusation continued to dog Bush and was now being leveled by bin Laden himself.

"The darkness of the black gold blurred his vision," he said of the president. "So the war went ahead, the death toll rose, the American economy bled, and Bush became embroiled in the swamps of Iraq that threaten his future."

This reference to "swamps" sounded suspiciously like the "quagmire" argument that Democrats had been making against Bush since the war began.

"In conclusion, I tell you in truth, that your security is not in the hands of Kerry, nor Bush, nor al Qaeda," bin Laden lectured. "No, your security is in your own hands. And every state that doesn't play with our security has automatically guaranteed its own security."

This was the first and only reference to Kerry in the entire fifteen-minute videotape and, notably, it was not a criticism of the Democrat. Yet this was the quotation most often cited by newspapers in the final weekend before the election. Journalists were not eager to report that the man who incinerated three thousand Americans on September 11 now clearly opposed a second Bush term. That might redound to the president's benefit, since polls showed Americans trusted Bush over Kerry by a wide margin when it came to fighting terrorism. So the press tried to muddy the waters by reporting over and over that bin Laden had said America's security "is not in the hands of Kerry or Bush." This gave the impression that bin Laden had no preference in the election, when in fact he clearly opposed Bush while remaining neutral on Kerry. Indeed, he had uttered well over a dozen specific denunciations of Bush and his administration during his diatribe.

"He certainly wants George Bush out of the White House," former New York mayor Rudy Giuliani said of bin Laden on NBC. "There's no question that he very much opposes George Bush, and I think there's a reason for that—because the man is on the run."

Yet Bush was loath to exploit the bin Laden video for political advantage.

"Let me make this very clear," he said the day the tape was released. "Americans will not be intimidated or influenced by an enemy of our country. I'm sure Senator Kerry agrees with this."

But instead of joining Bush on the high road, Kerry decided to politicize the bin Laden tape.

"I regret that when George Bush had the opportunity in Afghanistan at Tora Bora, he didn't choose to use American forces to hunt down and kill Osama bin Laden," he thundered.

Kerry's instincts to take the low road were borne out by a poll he commissioned over the weekend on the political impact of bin Laden inserting himself into the presidential campaign. Pollster Stanley Greenberg reported back to Kerry that the videotape made voters more likely to support Bush.

"The thing that I find amazing about it was that John Kerry's first response was to go conduct a poll to find out what he should say about this tape from Osama bin Laden," Vice President Cheney marveled at a stump speech in Iowa. "It's as though he didn't know what he believed until he has to go and check the poll, stick his finger in the air to see which way the political winds are blowing, and then make a decision and take a position and articulate a point of view."

He added, "George Bush doesn't need an opinion poll to know what he believes, especially about Osama bin Laden."

Inside the president's campaign, Bush told me there were "enormous amounts of discussion" about the tape, which he called "an interesting entry by our enemy into the campaign."

"What does it mean? Is it going to help? Is it going to hurt?" he said. "Anything that drops in at the end of a campaign that is not already decided creates all kinds of anxieties, because you're not sure of the effect."

"I thought it was going to help," he concluded. "I thought it would help remind people that if bin Laden doesn't want Bush to be the president, something must be right with Bush."

Mehlman agreed.

"It reminded people of the stakes," he told me. "It reinforced an issue on which Bush had a big lead over Kerry."

Indeed, the mainstream media became alarmed by the tape's potential to help Bush. Dan Rather's predecessor, Walter Cronkite, fretted about this unfortunate development on CNN's *Larry King Live*.

"I have a feeling that it could tilt the election a bit," said the former CBS anchorman, a self-described liberal. "In fact, I'm a little inclined to think that Karl Rove, the political manager at the White House, who is a very clever man, he probably set up bin Laden to this thing."

Ah, the old "Republican dirty tricks" argument. That meant the Democrats were truly worried.

CHAPTER ELEVEN

"SWINGING LIKE COUNT BASIE"

K arl Rove's hand was shaking so badly that Dan Bartlett had to hold the paper for him as he wrote down the devastating numbers from the first wave of exit polls. It was mid-afternoon on Election Day and the Bush aides were in the senior staff cabin of Air Force One as it ferried the president back to Washington at the conclusion of the long and grueling campaign. Rove was on the phone with Bush pollster Matthew Dowd, who had just received the first concrete indication of whether all their hard work would finally pay off. As the person most responsible for engineering the president's reelection, Rove was staggered by the news.

John Kerry was ahead by an astonishing twenty points in Pennsylvania, one of the three most important battleground states in the entire election. Sure, Bush had lost Pennsylvania to Al Gore in 2000, but the margin then had been a mere four points. Getting blown out by twenty would be a shocking humiliation, especially after the president had made countless trips to the state and spent millions of dollars there on television ads. Moreover, a loss in Pennsylvania meant Bush would have to carry both Florida and Ohio—the other two all-important states in the election. But according to the exit polls, he was down by three in Florida and four in Ohio.

As Rove scribbled more numbers, the news only got worse. Of the ten battleground states for which Dowd had results, Bush was ahead in only one—Colorado. The candidates were tied in Iowa, which Bush had won in 2000, but Kerry was leading everywhere else, including Michigan and New Mexico. In Wisconsin, which Bush had lost to Gore by barely a tenth of a point in 2000, Kerry was now ahead by an incredible nine points. In Minnesota, which Gore had won by two points, Kerry was dominating by a mind-blowing eighteen. Even in New Hampshire, which Bush had carried in 2000, Kerry was now winning by sixteen points. It was nothing short of a landslide.

"This is one of those moments when your head says one thing and your heart says something else," Rove told me. "On the one hand, your head says this can't be. I mean, it says *blowout*. And yet on the other hand, your heart says, Oh God, we're, we're—*we're done*."

Rove and Bartlett were soon joined by National Security Adviser Condoleezza Rice and Karen Hughes, an informal adviser to the president. Up until the phone call with Dowd, the mood on the plane had been upbeat. People had been playing cards, cracking jokes, letting off steam after the marathon campaign. But now each adviser's face went ashen at the crushing news. When Bush finally walked in, he could tell right away there was a problem.

"They don't look good," Rove said of the exit polls.

"How bad do they look?" Bush said.

"Well," Rove ventured, "something has got to be wrong with them."

Rove had once earned the presidential nickname "Turd Blossom" for his ability to turn disastrous political developments into hopeful opportunities. This time around, however, even Turd Blossom could find nothing but doom in the exit polls.

Bush acknowledged to me that the news was "a downer, because we had just worked our hearts out, coming down the stretch, felt good about it all—and then get this kind of cold water. On the other hand, it wasn't frigid, because something looked wrong."

The president made his skepticism clear after Rove finished running through the numbers.

"I don't believe it," he told his staff. "If this is what they've decided, fine. But I don't believe it."

"It's too early," counseled Bartlett, the White House communications director, who had worked with Bush for a decade, longer than any other aide. "Let's wait."

But Bush couldn't stop thinking about the stunning news.

"That doesn't seem right," he muttered as the plane touched down at Andrews Air Force Base near Washington.

"It doesn't matter whether they're right or wrong," countered Karen Hughes. "There are people still voting. When you come down the stairs of Air Force One, smile and wave."

So Bush plastered a fake smile across his face and waved at the handful of people who watched him make the short walk across the tarmac from Air Force One to Marine One. Minutes later, the helicopter deposited the presidential entourage on the South Lawn of the White House. It was time for another fake smile.

"There was a large crowd there," Bush explained to me. "And, you know, I was waving: 'Great to see you all!'"

The president's aides were putting on similarly brave faces for the short walk across the South Lawn, although they weren't very convincing.

"When the president arrived and came in, they had faux smiles coming from the helicopter into the White House," White House chief of staff Andy Card told me. "And when they reached the Diplomatic Room, you could see the upturned corners of the mouth turn down."

It was obvious to Bush and his entourage that the bad news had already begun to spread through the White House staff.

"You could go around and you could actually tell who had heard the exit polls. Nobody was talking about it, but you could tell who had heard," Card said. "I could feel the wave of disappointment building."

Even outside the White House, the exit polls were taking a psychological toll at the highest levels of the Bush campaign. Vice President Cheney, who was returning to Washington after stumping in Wisconsin, got the news from his daughter Mary, who was running his campaign.

"My family was panicked," Cheney told me. "When I got back and got on the ground, I could tell there was a sense of concern, shall I say, back at campaign headquarters."

As evidence, Cheney was asked to make a series of last-minute phone calls to live radio shows in an effort to get more Republicans to the polls. He agreed to make the calls, partly because his wife, Lynne, was so rattled by the exit polls.

"She was worried," the vice president told me. "My daughters were worried. But I wasn't really worried about it."

An old hand who had been through more presidential campaigns than most, Cheney had good reasons for his stoicism.

"First of all, I'd seen exit polls before that were wrong," he told me. "Second, I knew enough about polling and surveys that when you design a sample, to reach in partway through the sample and try to extract credible information makes no sense at all. It's screwy to begin with. So I blew it off."

Ken Mehlman told me, "I'll be honest with you, there were people in the campaign who were unhappy."

The campaign manager tried to remain upbeat when he found himself on a conference call with Bush and his father, who were at the White House.

"What do you think of all this?" the younger Bush asked.

"I don't believe the exit polls," Mehlman replied.

"Why?" Bush said.

"Because they're too skewed," Mehlman replied. "Here's what I know."

He then launched into a detailed analysis of various counties that was utterly incompatible with the exit poll results.

"Okay," Bush said. "That sounds good."

In fact, it sounded so good that Cheney confidante Mary Matalin soon called Mehlman and asked him to repeat his analysis to the vice president.

Meanwhile, Rove was also coming to the conclusion that the exit polls were screwy. The numbers were simply too different from all the polling that had been done in the final days of the campaign. For example, Kerry had been ahead of Bush by only a single point in each of three states—Pennsylvania, New Hampshire, and Wisconsin—according to RealClearPolitics, a website that averaged all the major polls. But now Kerry was dominating by margins of nine to twenty points. Furthermore, a second wave of exit polls showed Kerry winning the national popular vote by a single point, a reversal of pre-election polls that showed Bush winning by 1.5 points.

"The numbers were just nuts," Rove told me. "And you just sit there and say, this does not make sense. After fifteen minutes of looking at these exit polls, there was no doubt in my mind that there were huge, horrific problems with the data."

Card, who never put much credence in the exit polls in the first place, was equally skeptical, although much of his staff remained clearly devastated.

"I feel good about things—let's go out and feel good," Card told Rove. "So we did, we truly went out and felt good. We were trying to buck everybody up and cheer them up."

Unfortunately, the media was taking the exit polls very seriously. Over at the Ronald Reagan building, where White House correspondents were gathered to await election returns, they were all but writing the president's political obituary. The reporters were conveniently ignoring the atrocious track record of the exit polls, which had been commissioned by a media consortium consisting of ABC, CBS, NBC, CNN, the AP, and FOX News. These news organizations had used the exit polls—which were notoriously slipshod, unscientific, and skewed to favor Democrats—as an excuse to prematurely and erroneously declare Gore the winner of the all-important state of Florida on Election Night 2000. By calling the state even before the polls had closed, the media managed to depress Republican turnout and reduce Bush's margin of error in Florida from an estimated 10,000 votes to 537, plunging the nation into a thirty-six-day post-election nightmare known as the Recount Wars. The exit pollsters promised to fix the bugs in their system in time for the 2002 midterm elections, but the bugs only multiplied. Unable to guarantee the accuracy of their findings, exit pollsters stunned the political world on Election Night by announcing that they were scrapping the entire operation and issuing no results. Now, two years later, those same exit pollsters were predicting a Kerry landslide—and the mainstream media, all too eager to believe such an outcome, cast journalistic skepticism to the winds.

So did Kerry's senior political adviser, Bob Shrum, whose track record for getting Democratic presidential candidates elected was an abysmal zero for seven. Confident that his curse had finally been broken, he approached Kerry shortly after 7 p.m. and said with a reverent smile, "May I be the first to say 'Mr. President'?"

By this time, the exit polls had been plastered all over the Internet for more than five hours, even though the media outlets that commissioned them were supposed to keep the results secret until voting precincts closed. Giddy with the prospect of a Kerry presidency, news organizations leaked the numbers with reckless abandon. As a result, millions of Americans—many of whom had not yet voted—read during the course of the afternoon that Kerry had a virtual lock on the White House. Even overseas, Bush was being written off. British prime minister Tony Blair went to bed believing his Texan friend had lost the election.

While bloggers had a field day disseminating the exit polls, the news organizations that paid for the data were supposed to publicly pretend they had no idea which candidate was ahead. The talking heads on TV, while not overtly announcing that Kerry was cleaning Bush's clock, found roundabout ways of imparting this information to tens of millions of voters, including many who had not yet cast ballots. CBS managed to accomplish this before the polls closed in Florida, Pennsylvania, and numerous other states.

"I just got through to the Kerry campaign. I spoke with Joe Lockhart over there," announced Bob Schieffer to anchorman Dan Rather. "The Kerry people say that they feel pretty good right now. They think that they now have—and Lockhart says flatly—they now have a chance to win every battleground state."

Having blatantly parroted the Democratic spin, which just so happened to mirror the exit polls, Schieffer now went through the motions of dispensing an obligatory dollop of skepticism for the cameras.

"Now, we have to keep that in context," he cautioned. "That's coming from the Kerry campaign. But that's the story they're putting out right now."

Rather nodded sagely. Mindful of his own embarrassing performance on Election Night 2000 and his catastrophic use of forged documents just two months previously, the anchorman decided to echo Schieffer's profession of healthy skepticism.

"One's reminded of the old saying: don't taunt the alligator until after you've crossed the creek," Rather mused, prompting a puzzled look from Schieffer. "Apparently, Joe doesn't subscribe to that."

It was the first of the evening's many "Ratherisms," those cornball maxims calculated to give the notoriously stiff anchorman some desperately needed folksiness and down-home charm. More often than not, they struck viewers as forced or even bizarre.

"This race is hotter than a Times Square Rolex," he would exclaim as the night wore on. "Closer than Lassie and Timmy."

In case this reference to a fictional dog and her master last seen in a TV series forty years earlier was insufficiently dated, the anchorman reached back to the big band era to create more Ratherisms.

"The presidential race is swinging like Count Basie," he said, driving away the last remnants of CBS's youth demographic. "Humming along like Ray Charles."

Even conservative commentators like Bill Kristol on FOX News seemed deflated by the exit polls. This alarmed Rove, who was in the Old Family Dining Room of the White House, which he had turned into a command center, complete with banks of computer monitors displaying the latest raw returns. Rove remembered all too well the nightmare of four years earlier, when Republicans in Western states actually got out of line at polling places and went home after learning that Gore had supposedly carried Florida.

"I immediately began making phone calls to people who were connected to the networks about this," Rove told me. "And I'd say, 'This just does not make sense.' And they'd say, 'Oh, that's an interesting question. We'll talk to our fellows in New Jersey, where they're running the exit polling, and we'll get back to you.'

"And if they returned the call at all, after you made the complaint, they'd come up with an incredible explanation that had been given to them by the exit guys," he added. "They'd have the most insane set of excuses."

For example, Rove explained that when you averaged together all the polls that were taken in Pennsylvania during the final week of the campaign, Bush was only down by two percentage points, not twenty.

"And they'd say, 'Well, perhaps it could be that Kerry just won all the undecideds,'" Rove told me. "I said, 'Hey, give him all the undecideds. There were only four points of undecideds. Give him all four!'"

Rove also complained that the exit polls showed women comprising 59 percent of the electorate, a full seven points higher than in any previous election.

"They'd say, 'Well, the exit pollers suggest that Kerry may have succeeded in changing the nature of the electorate,'" Rove told me. "I'd say, 'He has succeeded in doing something that no presidential candidate in the history of America has ever come close to doing, and that is making women more than 53 percent of the electorate.'"

Rove was particularly incensed that the exit polls showed Bush losing the white male vote in Florida.

"I'd say, 'Does it make sense to you that white men are going for John Kerry in a southern state?'" he told me. "And they'd say, 'Well, the exit polling suggests his wartime service may have swung them.'"

While Rove browbeat the mainstream media, Mehlman mobilized the opposition media. He went on FOX News as many times as possible to refute the conventional wisdom of an imminent Kerry blowout. He and his underlings deluged talk-radio hosts and conservative bloggers with hourly phone calls aimed at rallying the rank-and-file Republicans.

"Our theory was that the MSM would do what it did, and so in our alternative universe, we needed to give people real information," Mehlman told me.

Over at the White House, in the private quarters known simply as "the residence," Bush was watching returns on television with a couple dozen friends and family members. They gathered in the first family's living room, also known as the West Sitting Hall, and enjoyed a buffet of crab cakes, lamb chops, beef tenderloin, smoked salmon, squash soup, shrimp, tamales, and sopaipillas. Occasionally Bush would wander downstairs to look over Rove's shoulder at the latest tallies coming across the computer screens. After scrutinizing the numbers right down to the precinct level, Bush would head back to the living room to rejoin his wife, daughters, parents, siblings, and confidants.

"We're very upbeat," the president told reporters who were briefly ushered into the room at 9:37 p.m. "I believe I will win."

The president's early skepticism of the exit polls was now being borne out by actual vote tallies, which told a much more encouraging story.

"We held our own in our states," he told me. "And the states where we're supposed to do well, we did real well in."

For example, Bush won West Virginia by a convincing thirteen points.

"It's a pretty good indicator," he told me. "And then Karl started calling me with some of these counties in Florida, precincts in certain counties. He had the 2000 to 2004 comparison, and man, we were romping."

At 11:39 p.m., the networks began declaring Bush the winner in Florida. Since Kerry had already won Pennsylvania, that meant the entire election would come down to Ohio, as most analysts had long predicted. The networks seemed in no hurry to declare a winner in this all-important state, even though Bush had been assured by aides before 10:30 p.m. that he would prevail there.

"There's a couple of key swing counties in Ohio," Rove told his boss, "running ahead of where we need you to be."

Bush told me, "I felt good about that."

Indeed, with nearly two-thirds of Ohio's precincts tallied, Bush was leading Kerry by five percentage points, fifty-two to forty-seven. Armed with this information, Andy Card placed a call to Kerry campaign manager Mary Beth Cahill shortly before midnight.

"Mary Beth, I don't know what your numbers are saying, but our numbers are looking very good," Card told her. "Should we work on scheduling a phone call? You want to line up a phone call?"

Cahill politely answered with a single word: "No."

"Okay, well, when you're ready, I'm ready," Card said before hanging up.

As Tuesday gave way to Wednesday, Bush told me he felt "like a marathon runner" who discovers that "the race never quite ends."

"I usually go to bed at 9:30 p.m., as you know, or 10 p.m.," he added. "And midnight came around. It just looked like it was going to drag on forever."

At 12:41 a.m., with 83 percent of Ohio's precincts counted, the president was beating Kerry by three percentage points, fifty-one to forty-eight. In terms of raw votes, Bush was ahead by nearly 140,000, an obviously insurmountable lead, so FOX News became the first network to declare him the winner in Ohio. That gave the president 266 electoral votes—or four shy of the 270 necessary for victory. But anyone with a rudimentary grasp of arithmetic knew that the president's reelection was in the bag. After all, in less than twenty minutes, the polls would close in Alaska, where Bush was trouncing Kerry by twenty-six points—a larger margin than Kerry enjoyed in any Democratic state. Alaska's three electoral votes would push the president's total to 269, or one shy of the magic number. But in this case, 269 was the same as a Bush victory. That's because even if Kerry swept the remaining states and matched the president's 269 electoral votes—a highly unlikely scenario—the tie would be broken by the GOP-controlled House of Representatives. Since each state would get one vote and Republicans controlled twenty-eight of the fifty states, the president would triumph with several votes to spare. Yet no one was even seriously contemplating this scenario, as it was obvious the president's electoral tally would eventually exceed 270. All he had to do was win one of three remaining states he had carried in 2000—Nevada, New Mexico, and Iowa. Bush was already beating Kerry by three percentage points, or more than 16,000 votes, in New Mexico. In short, it was impossible to imagine Kerry becoming president.

"BUSH WINS," blared the headline on the wildly popular Drudge Report website shortly before 1 a.m. Journalist Matt Drudge had been monitoring returns in key states and recognized the inevitability of the president's reelection. As usual, Drudge was way ahead of the mainstream media, which was being intensively lobbied by the Kerry campaign.

In fact, moments after FOX News declared Bush the winner of Ohio, Kerry campaign operatives frantically telephoned ABC, CBS, CNN, and NBC and implored them not to follow suit. All obeyed except NBC, which declared Bush the winner of Ohio at 12:59 a.m. One minute later, both NBC and FOX called Alaska for Bush and announced that the president had amassed 269 votes.

"This race is hotter than the Devil's anvil!" said Rather. "We don't know whether to wind a watch or bark at the moon!"

Card checked the latest tallies with the Ohio secretary of state and then shared them with Cahill in a second phone call.

"Mary Beth, our numbers have continued to hold," he told her. "Do they reflect your numbers?"

"They don't reflect our numbers," she replied. "We're getting different numbers."

"Well, I don't know where your numbers are coming from," Card said. "But our numbers are holding."

Shortly after this conversation, Cahill issued a defiant public statement that made it clear Kerry was refusing to face reality.

"The vote count in Ohio has not been completed," she said at 1:27 a.m. "There are more than 250,000 remaining votes to be counted. We believe when they are, John Kerry will win Ohio."

Cahill was referring to provisional ballots that had been distributed to people who were barred from casting regular ballots at polling places because of eligibility problems. The state planned to double-check the eligibility of these voters in the days after the election and then count the provisional ballots of those who had been disenfranchised.

But even if there really were that many provisional ballots, and even if all of them were legitimate—which was extremely unlikely—Kerry would have to win nearly 80 percent of them to overcome the president's 140,000-vote lead in Ohio. Clearly, Cahill was grasping at straws.

One hour later, John Edwards took the stage at Copley Square in Boston, where demoralized Kerry supporters had been standing in a chilly drizzle for hours. A disembodied voice over the public address system introduced Edwards as "the next vice president of the United States." Obviously, this would not be a concession speech. The crowd momentarily came to life as Edwards strode to the microphone, flashing his thousand-watt smile and violently flinging out his arms to project his upturned thumbs.

"It's been a long night," he said. "But we've waited four years for this victory—we can wait one more night."

Edwards then adopted Al Gore's mantra from the Recount Wars of 2000, causing maximum trepidation among Republicans.

"John Kerry and I made a promise to the American people that in this election, every vote would count and every vote would be counted," he said. "Tonight, we are keeping our word and we will fight for every vote. You deserve no less."

Edwards was choosing to ignore the math. At that moment, with 87 percent of the precincts tallied nationwide, Bush was beating Kerry by a whopping 3.6 million votes. There was no way on God's green earth that John Kerry could possibly win the popular vote, which Gore had won by a mere half million in 2000. Furthermore, Bush was maintaining his insurmountable lead in the all-important state of Ohio, where 97 percent of the precincts now had been counted. He was even ahead in Nevada, New Mexico, and Iowa, although Democratic officials in the latter two decided to stop counting for the night in order to buy Kerry some time. This gave the networks an excuse not to call these states, although New Mexico was eminently callable. Even before Edwards made his announcement, Bush was leading Kerry by a margin of 52 to 47 percent, with 93 percent of New Mexico's precincts reporting.

At 3:30 a.m., Bush noticed that his father was still wide awake in the residence, waiting for the sort of news he had never received a dozen years earlier. The son had been seared by that bitter defeat, although time had softened the blow.

"Ninety-two was a disappointment," Bush said of his father's loss. "But he taught me a really good lesson—that life moves on. And it's very important for those of us in the political arena, win or lose, to recognize that life is bigger than just politics."

Now the son, girding for the possibility of another post-election recount nightmare, fretted over his aging father.

"I was worried about him staying up too late," Bush said. "He was awaiting the outcome and was hopeful that we would go over and be able to talk to our supporters, and it just didn't happen that way."

Bush explained to me, "I think in his mind, there was just a little anxiety. He wanted it *then*, like most of the people who run for office, including me. It's nice to get the verdict, one way or the other, on Election Night—closure."

Yet closure was nowhere in sight and Bush figured his father needed some rest. He urged him to go to bed.

"Go on, nothing's going to happen," the son said. "I'm going to win."

But the father insisted on getting one last rundown of the battleground states.

"Okay, here's what Karl said," Bush replied before running down the numbers. "Dad, look, New Mexico is solid; Nevada is over; Iowa—I bet we win Iowa.

"We've won," he assured his father. "We're fine in Ohio—it's over 100,000 votes, Dad. And it's just a matter of letting people get a sense for the reality and people will do the right thing."

The son implored his father, "Go to bed."

The elder Bush finally obeyed, which only served to make the exhausted Card jealous.

"I've got to go to bed," he pleaded to Cahill in his third phone call. "But we're still pretty confident in our numbers."

"Well, I'm sorry, we just have different numbers," she said. "And we feel good about them."

"Okay," Card sighed.

At 3:44 a.m., CBS awarded Nevada to Bush, a call that was matched by CNN and ABC within the space of an hour. But these three networks still refused to call Ohio for Bush, since that would put the president over the magic number of 270 electoral votes. Meanwhile, both FOX and NBC—which had called Ohio hours earlier—refused to call Nevada, since that would mean handing the election to Bush. NBC was simply too biased and beholden to Kerry to call Nevada, just as CBS, CNN, and ABC were too biased and beholden to call Ohio. FOX, on the other hand, was motivated by fear. After all, FOX had been the first to declare Bush the winner on Election Night 2000, only to sheepishly reclassify the race as too close to call. Although FOX's initial call ultimately proved correct, the network had been heavily criticized, especially when word got around that Bush's first cousin, John Ellis, was in charge of FOX's decision desk on Election Night.

So from 4:39 a.m. forward, the talking heads on the networks hemmed and hawed and dithered and stalled and refused to call the presidential election of 2004. They utterly abdicated their traditional role of authoritatively projecting a winner and a loser. It was a far cry from 2000, when the networks had been all too eager to award the crucial state of Florida to Gore, even though polls in the state were still open, 96 percent of the precincts had not yet been tallied, and the final margin would come down to a mere 537 votes. Now they were unwilling to call Ohio, where 99.89 percent of the votes had been counted and Bush was ahead by nearly 140,000 votes.

"Why aren't they calling it?" Card cried in frustration. "Why aren't they calling it? What are they waiting for?"

Indeed, with virtually all votes counted across the nation, it was abundantly clear that Bush had decisively vanquished Kerry by a margin of 51 to 48 percent.

"I thought it was pretty ridiculous, given the 3 percent margin, that they wouldn't call it after the results were all in," Mehlman told me.

Rove and Bartlett were reduced to angrily telephoning the various networks and trying to shame them into performing their journalistic duty. But it was hopeless.

"Nobody wanted to call it so that we had won—not even FOX," Card told me. "Yes, we were frustrated at FOX. It was like, c'mon, are they just afraid to say it? I mean, it was almost like when one says it, they'll all say it. But since one won't say it, no one will say it."

But there was also something more sinister behind the networks' reluctance to call the race, according to Card.

"Some of the talking heads," he told me, "were rooting for a crisis in Ohio. It wasn't just that they were afraid to admit we had won."

As in 2000, the networks dragged their feet in awarding states to Bush and raced to award states to his Democratic opponent. This was true even when Bush won states by larger margins than Kerry. At 5 a.m. CNN made a decision that epitomized the media's blatant double standard. The network gave Kerry the closest state in the entire election, Wisconsin, even though the Democrat was ahead by only 13,000 votes and would ultimately prevail by less than half of a single percentage point. Yet CNN still refused to call Ohio for Bush, where he was ahead by two full percentage points, fifty-one to forty-nine, and led Kerry by some 140,000 votes—or more than ten times the margin in Wisconsin. Over and over, CNN and the rest of the networks sanctimoniously told viewers that Ohio was simply "too close to call."

"Given the small difference and given the provisional ballot issue, we're just not comfortable at CNN making this call," CNN's Judy Woodruff said. "We are being very cautious here."

Bush couldn't believe it. The networks were simply refusing to declare him the winner.

"I remember staring at the tube, watching the same thing cycle through," he told me. "It drug on. The evening drug on and on and on."

The president was itching to make the short drive over to the Ronald Reagan building in Washington, where his supporters had been waiting all night for a victory speech. But how could he claim victory if the networks refused to call the race and Kerry refused to concede? The president's aides weighed the pros and cons of giving Kerry some more time to come to grips with reality.

"It was a healthy debate," Card said. "Do we declare victory? Just do it unilaterally? Or do we say it looks good and invite them to concede? And Don Evans had a view and Karen Hughes had a view and Karl had a view. I had a view."

Ultimately, it was the president himself who settled the question of whether he would personally declare victory.

"I decided not to do that," he told me. "I felt like the facts would speak for themselves."

Bush figured his margin of victory in Ohio was big enough to preclude the sort of standoff that occurred in Florida, where his margin of victory had been just 537 votes.

"This one we knew there would be finality pretty quickly," he told me. "It's just such a difference from the 2000 campaign, where nothing happened Election Night."

Having decided to give Kerry some more time to do the right thing, Bush went to bed at 5 a.m., or seven hours after he normally turned in. Although he had opted not to personally declare victory, he authorized his staff to do so on his behalf as sort of a stopgap measure. So Card was dispatched to the Reagan building.

"We are convinced that President Bush has won reelection with at least 286 electoral votes," he told the cheering crowd. "And he also has a margin of at least three and a half million popular votes."

Breaking with tradition, the White House was announcing the election's winner before the networks.

"In Ohio, President Bush has a lead of at least 140,000 votes," Card said. "The secretary of state's office has informed us that this margin is statistically insurmountable, even after the provisional ballots are considered.

"So President Bush has won the state of Ohio!" Card exclaimed, prompting another cheer from the crowd. "President Bush has also been declared the winner in Nevada."

Card had done what no network had dared—state the obvious. By citing both Ohio (which had been called by FOX and NBC) and Nevada (which had been called by ABC, CBS, and CNN) Card illustrated the irrefutable proof of Bush's victory. But he went even further by claiming wins in Iowa and New Mexico, which is how he arrived at the final electoral vote tally of 286.

"President Bush decided to give Senator Kerry the respect of more time to reflect on the results of this election," Card concluded. "The president will be making a statement later today."

Translation: Kerry was delusional and Bush was giving him one last chance to save face. If Kerry persisted in this folly, the president would be forced to claim victory even without a concession from the loser.

Card went back to the White House, said good-bye to the staff, and headed home. He fell asleep around 6:30 a.m. and then arose an hour later. His first order of business was placing another phone call to Cahill, who was still clinging to the fiction that Kerry could somehow win Ohio. Card recited the latest numbers and reminded her of the math.

"Mary Beth, where are you getting your numbers?" Card asked.

"Well," she replied vaguely, "they're coming from our people."

"Get the numbers from the secretary of state's office," Card urged. "They're the ones that are official. Here's his phone number. Call him."

He proceeded to rattle off numbers for the secretary of state's office, home, and cell phone, as well as a number for his personal aide.

"If the numbers I've given you aren't consistent with the numbers you get from the secretary of state, let me know, call me back," Card said.

"Well," Cahill ventured. "If the numbers are what you say they are—and I'm not sure that they will be—but if they are, I will recommend my guy call your guy."

Over at the White House, Card's guy woke up at 7 a.m. after getting just two hours of sleep. By 8 a.m. he was in the Oval Office, where he soon received his father.

"We had a good talk," the son said. "There was some uncertainty about that morning as to when the election would actually end. And it wasn't clear at that point in time."

The elder Bush then departed for Houston, leaving his son to confer with various senior staffers who streamed in and out of the Oval Office for the next several hours. Bartlett was the first to poke his head in the office, followed by Card, Hughes, Rice, and Cheney.

Although there was still some Democratic uncertainty about the presidential election, it was indisputable that the GOP had made substantial gains in Congress. In the Senate, Republicans increased their majority from fifty-one votes to fifty-five. In the House, Republicans gained three seats, giving them a thirty-vote advantage over the Democrats, 232 to 202. It was the sixth consecutive GOP-controlled House, giving Republicans an uninterrupted reign of at least a dozen years. The last time that happened was the period from 1921 to 1933.

The president's coattails were undeniable. It was the second consecutive congressional election in which Bush had led the GOP to historic gains. In 2002, Republicans had padded their House majority by six seats and wrested the Senate away from Democratic control by picking up two seats. The success of the president, who campaigned tirelessly for his fellow Republicans, stood in stark contrast to the track record of his White House predecessors, who since World War II had lost an average of two dozen House seats in their first midterm elections. Bill Clinton had lost a staggering fifty-four House seats and nine Senate seats, along with Democratic control of both chambers. But Bush had picked up seats in his first midterms and now added to his majorities.

So the president spent some time calling the victorious Republicans and congratulating them. He telephoned Richard Burr, who had defeated former Clinton chief of staff Erskine Bowles for the North Carolina Senate seat being vacated by Kerry's running mate, John Edwards. He called his former secretary of housing and urban development, Mel Martinez, who had just become the nation's first Cuban American senator, winning the Florida seat vacated by Bob Graham, one of nine Democrats who had challenged Kerry in the presidential primaries. Bush also called David Vitter, who had just won the Louisiana Senate seat vacated by the retiring John Breaux, a Democrat. Vitter was the first Republican since Reconstruction to win a Senate seat in Louisiana, completing a GOP sweep of the South.

At 9:30 a.m., Bush received his regular intelligence briefing, followed by the regular FBI briefing. Then he resumed his visits with top advisers and made some more congratulatory phone calls to fellow Republicans.

He telephoned John Thune of South Dakota, who had pulled off the extraordinary feat of ousting Senate Minority Leader Tom Daschle, the top Democrat in Congress. It was the first time in fifty-two years that a Senate leader had been tossed out of office. Next to the presidential contest, Thune's victory was the most significant race of 2004. It was a crushing humiliation of the Democratic Party. Daschle's defeat came two years after he lost his job as majority leader in the Republican takeover of the Senate. He would be departing Washington along with Representative Richard Gephardt, who had abandoned his post as House Minority Leader after the GOP blowout in 2002. The Missouri Democrat decided to run for president rather than reelection in 2004 and had been decisively beaten by John Kerry. Gephardt and Daschle had been the most prominent Democrats when Bush came to Washington four years earlier. Now they were sent packing by the constantly "misunderestimated" president.

Bush also called Tom Coburn and Jim Bunning, who had won Senate races in Oklahoma and Kentucky, respectively. Finally, he congratulated Jim DeMint of South Carolina for winning the Senate seat that had been occupied for thirty-eight years by retiring Democrat Ernest "Fritz" Hollings. Bush urged DeMint to waste no time in pushing through a Republican legislative agenda.

"Now is the time to get it done," the president said.

At about 10 a.m., Rove arrived at the White House and joined the parade of top officials paying their respects to the president, including Secretary of Defense Donald Rumsfeld, chief speechwriter Michael Gerson, and press secretary Scott McClellan.

A short while later, Bush received word that Kerry would be calling him within the hour. The president spent that time huddling with Rove, Bartlett,

Hughes, McClellan, and Gerson. At 11:02 a.m., presidential assistant Ashley Estes informed Bush that Kerry was on the phone. Bush, who had been standing in the middle of the Oval Office holding court, went over and sat behind the desk once used by Kerry's idol—John F. Kennedy. He picked up the phone and listened to the words he had longed to hear since first telephoning Kerry back in March to welcome him to the campaign.

"Congratulations, Mr. President," Kerry said.

A visceral sense of relief flooded through George W. Bush's very bones. At long last, he had attained the prize that had eluded his father—a second term. And unlike his first victory four years ago, which had been tainted by the Recount Wars, this time Bush was armed with a mandate. Instead of losing the popular vote by half a million ballots, Bush had won it by a margin seven times that large. In fact, he had won more popular votes than any president in history. He had beaten Kerry, 51 to 48 percent, precisely the opposite outcome that had been predicted by the final wave of exit polls. Bush had won thirty-one states, compared to just nineteen for Kerry, which made the national map appear overwhelmingly red. The effect was even more dramatic on the county-by-county map, which made the entire nation look like a vast sea of red, broken only occasionally by splotches of blue along the coasts and in urban centers. Furthermore, Bush had increased his Electoral College victory from 271 votes against Gore to 286 against Kerry—just as Card had announced at the Reagan building. Although Bush had grown increasingly confident of victory over the previous twelve hours, Kerry's concession made it official.

"You were an admirable, worthy opponent," he told the Democrat. "You waged one tough campaign."

Kerry was equally gracious and the two men agreed to try to unite the nation now that the election was over.

"I hope you are proud of the effort you put in," Bush said. "You should be."

The phone call lasted less than five minutes and then Bush hung up and turned to his aides.

"We won, team," he marveled.

One by one, the president hugged his closest advisers—Rove, Bartlett, Hughes, and McClellan. He continued hugging other aides who walked into the Oval Office, including Card, Estes, Joe Hagin, and Blake Gottesman.

Bush then headed down the hall to Dick Cheney's West Wing office, but the vice president was just emerging from the elevator after a meeting in the underground Situation Room.

"Congratulations," Bush said to Cheney before adding mischievously, "I know, Dick, you're not a guy for hugs."

By this time, First Lady Laura Bush had called the Oval Office from the residence. So the president went up to tell her the good news and treat himself to a workout.

Unfortunately, his father had already departed for Houston.

"So I never got to see him face to face to watch his, I guess, pride in his tired eyes as his son got a second term," Bush lamented.

However, the two spoke by phone later in the day.

"He was very proud, very proud, and pleased, and relieved, relieved," the president told me. "I told him to get a nap."

When I caught up with Bush in the Oval Office, I asked him, quite simply, how he won.

"The presidential election is an election on leadership," he told me. "I'll let the experts decide how I won. I can just tell you it was important to be consistent in message, not waver in principle, make it clear to the American people that I was willing to make the tough decisions and stand by them."

It didn't take long for news of Kerry's phone call to reach the press. Armed with this information, CBS absurdly "declared" Bush the winner of Ohio at 11:14 a.m. Thirteen minutes later, FOX declared Bush the winner of Nevada. The disgrace of the television networks was now complete. After refusing to acknowledge the mathematical impossibility of Kerry's quest and ignoring the declaration of victory by the president's own chief of staff, the networks called the election for Bush only after the Democratic candidate gave them permission. So much for journalistic independence.

At 1 p.m., or just twenty-four hours after the exit polls predicted a Democratic landslide, Kerry publicly conceded the election in a speech to supporters at Faneuil Hall in Boston. The first order of business was dissuading the militants in his party from waging the sort of scorched-earth post-election political warfare that Al Gore had unleashed after the 2000 election.

"The outcome should be decided by voters, not a protracted legal process," he counseled. "I would not give up this fight if there was a chance that we would prevail. But it is now clear that even when all the provisional ballots are counted, which they will be, there won't be enough outstanding votes for us to be able to win Ohio. And therefore, we cannot win this election."

Indeed, Kerry ended up losing Ohio by nearly 120,000 votes. Having talked his supporters down from the ledge, he now apologized to them for losing the election.

"I'm sorry that we got here a little bit late and little bit short," he said. "And I wish—you don't know how much—that I could have brought this race home for you."

He added, "I did my best to express my vision and my hopes for America. We worked hard and we fought hard, and I wish that things had turned out a little differently."

Finally, Kerry called on fellow Democrats to "begin the healing."

"I pledge to do my part to try to bridge the partisan divide," he said. "I know this is a difficult time for my supporters, but I ask them, all of you, to join me in doing that. Now, more than ever, with our soldiers in harm's way, we must stand together and succeed in Iraq and win the War on Terror."

Bush let these words sink into the national consciousness for an hour before heading over to the Reagan building, where he was introduced to supporters by Cheney.

"This has been a consequential presidency," the vice president said, "which has revitalized our economy and reasserted a confident American role in the world. Yet in the election of 2004, we did more than campaign on a record. President Bush ran forthrightly on a clear agenda for this nation's future, and the nation responded by giving him a mandate. Now we move forward to serve and to guard the country we love.

"It has been my special privilege to serve as vice president alongside this exceptional American. He's a man of deep conviction and personal kindness. His leadership is wise, and firm, and fearless. Those are qualities that Americans like in a president—and those are the qualities we will need for the next four years. If ever a man met his moment as leader of this country, that man is George W. Bush."

Bush took the stage amid thunderous cheers. He thanked his supporters, praised his opponent, and bestowed a new nickname on Karl Rove that was much more dignified than "Turd Blossom." From now on, decreed the president, Rove would be known simply as "The Architect," the man who had drawn up the plans for a winning campaign. Rove had been helped by some unexpected allies, including the Swift Boat Veterans for Truth and, inadvertently, CBS News. He was also aided by the armies of conservatives who showed up at the polls to outlaw gay marriage in all eleven states where the issue was on the ballot. Bush ended up winning nine of those states, including the all-important state of Ohio. Naturally, the mainstream media professed shock that "moral issues" like gay marriage and abortion had played such a major role in the election. MSNBC's Chris Matthews actually suggested, without a trace of irony, that news organizations hire special correspondents to cover the red states as if they were foreign countries.

"America has spoken," Bush told his supporters when the cheers finally subsided at the Reagan building. "I'm humbled by the trust and the confidence of my fellow citizens. With that trust comes a duty to serve all Americans, and I will do my best to fulfill that duty every day as your president."

It wasn't long before Bush, a born-again Christian, was talking about prayer.

"There's an old saying: 'Do not pray for tasks equal to your powers; pray for powers equal to your tasks,'" he mused. "In four historic years, America has been given great tasks, and faced them with strength and courage. Our people have restored the vigor of this economy, and shown resolve and patience in a new kind of war. Our military has brought justice to the enemy, and honor to America. Our nation has defended itself, and served the freedom of all mankind.

"I'm proud to lead such an amazing country," concluded the weary but gratified president. "And I'm proud to lead it forward."

CHAPTER TWELVE

GEORGE W. BUSH HIGH SCHOOL

resident Bush waited until his Secret Service agent, Nick Trotta, opened the door of the limousine before stepping out with First Lady Laura Bush. They were in front of an old train station that had been converted into a fancy banquet hall in Santiago, Chile, site of the closing ceremonies for an international economic summit. The First Couple stepped through a wide doorway lined on both sides with beefy Chilean security agents. As soon as the Bushes entered the building, the Chileans closed ranks, blocking Trotta from trailing the president. It was their way of retaliating against the Secret Service, which had irritated them all week by insisting on controlling the president's space, even on Chile's sovereign soil. The payback went unnoticed by Bush, who disappeared inside the hall as the Chilean and American security forces scuffled in the doorway. One Secret Service agent was roughly shoved against a wall. A Chilean was unceremoniously placed in a half nelson. Tempers flared as muscle-bound men in dark suits with coiled wires coming out of their ears wrestled with each other in an extraordinarily tense fracas.

"You're not stopping me! You're not stopping me! I'm with the president!" bellowed one of the American agents.

Oblivious to the melee, Bush and his wife walked across a red carpet for staged photos with Chilean president Ricardo Lagos and his wife, Luisa Durán.

"You want us to pose here?" Bush queried with a smile, turning to face a sea of cameras.

At length, however, the president realized that he was no longer being shadowed by his Secret Service agent, which was roughly equivalent to anyone else realizing they had gone out in public without their pants. The discovery came while he and Laura were being led along another stretch of red carpet by Lagos. Bush noticed the hubbub in the doorway and, without a word to his wife or hosts, peeled off on his own and made a beeline for the fight. He waded into the scrum of men—most of whom had their backs to Bush—and tried to reach over their hulking masses. He was pointing at Trotta in a gesture that signified he should be allowed to pass. But no one seemed to realize the president of the United States had now joined the scrap, so they kept pushing and shoving and shouting and head-locking each other. Bush plunged deeper into the fracas, wedging his way between enormous bodies until he could extend his right arm toward Trotta's suit coat. Grabbing the fabric in his hand, the president began pulling his disheveled agent through the throng. He finally popped him out like a cork from a particularly unyielding bottle. Trotta adjusted his suit coat and fell in behind the president, who straightened a sleeve and strode back toward the dignitaries. Along the way, Bush smiled and arched his eyebrows at the astonished press, as if to say, "Can you believe this nonsense?"

The entire episode lasted just twenty seconds, and yet it spoke volumes about George W. Bush.

"All of us journalists agree that President Bush looked like a cowboy," whined reporter Marcelo Romero of Santiago's *La Cuarta* newspaper. "It was total breach of protocol. I've seen a lot of John Wayne movies, and President Bush was definitely acting like a cowboy."

And yet American reporters on the trip were bemused by the altercation. They watched it over and over again in the press center in Santiago, cheering whenever a cameraman brought in fresh videotape that showed the action from another angle.

"The president is someone who tends to delegate," deadpanned White House press secretary Scott McClellan. "But every now and then, he's a hands-on kind of guy."

The altercation, which occurred on November 20, neatly summed up the difference between Bush and Kerry. When Kerry collided with his own Secret Service agent while snowboarding, he fumed, "The son of a bitch knocked me over." But when Bush discovered Trotta was in trouble, he cast aside diplomatic protocols and instinctively rescued the man who had sworn to take a bullet for him.

Truth be told, the president had been feeling unusually expansive ever since vanquishing Kerry in the election. In fact, the day after Kerry conceded, Bush held a press conference that amounted to a victory lap. "Something refreshing about coming off an election," he exulted at a press conference. "You go out and you make your case, and you tell the people, 'This is what I intend to do.' And after hundreds of speeches and three debates and interviews and the whole process, where you keep basically saying the same thing over and over again, that when you win, there is a feeling that the people have spoken and embraced your point of view."

A reporter asked, "Do you feel more free, sir?"

"Do I feel free? Let me put it to you this way: I earned capital in the campaign, political capital, and now I intend to spend it. It is my style," the president enthused. "I'm going to spend it for what I told the people I'd spend it on, which is—you've heard the agenda: Social Security and tax reform, moving this economy forward, education, fighting and winning the War on Terror."

Although the War on Terror, especially the ongoing struggle in Iraq, had been the top issue of the presidential campaign, Bush now sounded like he was relegating it to last on his list of second-term priorities. Having vanquished Kerry by more than three million votes, he figured he had essentially won the Iraq debate and could move on to other initiatives.

"The Iraq issue is one that people disagreed with, and there's no need to rehash my case," he concluded. "I've got the will of the people at my back."

Besides, he was eager to conquer other worlds in his second term.

"We'll start on Social Security now," he said. "Reforming Social Security will be a priority of my administration."

But Democrats, still smarting from their electoral defeat, had no intention of handing Bush a legislative victory on a major issue like Social Security. In fact, they argued that he needed to be more "conciliatory" after such a divisive election. After all, clucked the mainstream media, Kerry would be president if just sixty thousand Ohioans had switched their votes. Democrats warned that Bush needed to "reach across the partisan divide" and rein in his aggressive foreign policy, especially since his preemptive invasion of Iraq had very nearly cost him the White House.

And so by the time Bush showed up at the Capitol to take the oath of office from frail-looking Supreme Court chief justice William Rehnquist, the Left expected to hear a "kinder, gentler" president who had been chastened by the bruising campaign. When Bush stepped to the microphone to deliver his second inaugural address, journalists and Democrats settled back for a speech that would no doubt be marked by compromise and cooperation.

Instead, they got George W. Bush on steroids.

For starters, the president made clear that his predecessors—both Bill Clinton and his own father, who were in attendance—had been asleep at the switch while the threat of global terrorism steadily gathered in the wake of the Cold War.

"After the shipwreck of Communism came years of relative quiet, years of repose, years of sabbatical—and then there came a day of fire," Bush said on the steps of the snow-covered Capitol. "Freedom came under attack."

As for who did the attacking, Bush was not about to give some mushy, politically correct explanation about terrorists being misunderstood freedom fighters. Instead, he denounced them as pure evil. His sweeping, apocalyptic rhetoric sounded like something out of Tolkien's epic *The Lord of the Rings*, with civilization itself being threatened by the dark lord Sauron of Mordor.

"As long as whole regions of the world simmer in resentment and tyranny—prone to ideologies that feed hatred and excuse murder—violence will gather, and multiply in destructive power, and cross the most defended borders, and raise a mortal threat. There is only one force of history that can break the reign of hatred and resentment, and expose the pretensions of tyrants, and reward the hopes of the decent and tolerant. And that is the force of human freedom."

Instead of apologizing for Iraq, Bush hailed its liberation—along with the liberation of Afghanistan—as a catalyst for something even greater: the democratization of the entire Middle East.

"Because we have acted in the great liberating tradition of this nation, tens of millions have achieved their freedom. And as hope kindles hope, millions more will find it. By our efforts, we have lit a fire as well—a fire in the minds of men. It warms those who feel its power, it burns those who fight its progress, and one day this untamed fire of freedom will reach the darkest corners of our world."

In addition to the altruistic merits of such a lofty goal, Bush cited a much more selfish reason to spread freedom—the protection of the United States. He came right out and said that if he stopped aggressively promoting democratization, America's very existence would be threatened.

"We are led, by events and common sense, to one conclusion: the survival of liberty in our land increasingly depends on the success of liberty in other lands. The best hope for peace in our world is the expansion of freedom in all the world," he said. "So it is the policy of the United States to seek and support the growth of democratic movements and institutions in every nation and culture, with the ultimate goal of ending tyranny in our world."

So much for Bush trimming his second-term sails. By calling for nothing less than "ending tyranny in our world," the president had shown an audacity that even his supporters had not expected. And by unapologetically reaffirming the moral clarity that had marked his presidency since September 11, Bush drove his detractors straight up the wall.

"We will persistently clarify the choice before every ruler and every nation: the moral choice between oppression, which is always wrong, and freedom, which is eternally right. America will not pretend that jailed dissidents pre-fer their chains, or that women welcome humiliation and servitude, or that any human being aspires to live at the mercy of bullies."

At this point, Bush could not resist gently tweaking his critics.

"Some, I know, have questioned the global appeal of liberty, though this time in history—four decades defined by the swiftest advance of freedom ever seen—is an odd time for doubt," he noted wryly. "Americans, of all peo-ple, should never be surprised by the power of our ideals."

By now it was clear this was the most idealistic inaugural address in decades. But Bush was just getting warmed up.

"A few Americans have accepted the hardest duties in this cause—in the quiet work of intelligence and diplomacy, the idealistic work of helping raise up free governments, the dangerous and necessary work of fighting our ene-mies," he said. "All Americans have witnessed this idealism, and some for the first time.

"I ask our youngest citizens to believe the evidence of your eyes. You have seen duty and allegiance in the determined faces of our soldiers. You have seen that life is fragile, and evil is real, and courage triumphs. Make the choice to serve in a cause larger than your wants, larger than yourself—and in your days you will add not just to the wealth of our country, but to its character."

Instead of being cowed by the moral relativists who had supported John Kerry, the president was proclaiming without embarrassment that "evil is real." What's more, he was appealing directly to the vaunted "youth vote" that Kerry had counted on to carry him into the White House. Bush was upping the rhetorical ante on an inaugural address delivered forty-four years earlier by President Kennedy, who had implored the nation's young people to "ask not what your country can do for you. Ask what you can do for your coun-try." Kerry, who had idolized Kennedy, now sat glumly in the reviewing stands, a forlorn expression on his long face.

The mainstream media was equally depressed by this soaring rhetoric from Bush, who in 2000 had called for a more "humble" foreign policy. How could the president have grown so cocky, especially with so many problems dogging his administration? People were dying in Iraq. Asia was reeling from a devastating tsunami. In fact, the Left had accused Bush of being slow to respond and Americans of being "stingy" in the relief effort. Closer to home, half the president's cabinet had resigned after the election, leaving the White House scrambling for replacements. And yet Bush had the audacity to do something the press almost never did—step back and focus on the big picture.

"From the perspective of a single day, including this day of dedication, the issues and questions before our country are many," he explained. "From the viewpoint of centuries, the questions that come to us are narrowed and few. Did our generation advance the cause of freedom? And did our character bring credit to that cause?"

Bush made clear he was determined to answer such questions in the affirmative. Along the way, he articulated an unflinching optimism not seen since Ronald Reagan.

"We go forward with complete confidence in the eventual triumph of freedom," he concluded. "History has an ebb and flow of justice, but history also has a visible direction, set by liberty and the Author of liberty.

"When the Declaration of Independence was first read in public and the Liberty Bell was sounded in celebration, a witness said, 'It rang as if it meant something.' In our time it means something still.

"America, in this young century, proclaims liberty throughout all the world, and to all the inhabitants thereof. Renewed in our strength—tested, but not weary—we are ready for the greatest achievements in the history of freedom."

The mainstream media, while dazzled by the sheer eloquence of the speech, nonetheless found plenty to dislike about it. *Roll Call* executive editor Mort Kondracke called Bush's second inaugural address "one of the most exhilarating ever delivered—but also one of the most disconcerting." He added, "The address was soaringly eloquent, audaciously idealistic and deeply reverent. Yet its content was so breathtakingly ambitious as to verge on hubris." The headline over Kondracke's column called the speech "scary."

Over at ABC News, self-described liberal Democrat George Stephanopoulos sniped that the president had delivered a speech filled with "idealism, not realism." *New York Times* reporter Todd Purdum, husband of former Clinton White House press secretary Dee Dee Myers, complained that Bush saw the world in "black and white." He added archly, "There remains a wide gulf between his eloquent aspirations and the realities on the ground."

NBC's Norah O'Donnell told radio talk-show host Don Imus, a Democrat who voted for Kerry, that she felt conflicted by the speech.

"It was beautifully soaring rhetoric and lyrical, but there was no specificity," she opined. "Kind of made you long for, perhaps, sort of some blunt rhetoric from a McCain-type."

Former White House speechwriter Peggy Noonan, who wrote the elder President Bush's 1989 inaugural address, evidently did not like her old boss's tenure described as "years of repose, years of sabbatical." She belittled George W. Bush's call for ending global tyranny as "somewhere between dreamy and disturbing. Tyranny is a very bad thing and quite wicked, but one doesn't expect we're going to eradicate it any time soon." She added condescendingly, "This is not heaven, it's earth."

But the ultimate rebuttal to Bush's inaugural came from Iraq's top terrorist, Abu Musab al-Zarqawi, the thug who had sawed off Nicholas Berg's head in May to avenge the humiliation of Iraqi prisoners at Abu Ghraib. Three days after the president pledged to spread democracy throughout the Middle East, al-Zarqawi vowed to stop it cold.

"We have declared a bitter war against the principle of democracy and all those who seek to enact it," al-Zarqawi railed in an audiotape broadcast on the Internet.

The rant was aimed at dissuading Iraqis from voting in that nation's first free elections in more than half a century. Scheduled for January 30, the parliamentary elections would be the first real test of the grand strategy Bush had laid out in his inaugural.

"Candidates in elections are seeking to become demi-gods, while those who vote for them are infidels," al-Zarqawi seethed. "And with God as my witness, I have informed them of our intentions."

That was a quaint euphemism for overtly threatening to murder voters and their entire families in the most gruesome fashion imaginable. Al-Zarqawi and his fellow terrorists actually put the threat in writing and disseminated it in the form of leaflets that were strewn through the streets of Iraq in the run-up to the voting.

"This is a final warning to all of those who plan to participate in the election," the leaflets read. "We vow to wash the streets of Baghdad with the voters' blood." The killers added, "To those of you who think you can vote and then run away, we will shadow you and catch you. And we will cut off your heads and the heads of your children."

Bush was asked about these threats at a press conference on January 26, just hours after a Marine helicopter crashed in an Iraqi sandstorm, killing all thirty-one aboard. With another half dozen troops killed elsewhere in combat, it was the single deadliest day for U.S. forces in the twenty-two months since they liberated Iraq.

"Mr. President, the insurgents in Iraq are threatening to kill anyone who comes out to vote on Sunday," said a reporter in the James S. Brady briefing room. "Do you think they'll succeed in killing or scaring away enough people so that the elections will be rendered seriously flawed or not credible?"

"We anticipate a lot of Iraqis will vote," Bush replied. "Surveys show that the vast majority of people do want to participate in democracy. And some are feeling intimidated. I urge all people to vote. I urge people to defy these terrorists."

The next reporter pressed Bush to define a "credible" level of voter turnout, but the president was not about to fall into the expectations trap. Journalists and Democrats were already making pessimistic predictions that fewer than half of Iraq's fourteen million eligible voters would be brave enough to show up at the polls. Bush was not about to make an overly optimistic prediction that would surely be thrown back in his face the moment it was proven wrong.

"I am impressed by the bravery of the Iraqi citizens," he said. "I anticipate a grand moment in Iraqi history. If we'd been having this discussion a couple of years ago and I'd have stood up in front of you and said the Iraqi people would be voting, you would look at me like some of you still look at me—with a kind of blank expression."

A third reporter raised a criticism that was all too familiar to Bush.

"Mr. President, Senator Ted Kennedy recently repeated his characterization of Iraq as a 'quagmire' and has called it your Vietnam," the journalist said. "What kind of an effect do you think these statements have on the morale of our troops and on the confidence of the Iraqi people that what you're trying to do over there is going to succeed?"

"I think the Iraqi people are wondering whether or not this nation has the will necessary to stand with them as a democracy evolves," Bush lamented. "The enemy would like nothing more than the United States to precipitously pull out and withdraw before the Iraqis are prepared to defend themselves. Their objective is to stop the advance of democracy. Freedom scares them.

"Zarqawi said something interesting the other day," Bush mused. "He was talking about democracy and how terrible democracy is. We believe that people ought to be allowed to express themselves, and we believe that people ought to decide the fates of their governments."

In the end, the citizens of Iraq sided with Bush over al-Zarqawi. Some 8.5 million Iraqis braved the threat of violence by hiking to their local polling places, casting ballots, and then dipping the index fingers of their right hands into purple ink to signify that they had voted. An astonishing 60 percent of eligible voters turned out, exceeding even the most optimistic expectations in both Iraq and America. It was a major milestone in Iraq's journey from dictatorship to democracy.

"I would have crawled here if I had to," a one-legged Iraqi told the *Times* of London at a Baghdad polling station. "I don't want terrorists to kill other Iraqis like they tried to kill me."

The man, named Samir Hassan, added, "Today I am voting for peace. It is the only way—we must vote against them."

A woman named Fathiya Mohammed was equally defiant.

"Am I scared? Of course I'm not scared. This is my country," she told the paper at a polling station in the small town of Askan.

"This is democracy," she added. "This is the first day I feel freedom."

That's because past elections in Iraq had been a cruel joke, with fully 100 percent of the voters choosing the only name on the ballot—Saddam Hussein. Now voters luxuriated in a list of 111 political parties that fielded candidates for provincial parliaments. Voters also chose a transitional national assembly and empowered it to write the nation's constitution. The plan was for Iraqis to return to the polls in October to ratify the constitution and again in December to choose a permanent national assembly, thereby officially ending the temporary government established by U.S. envoy Paul Bremer after Iraq's liberation.

When the polls finally closed, President Bush stepped into the Cross Hall of the White House to congratulate the Iraqis.

"Today the people of Iraq have spoken to the world, and the world is hearing the voice of freedom from the center of the Middle East," he said. "In great numbers, and under great risk, Iraqis have shown their commitment to democracy.

"By participating in free elections, the Iraqi people have firmly rejected the anti-democratic ideology of the terrorists. They have refused to be intimidated by thugs and assassins. And they have demonstrated the kind of courage that is always the foundation of self-government."

Even the Bush-hating editorial page of the *New York Times* had to admit it was "a remarkably successful election day," adding, "We rejoice in a heartening advance by the Iraqi people."

Other Bush critics were less effusive. Former president Jimmy Carter refused to comment on the success of the election because he had wrongly predicted back in September that it would fail. "I personally do not believe they're going to be ready for the election in January," he told Katie Couric on NBC's *Today Show*. "There's no security there." Yet Iraqi and American troops provided an abundance of security at the polling places, keeping violence to a minimum. After ten days of post-election taunts from the *Washington Times* and the *Wall Street Journal*, Carter finally broke his silence and grudgingly acknowledged that the election "was a surprisingly good step forward." It was a remarkable admission from a man who, like Ted Kennedy and so many other Democrats, branded Iraq "as much of a quagmire as was Vietnam."

Three days after the Iraqi elections, Bush traveled to the other end of Pennsylvania Avenue to deliver his State of the Union address. Near the end of the speech, he introduced an Iraqi woman who had been invited to sit with First Lady Laura Bush in the House chamber's balcony box. Bush proceeded to quote the woman, Safia Taleb al-Suhail, a leading democracy advocate.

"We were occupied for thirty-five years by Saddam Hussein—that was the real occupation," she said. "Thank you to the American people who paid the cost, but most of all, to the soldiers."

Safia smiled modestly at the sound of her own words being read by the president. But Bush was not finished.

"Eleven years ago, Safia's father was assassinated by Saddam's intelligence service," he said. "Three days ago in Baghdad, Safia was finally able to vote for the leaders of her country—and we are honored that she is with us tonight."

The president gestured to Safia and the chamber exploded in cheers and applause. Everyone jumped to their feet to give an extended ovation to this brave Iraqi, who held aloft her ink-stained finger to confirm that she had indeed voted. In a show of solidarity, Republican members of Congress had dyed their own fingers and now raised them triumphantly. Safia, clearly moved, now raised a second finger to signify *V* for victory. The place went wild.

When the applause finally subsided and everyone sat down, Bush emphasized that the Iraqi elections would not have been possible without the heroic sacrifice of U.S. troops, especially those who had died in battle. He singled out Marine Corps sergeant Byron Norwood of Pflugerville, Texas, whose mother sent the president a letter after her son was killed by sniper fire during the U.S. assault on the terrorist stronghold of Fallujah. With the nation watching and listening, Bush quoted from that letter.

"When Byron was home the last time, I said that I wanted to protect him like I had since he was born," the mother had written. "He just hugged me and said, 'You've done your job, Mom. Now it is my turn to protect you.'"

Bush gestured again to the balcony box, only this time he singled out an American woman and her husband, sitting directly behind Safia and the First Lady.

"Ladies and gentlemen, with grateful hearts, we honor freedom's defenders and our military families, represented here this evening by Sergeant Norwood's mom and dad, Janet and Bill Norwood," said the president, who seemed on the verge of tears.

Another standing ovation. Laura Bush turned around and shook Bill's hand. He and his wife, embarrassed by all the attention, rose and looked at each other helplessly. They seemed unsure of what to do with their hands, since they were the only ones not clapping. Janet nervously fingered a metal bead chain lanyard that contained the dog tags her son had been wearing when he was killed. One of the tags had Byron's photo on the front and an eagle image on the back, along with the inscription "Freedom is never free." After an awkward moment, Janet and Bill each slipped an arm behind the other's back and Janet rested her head on Bill's beefy shoulder. The applause rose, accompanied by whistles, whoops, and cheers—the place was really rocking.

As the ovation thundered in her ears, Janet looked down at Safia and smiled. The two women, each of whom had suffered a devastating loss in the struggle for a free Iraq, had met just before the president began his speech. Safia had overheard Washington mayor Anthony Williams introduce himself to Janet, who was pining for her late son.

"I wish that he was alive, so that he could see the success that he and his colleagues helped with the election," Janet told the mayor.

When that conversation ended, Bush had still not entered the chamber. So Safia introduced herself to the woman who had suffered so much for the cause of Iraqi democracy.

"I'm Safia from Iraq. I heard what you said, and I'm here to tell you how grateful we are," she said. "Hopefully, one day I can invite you to Iraq."

"Is your finger purple?" Janet asked.

Safia revealed her ink-stained digit, which Janet grabbed and held on to for dear life. The women formed an instant bond. Norwood dug out some photos of Byron just before his death in Iraq. Safia pored over the images and jotted down her phone number and e-mail address. Janet reciprocated just as the First Lady arrived and the president's speech began. When Bush got to the part about Safia, no one in the chamber applauded more earnestly than Janet.

And now that the president was singling out Janet for recognition, the bereaved mother looked to her new Iraqi friend for moral support. As the cheers intensified, Janet bent down to hug Safia. The women wrapped their arms around each other for what seemed like a long time. They buried their heads in each other's shoulders and patted each other gently on the back. After finally breaking their embrace, they were unable to pull away from each other. Byron's dog tags, which Janet had been clutching in her left hand, had somehow become entangled in Safia's right sleeve. It took a moment to figure out what bound them together. At length, Safia held out her right hand—the one with the ink-stained finger—while Janet worked to free the dog tags from her sleeve. The moment stretched out as thirty-eight million Americans sat glued to their television sets. No one was paying the slightest attention to Bush, who folded his hands on the lectern and gazed over at the entangled women like everyone else. Laura kept the applause going as she beamed at her flummoxed guests, who smiled sheepishly. By the time they finally separated and sat down, they had received an ovation that lasted nearly a minute and a half—the longest of the evening. And they had inadvertently created an electrifying moment that would be remembered long after the president's lofty words were forgotten.

Incredibly, some members of the mainstream media suggested this spontaneous moment had actually been staged by the White House for political gain. Chris Matthews of MSNBC's *Hardball* actually floated the theory that "President Bush used this to push his numbers on Social Security reform, just to get his general appeal up a bit, a couple of points." The hug was dismissed as a "bit of theater" by left-wing actress Janeane Garofalo, who hosted a talk show on the liberal radio network Air America. Appearing on MSNBC, Garofalo also said it was "disgusting" for the "ink-fingered Republicans" to show solidarity with Iraqi voters. To mock the lawmakers, she flashed a Nazi salute on national television.

Yet it was hard to ignore the winds of change that were beginning to blow through the Middle East. It was even harder to make the case that Bush had nothing to do with those changes. His aggressive push for democratization, coupled with his stubborn intolerance for tyrants, was beginning to bear fruit.

The most obvious example was Afghanistan, which U.S. forces had liberated after al Qaeda attacked America. The liberation paved the way for Afghanistan to hold its first-ever presidential election in October 2004. More than eight million Afghans turned out to elect Hamid Karzai, a staunch U.S. ally.

One month later, Bush seized another opportunity to help democratize the Middle East when Palestinian leader Yasser Arafat died. All through his first term, Bush had refused to meet with Arafat, calling him an "obstacle to peace." Unlike President Clinton, who met with Arafat more than any other leader during his eight years in the White House, Bush simply would not reward the Palestinian's bad behavior. But now that Arafat was gone, Bush saw a chance to get behind a Palestinian leader who was more serious about reform. On January 9, Palestinians cast ballots in their first presidential election in nine years. The winner was Mahmoud Abbas, who was immediately hailed by Bush as a constructive partner in the peace process.

Amazingly, in the space of less than four months, historic elections had been successfully completed in three Middle Eastern hot spots—Afghanistan, Iraq, and the Palestinian territories. More than seventeen million Middle Easterners, men and women alike, had done something that most of them had never before contemplated—cast ballots for leaders of their choice in fair, democratic elections.

Still, this did not satisfy Condoleezza Rice, who was promoted from national security adviser in the first Bush term to secretary of state in the second, to replace the retiring Colin Powell. On February 8, during a visit to

Paris, Rice hailed "the elections that have taken place in the Palestinian territories, in Iraq and Afghanistan." She then added that there should be "a fourth free election in the Middle East, and that should be Lebanon."

Unfortunately, Syria—a state sponsor of terror and Ba'ath Party dictatorship (like Saddam Hussein's Iraq)—was suffocating Lebanon and preventing free and fair elections. Syrian president Bashar al-Assad kept 14,000 troops, countless intelligence operatives, and a puppet president, Emile Lahoud, in Lebanon.

"Lebanon is a fledgling democracy in that region and they need to be left to their work [without] foreign interference," Rice scolded. "It is time for Syria to demonstrate that it does not want to be isolated, that it does not want to have a bad relationship with the United States."

Rice was taking a harder line against Syria than had her predecessor. Appalled by Syria's bullying of Lebanon and its harboring of terrorists, who were allowed to pass freely into Iraq and Israel, Rice sought ways to ratchet up pressure on Damascus.

In September 2004, the United Nations Security Council had passed a resolution calling for all "foreign forces to withdraw from Lebanon." Though the United Nations could not even bring itself to name Syria as the only foreign force in Lebanon, the response from Damascus was swift and defiant. The day after the UN resolution was passed, Syria strong-armed Lebanon's parliament into extending Lahoud's term as president. In protest, Lebanon's prime minister, Rafik Hariri, resigned. The United States stood with Hariri, demanding that Lebanon's sovereign independence be honored.

President Bush had already halted all flights between the United States and Syria and cut off all American exports to Syria, except for food and medicine, as part of the Syria Accountability Act, which he had signed into law on December 12, 2003. The act called on Damascus to "end its occupation of Lebanon." Now Rice was threatening to impose even greater sanctions.

"Syria has been unhelpful," Rice said. "It is out of step with where the rest of the region is going."

That turned out to be the understatement of the week. On February 14, an enormous explosion destroyed a motorcade as it drove through Beirut. When the smoke cleared, Hariri had been assassinated. Syria denied responsibility, but the next day, a furious Bush ordered the U.S. ambassador to return from Damascus for urgent consultations. The White House issued a statement vowing to help "restore Lebanon's independence, sovereignty, and democracy by freeing it from foreign occupation."

Undaunted, Syria and Iran announced they were forming a "united front" against the United States and other "common threats." But the Bush administration refused to back down from its demand for a pullout from Lebanon.

"There is no doubt that the conditions created by Syria's presence there have created a destabilized situation in Lebanon," Rice said. "Syria is interfering in the affairs of Lebanon."

She added ominously, "The United States does not like the direction of U.S.–Syrian relations, and we will continue to consider what other options are at our disposal."

One such option was for Bush to use his bully pulpit to browbeat the Syrians.

"We expect them to find and turn over former Saddam regime supporters, send them back to Iraq," he said in a press conference on February 17.

The pressure worked. Within a matter of days, Syrian officials arrested Saddam Hussein's half-brother, Sabawi Ibrahim al-Hassan, one of the most wanted leaders of Iraq's bloody insurgency, and turned him over to Iraqi authorities. This blatant capitulation did not go unnoticed by ordinary Lebanese citizens, who smelled fear among their Syrian overlords for the first time in years. Emboldened by this fear and driven by their own anger, Lebanese men and women began to do something that had been previously unthinkable—they protested against Syria's occupation. Day after day, tens of thousands of Lebanese marched through the streets in open defiance of a government that would normally crush such dissent. They carried banners that proclaimed "Enough!" and "We want the truth!"

Their leader was Druze patriarch Walid Jumblatt, a one-time supporter of the Syrian occupation who, like Hariri, had eventually turned against Damascus. As head of the Progressive Socialist Party, Jumblatt often railed against America and Israel. But now he had to give credit where credit was due.

"It's strange for me to say it, but this process of change has started because of the American invasion of Iraq," he told David Ignatius of the *Washington Post* on February 21. "I was cynical about Iraq. But when I saw the Iraqi people voting three weeks ago, eight million of them, it was the start of a new Arab world."

He added, "The Syrian people, the Egyptian people, all say that something is changing. The Berlin Wall has fallen. We can see it."

That same day, Bush gave a speech in Brussels reiterating his demand that Syria "end its occupation of Lebanon."

"Our shared commitment to democratic progress is being tested in Lebanon—a once thriving country that now suffers under the influence of an oppressive neighbor," the president told European leaders. "The Lebanese people have the right to be free."

The demonstrations in Lebanon grew larger by the day. Tens of thousands of Christians, Druze, and Muslims—including both Sunnis and Shi'a—marched shoulder to shoulder in unprecedented solidarity against the Syrian-backed government. Never before had the entire population of a Middle Eastern nation risen up against its oppressors.

On February 28, the Lebanese government, including Hariri's Syrian-backed replacement, caved in to the demands of reformers and resigned. The demonstrators exploded with joy.

"I love America!" an Arab Christian named Sady cried to a reporter from the *Washington Times*. "Tell Bush to come here! Thank him!"

The stunning development whetted the appetites of the protesters for further reform. Their daily demonstrations grew larger still. They pressed for a full withdrawal of Syrian troops and intelligence operatives. Even some intellectuals in Damascus began talking openly about reforming their own country.

"Something profound's going on right now, and what it really is, more than anything else, is a loss of fear," Dennis Ross, who had been the Middle East envoy for President Clinton and the elder President Bush, told me. "Every Arab regime has ruled basically through coercion and intimidation, and suddenly the fear factor is eroding."

Middle East analyst Marc Ginsberg, who was Clinton's ambassador to Morocco, said George W. Bush "deserves credit" for aggressively trying to spread freedom in the region. He said the catalyst for reform had been the Iraq election, which of course would not have been possible without the U.S.-led liberation.

"That vote had enormous emotional ramifications for the people in that region, who were really taken aback by what they saw," Ginsberg told me. "Every Arab newspaper that I'm reading now uses the phrase 'Why there and not here?'"

Bush had always felt confident that his push for democratization in the Middle East would bear fruit, although perhaps not this quickly.

"I was pleased," he told me. "Successful democracies in the Middle East will cause others to want to seek a different way, a different form of government than that which some people live under. It will help slip the yoke sooner."

This rapid slipping of the yoke left many Democrats in America feeling deeply conflicted. After all, they had spent nearly two years arguing that no good would ever come of the Iraq war. Comedian Jon Stewart, who had opposed the war and supported Kerry, now gave grudging credit to Bush for having instigated the surprising developments rippling through the Middle East. He made his opinion known while interviewing a former Clinton foreign policy adviser, Nancy Soderberg, who was promoting her new Bush-bashing book, *The Superpower Myth*. With a foreword by Clinton himself, the tome hit bookstores just in time for events in the Middle East to utterly disprove Soderberg's premise—that the president's push for democratization was doomed to fail.

"What I argue is that the Bush administration fell hostage to the super-power myth, believing that because we're the most powerful nation on earth, we were all-powerful, could bend the world to our will and not have to worry about the rest of the world," Soderberg began on the *Daily Show*, Stewart's wildly popular Comedy Central program. "I think what they're finding in the second term is, it's a little bit harder than that, and reality has an annoying way of intruding."

"I don't care for the way these guys conduct themselves," Stewart said of the Bush administration. "But boy, when you see the Lebanese take to the streets and all that, and you go, 'Oh my God, this is working,' and I begin to wonder."

"As a Democrat, you don't want anything nice to happen to the Republicans, and you don't want them to have progress," Soderberg admitted. "What's happening in Lebanon is great, but it's not necessarily directly related to the fact that we went into Iraq militarily."

But Stewart wasn't buying that argument.

"Do you think that the people of Lebanon would have had, sort of, the courage of their conviction, having not seen—not only the invasion but the election which followed?" he said. "It's almost as though that the Iraqi election has emboldened this crazy—something's going on over there. I'm smelling something."

The comedian theorized that the Bush administration's kindling of democracy in the Middle East had been inadvertent.

"Do they understand what they've unleashed?" he said. "If they had just come out at the very beginning and said, 'Here's my plan: I'm going to invade Iraq. We'll get rid of a bad guy because that will drain the swamp'; if they hadn't done the whole 'nuclear cloud,' you know; if they hadn't scared the pants off of everybody, and just said straight up, honestly, what was going on; I think I'd almost—I'd have no cognitive dissonance, no mixed feelings."

"The truth always helps in these things, I have to say," conceded Soderberg, who went on to acknowledge another hopeful development for Bush officials. "They may well have a chance to do a historic deal with the Palestinians and the Israelis. These guys could really pull off a whole series of Nobel Peace Prizes here. It may well work."

"This could be unbelievable!" Stewart cried in mock dismay, burying his head in his hands. "Oh my God!"

"It's scary for Democrats, I have to say," Soderberg allowed.

"Pretty soon, Republicans are gonna be like, 'Reagan was nothing compared to this guy,'" Stewart lamented of Bush. "Like, my kid's gonna go to a high school named after him, I just know it."

"Well, there's still Iran and North Korea, don't forget," Soderberg said. "There's hope for the rest of us."

"Iran and North Korea, that's true!" said Stewart, crossing his fingers. "That is true."

When the audience laughed, he hastened to add that there was actually a kernel of truth in what Soderberg had said. Perhaps North Korea or Iran, a pair of rogue regimes that were pursuing nuclear weapons, would detonate one of their bombs and somehow embarrass Bush politically. This is what the Democrats had been reduced to in the opening months of the president's muscular second term.

Despite Stewart's obvious sympathies for his guest, his intellectual honesty compelled him to debunk the premise of her exquisitely ill-timed book.

"This is the most difficult thing for me," he said. "I don't care for the tactics. I don't care for this, the weird arrogance, the setting up. But I gotta say, I haven't seen results like this ever in that region."

"There's always hope that this might not work," Soderberg said.

But Stewart was no longer listening to his guest.

"It's almost like we're not going to have to invade Iran and Syria," he said. "They're gonna invade themselves at a certain point."

"I think it's moving in the right direction," conceded Soderberg, now utterly defeated. "I'll have to give them credit for that. We'll see."

Indeed, within a week, the world saw Bashar al-Assad agree to withdraw all Syrian troops and security forces from Lebanon, under pressure from Bush and Rice. The administration also turned up the heat on other Middle

Eastern tyrannies. Rice canceled a visit to Egypt to protest the imprisonment of a dissident. One day later, Egyptian president Hosni Mubarak announced he would allow rivals to challenge him for the presidency for the first time. He even released the dissident. And while no one expected that Mubarak would allow a serious challenge to his presidency, it was at least modest progress. Rice pushed for reform in Saudi Arabia and the Gulf monarchy took a small step forward by allowing municipal elections, though women were barred from voting. Still, the breezes of freedom were beginning to blow, even in the most hard-line outposts of old-school authoritarianism.

"The chances of democratic progress in the broader Middle East have seemed frozen in place for decades," Bush said on March 8. "Yet at last, clearly and suddenly, the thaw has begun.

"The people of Afghanistan have embraced free government, after suffering under one of the most backward tyrannies on earth. The voters in Iraq defied threats of murder, and have set their country on a path to full democracy. The people of the Palestinian territories cast their ballots against violence and corruption of the past. And any who doubt the appeal of freedom in the Middle East can look to Lebanon, where the Lebanese people are demanding a free and independent nation."

Having spent years being pilloried for his insistence on toppling Saddam Hussein, Bush now savored the prospect of other dominoes beginning to fall.

"Across the Middle East, a critical mass of events is taking that region in a hopeful new direction," he said. "Pervasive fear is the foundation of every dictatorial regime—the prop that holds up all power not based on consent. And when the regime of fear is broken, and the people find their courage and find their voice, democracy is their goal, and tyrants, themselves, have reason to fear."

At a press conference on March 16, I put President Bush on the spot by asking how much of the credit his administration deserved for the winds of change in the Middle East.

"Mr. President, you faced a lot of skepticism in the run-up to the Iraq war, and a lot of criticism for miscalculating some of the challenges of postwar

Iraq," I began. "Now that the Iraq elections seem to be triggering signs of democratization throughout the broader Middle East, do you feel any sense of vindication?"

"I fully understand that as long as I'm the president I will face criticism—it's like part of the job. Frankly, you wouldn't be doing your job if you didn't occasionally lay out the gentle criticism," he said. "So that doesn't bother me, Bill. And, therefore, since it doesn't bother me and I expect it, I don't then seek vindication."

Bush added that he had recently read a new book on George Washington, *His Excellency* by Joseph J. Ellis, and knew that historian David McCullough had another book on Washington coming out soon, titled *1776*.

"What's interesting is George Washington is now getting a second, or third, or fifth, or tenth look in history," Bush said. "People are constantly evaluating somebody's standing in history, a president's standing in history, based upon events that took place during the presidency, based upon things that happened after the presidency, based upon—like in my case, hopefully, the march of freedom continues way after my presidency. And so I just don't worry about vindication or standing.

"The other thing, it turns out, in this job you've got a lot on your plate on a regular basis," he added. "You don't have much time to sit around and wander, lonely, in the Oval Office, kind of asking different portraits, how do you think my standing will be?"

This prompted knowing laughter from the press, which still remembered the lonely wanderings of Bill and Hillary Clinton. Just two months after taking office, Bill told Dan Rather that he would wander out on a White House balcony in the wee hours of the morning and gaze wistfully at the Jefferson Memorial in the distance, "just thinking about problems and wishing that Thomas Jefferson could come alive and talk to me about them." And who could forget Hillary famously admitting to imaginary conversations with Eleanor Roosevelt? But such self-indulgent musings were anathema to Bush, who was notoriously averse to public introspection. He considered his time in office far too brief for anguished navel-gazing.

"I've got a lot to do," he said. "I like to make decisions, and I make a lot of them."

Bush finally deflected the question of vindication by focusing instead on the brave souls who had cast ballots in Iraq.

"Look, the people who deserve the credit in Iraq are the Iraqi citizens that defied the terrorists," he said. "Imagine what it would be like to try to go vote, thinking that there could be a suicide bomber standing next to you in line, or somebody would lob a shell or a mortar at you. The courage of the Iraqi citizens was just overwhelming."

In the end, while Bush was unwilling to muse over his own legacy, he was more than willing to ponder what the Iraqis had unleashed through the simple act of voting.

"It was a powerful moment in the history of freedom," he beamed. "People in the world got to see what it means for a group of people that have been downtrodden to rise up and say, I want to be free."

CHAPTER THIRTEEN

"A Mixed Legacy"

"I never thought I'd be on this plane again," Bill Clinton told me aboard Air Force One. "They have turkey burgers too, which they didn't have when I was here. If they'd been serving me turkey burgers, I might not have had heart surgery."

The plane was about to land, but Clinton and I were still standing. So I braced my back against the bulkhead and, facing the recent heart surgery patient, placed a hand on his shoulder in case he pitched forward. He kept right on talking. This was like the old days, when he could hold court with reporters on that ultimate presidential perk, Air Force One. Now he was back as a guest of President Bush, flying to Rome for the funeral of Pope John Paul II. Clinton would have made his way to the press cabin earlier, but Bush's aides held him back until after the elder President Bush (George H. W., known as "41," as in the forty-first president of the United States) had chatted with reporters. "Forty-One" had been in no hurry to do so; he had waited until the plane was in Italian airspace. Now Clinton was making the most of his limited time, eventually sitting on the arm of my chair while I remained standing as the wheels of the 747 touched down on the tarmac in Rome.

"So much has been said and written about Pope John Paul," I said. "How would you sum up the significance of his life?"

"I'm not Catholic, but I went to Catholic grade school and I went to Georgetown and I studied with the Jesuits," said the Baptist ex-president. "I'm very interested in the Catholic church and its whole history."

Clinton then proceeded to recite much of that history, along with a great many things about John Paul II. Although he had high praise for the pontiff, the Democrat could not resist leveling a few criticisms. He complained that the pope had "centralized authority in the papacy again and enforced a very conservative theological doctrine." Referring to abortion, Clinton added, "Obviously we had a few disagreements." The former president even critiqued John Paul's administrative accomplishments.

"The number of Catholics increased by 250 million on his watch, but the numbers of priests didn't," Clinton lamented. "He's like all of us—he may have a mixed legacy."

This immediately struck me as newsworthy. While one could certainly argue the intellectual merits of Clinton's critique, his timing was politically indefensible. The pope had not even been buried yet. His body was lying in state at St. Peter's Basilica, which Clinton and the other presidents would be visiting in mere minutes. Mourners were lined up by the thousands to pay their final respects to one of the greatest men of the twentieth century. Millions more were riveted to televised coverage of the wake. And here was Bill Clinton, the impeached former president, best known for having sex with an intern in the Oval Office on Easter Sunday, complaining that Pope John Paul II had a "mixed legacy."

I knew I had a dynamite story for my newspaper, the *Washington Times*. But I also knew the other reporters aboard Air Force One would downplay the "mixed legacy" remark. And so, in an effort to build support for my angle, I e-mailed the quote to Matt Drudge after I got off the plane in Rome. Drudge immediately posted the entire quote, in full context, on his influential website and slapped a banner headline on top: "CLINTON: POPE 'MAY HAVE MIXED LEGACY.'"

Although Drudge accurately marked the post as "exclusive," it was quickly disseminated throughout the blogosphere. On Free Republic alone, hundreds of bloggers expressed their outrage over the former president's staggering insensitivity and narcissism. The outrage only intensified the next morning, when the *Washington Times* published my story.

"VATICAN CITY—President Bush, joined by two of his predecessors, knelt in prayer before the body of Pope John Paul II yesterday after former president Bill Clinton said the pontiff 'may have a mixed legacy.'"

The producers at FOX News Channel read the story and called me in Rome, where I did a telephone interview with the *FOX & Friends* morning show. Then talk radio picked up the Clinton quote and had a field day. By afternoon, the flap was all over the cable news channels, including CNN.

In the old days, when all news was essentially controlled by ABC, CBS, NBC, and the *New York Times*, this story would never have appeared. The liberal press would not have cast one of its icons in such an unflattering light. But now, thanks to the *Washington Times*, the Drudge Report, the blogosphere, talk radio, and FOX News, Clinton's ruminations were brought to the attention of millions of Americans. This "opposition media" had been particularly successful since Bush came into office. FOX News was now crushing CNN, the former ratings leader in cable news, twenty-four hours a day. More Americans checked the Drudge Report each day than the website of the vaunted *Washington Post*. And an obscure blogger, the very symbol of the nascent opposition media, had toppled a mighty anchorman, the ultimate dinosaur of the mainstream media.

Dan Rather had been forced off the air on March 9, a full year before his scheduled retirement, depriving him of the chance to say he had spent a quarter of a century in the anchor chair of the CBS *Evening News*. His colleague Mary Mapes was, in her own words, "spectacularly, publicly, embarrassingly fired" after fifteen years as a star producer. Senior vice president Betsy West, along with top producers Josh Howard and Mary Murphy, were forced to resign.

The internal investigation that CBS commissioned after the forged National Guard memos story resulted in a scathing 224-page report written by former attorney general Dick Thornburgh and former AP president Louis Boccardi. The report excoriated the network for its "myopic zeal" in trying to nail Bush and its "rigid and blind defense" of an obviously indefensible broadcast. The only one who managed to hang on to his job was CBS News president Andrew Heyward, although his days appeared numbered. Heyward's boss, CBS chairman and CEO Leslie Moonves, was making ominous rumblings about "lapses every step of the way." There was even talk of canceling the Wednesday edition of *60 Minutes*, the program that had aired not only Memogate, but the Abu Ghraib photos. The show's ratings were in the tank.

"I find it interesting that the old way of gathering the news is slowly but surely losing market share," Bush told me. "It's interesting to watch these media conglomerates try to deal with the realities of a new kind of world.

"It's the beginning of the twenty-first century; it also happens to be the beginning of—or near the beginning—of a revolution in newsgathering and dissemination," added the president who took office at the turn of the century. "Not in newsmaking—that tends to be pretty consistent."

Having been treated unfairly by the mainstream media for years, Bush was heartened by the rise of the opposition press.

"I think what's healthy is that there's no monopoly on the news," he told me. "There's competition. There's competition for the attention of, you know, 290 million people, or whatever it is.

"And the amazing thing about this world we live in is that there's a kind of free-flowing, kind of bulletin board of ideas and thoughts out there in the ether space, sometimes landing on somebody's desk and sometimes not, but always available. It's a very interesting period.

"I happen to think it's healthy for the country. I'm a person who believes that the more Internet traffic there is in a tyrannical society, the more likely it is somebody is going to be free. I like the idea—I'm an advocate."

So was Karl Rove, who viewed the Memogate fiasco as emblematic of "the failure of the mainstream media."

"The whole incident in the fall of 2004 showed really the power of the blogosphere," Rove told me. "Because in essence you now have an army of self-appointed experts looking over the shoulder of the mainstream media and bringing to bear enormously sophisticated skills, as well as very analytical and determined voices who now have an outlet. The world now has a cheap and inexpensive way of bringing their arguments to the attention of other people."

Although Rove viewed the blogosphere as truly revolutionary, he also saw its darker side.

"There is so much ugliness and viciousness and fundamental untruths that the blogosphere transmits," he told me. "There's a lot of junk in there. And so it does have a good effect in that it puts more eyes on the document, if you will. It puts forth more voices that are trying to arrive at what, quote, the truth is," he added. "But it also is a vehicle for ugly rumors, for scurrilous personal attacks, an avenue for the creation of urban legends which are deeply corrosive of the political system and of people's faith in it."

By the time Air Force One departed Rome for Washington after the pope's funeral, the opposition press had forcibly injected the "mixed legacy" story into the mainstream media's bloodstream. My fellow reporters on the plane, who had initially downplayed or even ignored Clinton's remark, were now all over it. In fact, it was the first question posed to Bush when he invited the press into the plane's conference room shortly after takeoff.

"Your predecessor suggested that the pope would leave a mixed legacy," said Tom Raum of the Associated Press. "Do you also think it will be a mixed legacy?"

Having expected such a question, the president quickly distanced himself from Clinton's assessment.

"I think Pope John Paul II will have a clear legacy of peace, compassion," he said. "A strong legacy of setting a clear moral tone."

Raum and the other reporters scribbled furiously, knowing they had a fresh angle to the story: Bush and Clinton disagreeing over whether the pope had a "mixed legacy."

"This will be one of the highlights of my presidency, to have been at this great ceremony," Bush continued. "A moment in my life that will strengthen my faith and my belief."

The Methodist president, who described himself as a born-again Christian, was deeply impressed by the sheer grandeur and pageantry of the high Catholic Mass and funeral. Sure, he had been to Mass before, but never a three-hour requiem extravaganza—almost entirely in Latin—in an emotionally charged St. Peter's Square.

"I knew the ceremony today would be majestic, but I didn't realize how moved I would be by the service itself, by the beautiful music. I was struck by the fact that the sound was so clear in this huge facility. It was as if we were inside the cathedral listening—and the voices were so pure," he marveled. "And then I think the thing that struck all our delegation most intensely was the final scene of the plain-looking casket—one of three, by the way: lead, wood, and wood—being carried and held up for the seal to be seen, and then the sun pouring out."

Indeed, the sun had broken through the clouds, as if on cue, just as the casket was raised aloft. Bush considered it nothing less than a sign from God.

"The Lord works in mysterious ways, and during all our life's journeys we're enabled to see the Lord at work if our eyes are open and our hearts are open," he observed. "You can look at the coffin being held—with the sun shining on it—any way you want. I happen to feel it was a special moment that was part of a special ceremony for a special person. And it helped strengthen my faith."

Similarly, Bush said his faith had been strengthened by years of witnessing the energetic pope stubbornly refuse to be slowed down by failing health. The president related this to his own optimism in the face of constant political attack.

"It is a clear example of Christ's influence in a person's life that he maintained such a kind of hopeful, optimistic, clear point of view amidst struggles—in his case, physical struggles," he said. "A lot of Christians gain great strength and confidence from seeing His Holiness in the last stages of life."

This optimism wasn't the only trait Bush admired in the pope. The president also appreciated John Paul's athleticism as a young man and his unyielding advocacy for human freedom.

"I mean, here's a person who has shown that a single individual can make a big difference in history and that, in my judgment, he received his great power and strength from the Almighty," he said. "Millions of Catholics and millions of others admired his strength and his purpose and his moral clarity."

Bush himself was often accused of seeing his presidency in messianic terms. Although he always brushed off suggestions that he had been placed in the White House by divine intervention in order to wage a righteous war on terror, the president was not afraid to talk openly about the power of prayer. Moreover, his second inaugural address made clear that his presidency stood for moral clarity, which was one of the reasons he admired the pontiff so much.

"I would define Pope John Paul II as a clear thinker who was like a rock," he said. "And tides of moral relativism kind of washed around him, but he stood strong as a rock."

Perhaps the president should have ended his discussion of morality and faith right there. But the press, always on the lookout for opportunities to caricature Bush as a Bible-thumping zealot, had one more question about religion. A reporter asked "if there was ever a moment where you ever had any doubts in your own faith."

"I think a walk in faith constantly confronts doubt, as faith becomes more mature," he began. "And you constantly confront, you know, questions."

Uh-oh. Bush didn't like the way that came out.

"My faith is strong," he corrected. "Today's ceremony, I bet you for millions of people, was a reaffirmation for many—and a way to make sure doubts don't seep into your soul."

All this talk about doubts seeping into souls was not exactly where Bush wanted to end. It was too easy to imagine the press running with the headline "Returning from Pope's Funeral, Bush Doubts His Faith." So he plowed ahead.

"Whether the moment be majestical or whether the moment be a part of just an average—your average moment in life—you can find ways to strengthen your faith. And it's necessary to do so, in my judgment," he said. "There is a—it's called a 'walk,' it's not called a 'moment' or a 'respite,' it's a walk. It's a constant maturing of an understanding of a . . ." Bush went on for some time, anxious to demonstrate that his faith in God was unwavering. He was painfully aware that religion was a minefield in Washington politics. Just weeks earlier, he had signed a bill aimed at saving the life of Terri Schiavo, a brain-damaged Florida woman whose feeding tube had been disconnected in a bitter family dispute. The bill, passed in an emergency session of Congress, allowed Schiavo's parents to sue in federal court for the feeding tube to be reinserted over the objections of Schiavo's husband.

"In cases like this one, where there are serious questions and substantial doubts, our society, our laws, and our courts should have a presumption in favor of life. This presumption is especially critical for those like Terri Schiavo, who live at the mercy of others," Bush said at the time. "I will continue to stand on the side of those defending life for all Americans, including those with disabilities."

Although Democrats had done nothing to stop passage of the bill, they went on to demonize Republicans as needlessly meddling in a family's anguished dilemma. The strategy paid political dividends. Soon polls were showing strong disapproval of Republicans as the heartbreaking drama played out across the cable news channels. When Schiavo finally died on March 31, Democrats vowed to turn the case into a political rallying cry against Republicans in the 2006 congressional elections.

Fortunately for Bush, the handful of reporters on Air Force One had moved on from the Schiavo case. They wanted to know how the president could possibly implement his Social Security reform plan in the face of stubborn Democratic opposition. Ever since the beginning of the year, Bush had been crisscrossing the nation in a fruitless effort to drum up support for his plan. He warned that the Social Security system would go broke if fundamental changes were not implemented. Bush bet an enormous amount of his political capital on reforming Social Security. But it was looking more and more like a losing bet. At least there was a silver lining. Bush figured the Democrats' obstructionism could be used against them in the 2006 elections, just as Democrats believed the Schiavo case could be used against the GOP.

"I happen to believe that not dealing with the problem will create political consequences when the public realizes how serious the problem is," he said of Social Security. "If you don't deal with the problem, or you go home and say, 'I'm not dealing with the problem,' there will be a political consequence."

This went to the very heart of the president's self-image as a strong leader, even if he didn't always end up prevailing.

"I have an obligation to set agenda items," he said. "I feel I got elected for a reason. My nature is such that if I came to Washington and saw a problem and didn't deal with it, I wouldn't feel very good about myself. I want it to be said that George W. Bush got elected and did what he said he was going to do."

Before he dismissed the Fourth Estate, Bush took one last shot at reaffirming his rock-solid religious faith. For some reason, he couldn't shake the feeling that some reporter would figure out a way to portray him as a doubting Thomas.

"When you discuss religion—on doubt—there is no doubt in my mind there is a living God. And no doubt in my mind that the Lord, Christ, was sent by the Almighty. No doubt in my mind about that. When I'm talking about doubts, I'm talking about the doubts that an individual struggles with in his or her life. That's important for you to make sure you get that part of the dialogue correct, if you don't mind."

"Thank you," a reporter said.

"Got it?" said Bush, still not satisfied. "Everybody got it correct? All right."

As long as he was amending his answers, the president figured he might as well take a final crack at distancing himself from Clinton, who was flying home on another plane.

"Let me make sure I go back to the first answer on His Holiness," Bush said. "I think my answer was, is that—what did I say?"

"I asked if you thought it was a 'mixed message,'" said Raum, rifling through his notebook. "And you said, 'I think John Paul II will have a clear legacy of peace.'"

"A clear and excellent legacy, if you don't mind adding the word 'excellent,'" the president said.

"Clear and excellent," murmured Raum, still scribbling.

"Yes," Bush said. "In other words, a strong legacy. I wanted to make sure there was a proper adjective to the legacy I thought he left behind. It was more than just 'clear.'"

"You said 'strong,' too, in that answer," interjected Scott McClellan, the president's press secretary.

"Okay," Bush said.

"Yes, you said, 'strong legacy of setting a clear moral tone,'" Raum confirmed.

"Fine, okay, good," the president concluded with a mischievous smile. "So off we go."

CHAPTER FOURTEEN

"A Magical, Mystical Kingdom of Journalistic Knights"

W hile President Bush was in Rome, Mary Mapes received a phone call from Dan Rather.

"I have some news for you," the ex-anchorman said playfully.

"Now what?"

Rather revealed that he and Mapes had just won a coveted Peabody Award for broadcasting the photos of U.S. troops mistreating prisoners at Abu Ghraib. It was a bittersweet moment for Mapes, who had soared to such glorious journalistic heights on the Abu Ghraib story only to crash and burn so spectacularly on the Memogate story.

"I was happy to get the news, especially from someone I love and respect so much," Mapes told the *New York Times*. "I think there is at least context here, if not vindication. And I am happy for my colleagues at CBS. I have always tried to separate the people who flicked me like a piece of lint off their shoulder when things were tough and the people that I worked with, who I remain very proud of."

Mapes and Rather were not the only journalists to win awards for their coverage of Abu Ghraib, which was now considered a watershed exposé in modern American journalism. Eleven days later, the Society of Professional Journalists announced that Michael Isikoff of *Newsweek* had won an award for his own coverage of the scandal. The magazine could not resist a bit of bragging.

"Isikoff obtained exclusive internal White House, Justice Department, and State Department memos showing how decisions made at the highest levels of the Bush administration led to abuses in the interrogation of terror suspects," *Newsweek* crowed on its website.

Not one to rest on his laurels, Isikoff was already working on his next blockbuster story about American authorities abusing prisoners in the War on Terror. Only this time around, instead of focusing on Abu Ghraib, Isikoff set his sights on the U.S. detention facility at Guantanamo Bay, a U.S. naval base at the southern tip of Cuba. The site housed hundreds of prisoners who had been captured on the battlefields of Afghanistan and other Middle Eastern countries. The Left was forever complaining that these prisoners, who had been caught trying to kill Americans, were being held indefinitely and without proper legal representation. But Isikoff took the debate to an entirely new level with a story he published on May 1.

"Sources tell *Newsweek*," he wrote, "interrogators, in an attempt to rattle suspects, flushed a Koran down a toilet."

Muslims in the Middle East were outraged to learn that U.S. officials had desecrated their holiest book. Their outrage quickly escalated into violence.

"By the end of the week, the rioting had spread from Afghanistan throughout much of the Muslim world, from Gaza to Indonesia," wrote *Newsweek* assistant managing editor Evan Thomas, who described his own magazine as "liberal."

"Mobs shouting 'Protect our Holy Book!' burned down government buildings and ransacked the offices of relief organizations in several Afghan provinces. The violence cost at least fifteen lives, injured scores of people, and sent a shudder through Washington, where officials worried about the stability of moderate regimes in the region."

Reporters immediately began to hyperventilate about the episode turning into another Abu Ghraib scandal. The Pentagon launched an exhaustive investigation, interviewing Guantanamo officials and examining 25,000 pages of documents.

"Despite our review of the situation, we can't find anything to substantiate the allegations that appeared in *Newsweek* magazine," said General Richard Myers, chairman of the Joint Chiefs of Staff. "More than one detainee tore pages out of the Koran and put it in the toilet in protest—to stop up the toilet. But we've not found any wrongdoing on the part of U.S. service members."

On May 13, Pentagon spokesman Larry Di Rita complained to *Newsweek* that the story did not appear to be true. The next day, Isikoff called his original source, who now said he "could no longer be sure" of the story, according to *Newsweek*.

"People are dead because of what this son of a bitch said," Di Rita seethed when the magazine backpedaled. "How could he be credible now?"

Newsweek editor Mark Whitaker explained that Isikoff's "information came from a knowledgeable U.S. government source, and before deciding whether to publish it we approached two separate Defense Department officials for comment. One declined to give us a response; the other challenged another aspect of the story but did not dispute the Koran charge."

It was the same dodge CBS had employed in the Memogate story—the administration didn't aggressively challenge the information, so it must be true.

"We regret that we got any part of our story wrong, and extend our sympathies to victims of the violence and to the U.S. soldiers caught in its midst," Whitaker finally wrote in an online statement on May 15, two weeks after the bogus story was published.

"Obviously we all feel horrible about what flowed from this," Isikoff told the *Washington Post*. "But it's important to remember there was absolutely no lapse in journalistic standards here."

This astonishing assertion perfectly summed up the mainstream media's staggering arrogance. The Koran-in-the-toilet allegation had come from a single source, yet Isikoff falsely claimed multiple "sources" in his original story. It was the same falsehood employed by CBS, which claimed the Memogate documents had come from "unimpeachable sources," when in reality they had come from one source, Bill Burkett, who was eminently impeachable. Like Burkett, *Newsweek*'s lone source changed his tune as soon as the information was exposed as fraudulent. And like CBS, *Newsweek* waited more than ten days to apologize.

"I think it was Mark Twain who said that something that's not true can speed around the world three or four times in a matter of seconds, while truth is still trying to put their boots on," lamented Defense Secretary Donald Rumsfeld the next day. "People lost their lives. People are dead. And that's unfortunate. And people need to be very careful about what they say."

Alas, Whitaker did not heed this advice. Hours after posting his online apology, he began to have second thoughts.

"We're not retracting anything," he defiantly told the *New York Times*. "We don't know for certain what we got wrong."

This infuriated White House press secretary Scott McClellan.

"I find it puzzling that *Newsweek* now acknowledges that the facts were wrong, and they refuse to offer a retraction. There is a certain journalistic standard that should be met, and in this case it was not met. The report was not accurate, and it was based on a single anonymous source who cannot personally substantiate the report, so they cannot verify the accuracy of the report," he told reporters. "I mean, this report has had serious consequences. It has caused damage to the image of the United States abroad. People have lost their lives. It has certainly caused damage to the credibility of the media, as well—and *Newsweek* itself."

Later that afternoon, *Newsweek* capitulated. Whitaker issued a grudging, one-sentence statement.

"Based on what we know now, we are retracting our original story that an internal military investigation had uncovered Koran abuse at Guantanamo Bay," he wrote.

The White House called the retraction a good first step and expressed hope it would not be the last.

"We would encourage *Newsweek* to do all that they can to help repair the damage that has been done, particularly in the region," McClellan said. "*Newsweek* can do that by talking about the way they got this wrong, and pointing out what the policies and practices of the United States military are when it comes to the handling of the holy Koran. The military put in place policies and procedures to make sure that the Koran is handled with the utmost care and respect. And I think it would help to point that out, because some have taken this report—those that are opposed to the United States—some have taken this report and exploited it and used it to incite violence."

This was too much for the other members of the mainstream media in the James S. Brady briefing room. ABC's Terry Moran simply could not bear to watch the Bush White House seize the moral high ground from one of his brethren.

"With respect, who made you the editor of *Newsweek*?" snapped Moran, who admitted that same week to radio host Hugh Hewitt there was "a deep anti-military bias in the media." "Do you think it's appropriate for you, at that podium, speaking with the authority of the president of the United States, to tell an American magazine what they should print?"

The *New York Times* was even more indignant.

"What specifically are you asking *Newsweek* to do?" *Times* reporter Elisabeth Bumiller demanded of McClellan. "Are you asking them to write a story about how *great* the American military is? Is that what you're saying here?"

Other journalists went so far as to suggest a grand conspiracy by the diabolical Bush administration, which somehow leaked bogus information so that it would explode in *Newsweek*'s face.

"Something smells funny to me," groused Keith Olbermann on MSNBC's *Countdown*. "Do you sense the same thing?"

"I certainly do," replied political analyst Craig Crawford, who saw dark parallels to the Memogate fiasco. "It does make you wonder if sometimes they set up the news media."

Well, it hadn't taken long for the press to blame the whole thing on Republican dirty tricks. "The dots connect," Crawford inveighed.

"It gives the administration the upper hand here in saying that the media screwed up," he added. "When the media stumbles in any way—no matter how insignificant—they try to push them right off the cliff, and that's what's happening here."

Amazingly, Crawford considered it "insignificant" that fifteen people had been killed and hundreds more hurt. Olbermann took the conspiracy theory even further in a blog posting on MSNBC's website.

"This one went similarly to the way the Killian memos story evolved at the White House," he wrote. "The news organization turns to the administration for a denial. The administration says nothing. The news organization runs the story. The administration jumps on the necks of the news organization with both feet—or has its proxies do it for them. That's beyond shameful. It's treasonous."

Such were the upside-down sensibilities of the mainstream media. *Newsweek* runs an anti-American fabrication that gets fifteen people killed— and the press accuses the White House of treason.

Over at CBS, Dan Rather's replacement seemed more upset with Scott McClellan than with Michael Isikoff.

"Admittedly, this is a very serious mistake that *Newsweek* has made and apologized for and retracted," said anchorman Bob Schieffer. "But I must say I can never recall a White House telling a news organization to go report X, Y, or Z."

The next day, CBS announced it was canceling the Wednesday edition of *60 Minutes*, the show that had broken both the Abu Ghraib and Memogate stories. Since this was the only show where Rather was still allowed to work,

CBS agreed to find room for him at the Sunday edition of *60 Minutes*. But it was strictly an act of charity. The entire world now regarded Rather as little more than a toothless tiger.

"What is the chance that management will allow you now to go off and do a major investigative story that takes on the administration?" sympathized liberal Tina Brown on CNBC. "I mean, after the flap over the National Guard story, do you feel inhibited?"

"No, no," Rather insisted. "I don't feel any pressure not to do such stories."

"Let's be realistic though. What are the realistic chances that you're going to be able to do a story that really shakes and rattles the Bush administration?"

"Excellent," Rather said with a straight face. "CBS News has a culture, has a history that—for those of us who work here, it's very real—that we see it as a sort of magical, mystical kingdom of journalistic knights. And I know I can mentally hear people rolling their eyes—that's the way we feel."

While Dan Rather was musing about his "magical kingdom" and *Newsweek* and its media allies were blithely besmirching the Bush administration and the military, the U.S. military itself was actually making remarkable progress in Iraq. American troops were training their Iraqi counterparts to assume more security responsibilities. The transitional assembly that had been elected in January was busily hammering out a constitution that would satisfy Shi'a, Sunnis, and Kurds. There was a healthy give and take to the negotiations, not unlike the process undertaken by America's founding fathers.

Tragically, however, insurgents continued to kill GIs and innocent civilians whenever possible, mostly in roadside bombings. Masterminding the carnage was Abu Musab al-Zarqawi, the al Qaeda leader who had murdered Nicholas Berg in retaliation for the broadcast of the Abu Ghraib photos. Still, it was difficult to make the case that the Jordanian-born terrorist was actually winning the struggle. After all, he had tried to stop Iraqis from voting back in January by threatening to behead them and their children, only to watch 8.5 million cast ballots anyway. Indeed, al-Zarqawi's frustration had originated at least a year before the elections, as evidenced by a letter he wrote to his al Qaeda masters in Afghanistan.

"Our enemy is growing stronger day after day, and its intelligence information increases," al-Zarqawi complained in the letter, which was intercepted by U.S. forces in January 2003. "By god, this is suffocation!"

He was especially incensed that Americans were gradually standing up Iraqi security forces.

"With the spread of the army and police, our future is becoming frightening," he wrote, adding that if it continued, "we will have to pack our bags and break camp for another land."

By July 2005, al Qaeda's plight had grown even more desperate, as evidenced by a response to al-Zarqawi's letter of complaint. The response—also intercepted by U.S. forces—was written by Osama bin Laden's second in command, Ayman al-Zawahiri, who was hiding out in the no-man's land along the Afghanistan–Pakistan border. The first point al-Zawahiri made to his underling was that things were tough all over.

"The real danger comes from the agent Pakistani army that is carrying out operations in the tribal areas, looking for mujahedeen," al-Zawahiri wrote. "My dear brother, we are following your news, despite the difficulty and hardship."

But the senior terrorist soon made clear that al-Zarqawi was only making things harder on himself by videotaping the gruesome beheadings of hostages. Al-Zawahiri said such in-your-face brutality was alienating the Muslim masses.

"We don't need this," he scolded. "We can kill the captives by bullet."

Al-Zawahiri told his underling that he needed to do a better job winning over "the hearts and minds" of ordinary Muslims. This could prove "a decisive factor between victory and defeat," he added.

"We are in a battle," he said. "More than half of this battle is taking place in the battlefield of the media."

It didn't help that al-Zarqawi kept blowing up innocent Shi'a Muslims in mosques and other holy sites, al-Zawahiri said. Sure, in an ideal world, it would be great to exterminate the Shi'a so that the Sunnis could retake control of Iraq, but that simply wasn't in the cards.

"And can the mujahedeen kill all of the Shi'a in Iraq?" he asked rhetorically. "Has any Islamic state in history ever tried that?"

Besides, al-Zawahiri argued, insurgents were already spread too thin across Iraq.

"Is the opening of another front now—in addition to the front against the Americans and the government—a wise decision? Or does this conflict with the Shi'a lift the burden from the Americans by diverting the mujahedeen to the Shi'a, while the Americans continue to control matters from afar?"

Having witnessed the swift destruction of the Taliban by U.S. forces that swept into Afghanistan in the immediate aftermath of the September 11 attacks, al-Zawahiri was hoping to avoid a rerun in Iraq.

"We don't want to repeat the mistake of the Taliban, who restricted participation in governance to the students and the people of Kandahar alone. They did not have any representation for the Afghan people in their ruling regime, so the result was that the Afghan people disengaged themselves from them.

"Even devout ones took the stance of the spectator and, when the invasion came, the emirate collapsed in days, because the people were either passive or hostile. Even the students themselves had a stronger affiliation to their tribes and their villages than their affiliation to the Islamic emirate or the Taliban movement or the responsible party in charge of each one of them in his place. Each of them retreated to his village and his tribe, where his affiliation was stronger!!"

Having dispensed this practical advice, al-Zawahiri moved to a more important discussion: laying out an overarching strategy against the infidels of the West. He regarded Iraq as the central battleground in a much broader war that spanned the entire globe.

"As for the battles that are going on in the far-flung regions of the Islamic world—such as Chechnya, Afghanistan, Kashmir, and Bosnia—they are just the groundwork and the vanguard for the major battles which have begun in the heart of the Islamic world," al-Zawahiri explained. "It has always been my belief that the victory of Islam will never take place until a Muslim state is established in the manner of the Prophet in the heart of the Islamic world."

Since Iraq was in the heart of the Islamic world, it was where the terrorists had decided to make their stand. This was precisely the argument that Bush had been making, despite efforts by Democrats to decouple Iraq from the broader War on Terror.

"We must think for a long time about our next steps and how we want to attain it," al-Zawahiri said. "And it is my humble opinion that the Jihad in Iraq requires several incremental goals. The first stage: expel the Americans from Iraq. Things may develop faster than we imagine. The aftermath of the collapse of American power in Vietnam—and how they ran and left their agents—is noteworthy. Because of that, we must be ready starting now, before events overtake us, and before we are surprised by the conspiracies of the Americans and the United Nations and their plans to fill the void behind them. We must take the initiative and impose a fait accompli upon our enemies, instead of the enemy imposing one on us, wherein our lot would be to merely resist their schemes."

Comparing Iraq to Vietnam was one area where al-Zawahiri and the Democrats agreed. The terrorist was counting on Democrats in Congress to press successfully for a cut-and-run policy in Iraq, as they had in Vietnam.

"The second stage: establish an Islamic authority or emirate," he continued. "Then develop it and support it until it achieves the level of a caliphate over as much territory as you can, to spread its power in Iraq, i.e., in Sunni areas.

"The third stage: extend the jihad wave to the secular countries neighboring Iraq.

"The fourth stage," al-Zawahiri concluded. "The clash with Israel, because Israel was established only to challenge any new Islamic entity."

Bush was both fascinated and appalled by this strategy.

"The Zawahiri letter is a very important letter for people to analyze and people to take very seriously," he told me. "The enemy—those who want to establish the caliphate from Indonesia to Spain—understand the stakes."

Having spelled out this grand strategy for taking over the entire Middle East in the biggest and most megalomaniacal power grab since Hitler and

Stalin, al-Zawahiri closed his letter on a rather mundane note. In fact, it was a little embarrassing, when you got right down to it. After all, he was the second in command to Osama bin Laden, the world's most wanted man, the leader of the most feared terrorist network on earth, a millionaire many times over. Al-Zarqawi, by contrast, was a mere employee who happened to run the al Qaeda franchise in Iraq, where he scraped by like a hunted animal, barely staying one step ahead of the Americans.

And yet it seemed the Americans, in addition to achieving dramatic military gains against al Qaeda, had also managed to sever various streams of cash that were the very lifeblood of the terrorist network. So al-Zawahiri, in a supremely awkward aside, was reduced to putting the arm on al-Zarqawi.

"Many of the lines have been cut off," he said of his cash supply. "Because of this, we need a payment while new lines are being opened."

Alas, the great and powerful al-Zawahiri sounded more like a common deadbeat whose electricity was about to be turned off.

"So, if you're capable of sending a payment of approximately $100,000," he pleaded, "we'll be very grateful to you."

CHAPTER FIFTEEN

POTUS Does SCOTUS

Four-year-old Jack Roberts was singularly unimpressed with the most powerful man on the planet. He sauntered right up to the "blue goose"—the armored presidential lectern—while George W. Bush was making a momentous announcement to the nation. Tens of millions of Americans were riveted to their television sets for a prime-time address of historic import, and there was Jack, the very picture of insouciance, dressed in a seersucker suit with short pants and saddle shoes, break-dancing in the State Dining Room of the White House. His mother, Jane, was frozen in place a few steps from the president, a stricken look on her face. She clutched the hand of her five-year-old daughter, Josie, whose expression said, "Jack's misbehaving and Mommy's upset, but there's nothing anyone can do about it." The family's mortification only deepened when Jack blithely dropped to his hands and knees and began crawling around the floor as the president plowed ahead with his boring announcement. Something about Daddy, who was standing safely on the other side of the blue goose, getting a new job. Jack couldn't care less. He was having too much fun exploring this grand room, with its fancy pillars and big fluffy curtains and high ceilings that echoed when he laughed. He couldn't understand it when Mommy grabbed his hand and admonished him to stand still. Brimming with youthful exuberance, Jack was finally led from the room while the man behind the blue goose kept droning on about Daddy.

"One of the most consequential decisions a president makes is his appointment of a justice to the Supreme Court," Bush was saying. "When a president chooses a justice, he's placing in human hands the authority and majesty of the law. The decisions of the Supreme Court affect the life of every American. And so a nominee to that court must be a person of superb credentials and the highest integrity, a person who will faithfully apply the Constitution and keep our founding promise of equal justice under law. I have found such a person in Judge John Roberts."

This was the most important domestic imperative of Bush's second term—reshaping the U.S. Supreme Court. As far as he was concerned, it was in dire need of reshaping. Despite the fact that seven of the court's nine justices had been appointed by Republicans, only three of those had turned out to be conservatives—Antonin Scalia, Clarence Thomas, and William Rehnquist. Two of the others—Anthony Kennedy and Sandra Day O'Connor—were certified moderates. Worst of all, the remaining two—John Paul Stevens and David Souter—had ended up as liberals. When you added in the only two justices appointed by a Democrat—Ruth Bader Ginsburg and Stephen Breyer—liberals outnumbered conservatives four to three, leaving a pair of swing votes with extraordinary influence over the most consequential rulings of the era.

One of those swing votes, O'Connor, was stepping down, creating the first vacancy in eleven years. This gave Bush a historic opportunity to alter the balance of the Court. If he succeeded, conservatives would achieve parity with liberals on the bench, four to four—assuming, of course, that Roberts turned out to be a true conservative. Having been burned so many times before, conservatives were wary of yet another Republican "stealth" candidate. "No more Souters" was their battle cry. Conservatives still resented Bush's father for installing Souter back in 1990. Republican presidents were notoriously timid about nominating demonstrably conservative candidates; their goal was to avoid a fight with Senate Democrats, and so they preferred candidates without a "paper trail." By contrast, Democratic presidents had no compunction about nominating overtly liberal justices. President Clinton had treated the far-left ideology of Ruth Bader Ginsburg, a former lawyer for the ultra-liberal American Civil Liberties Union, as a non-issue, and Republicans had played along. During her hearings before the Senate Judiciary Committee in 1993, Ginsburg refused to answer questions about how she might rule on hot-button issues. Untroubled by this ominous silence, Republicans joined with Democrats to confirm her nomination by an overwhelming vote of 96–3.

While Roberts was not as demonstrably conservative as Ginsburg was liberal, at least he wasn't a blank slate like Souter had been. Republicans were somewhat heartened to learn that the fifty-year-old Roberts was a brilliant lawyer who had once worked in the Reagan administration and had even clerked for Rehnquist at the Supreme Court. These and other credentials were eagerly touted by Bush as a way of assuring conservatives that Roberts wouldn't go wobbly.

"He's a man of extraordinary accomplishment and ability," the president said in the State Dining Room. "He has a good heart. He has the qualities Americans expect in a judge: experience, wisdom, fairness, and civility. He has profound respect for the rule of law and for the liberties guaranteed to every citizen. He will strictly apply the Constitution and laws, not legislate from the bench."

This was meant to further assuage conservatives who were fed up with liberal judicial activism. They were appalled when the Massachusetts Supreme Court ordered the state's legislature to write a law legalizing gay marriage in 2004. They were outraged when the Ninth U.S. Circuit Court of Appeals in San Francisco banned schoolchildren from reciting the Pledge of Allegiance because it contained the words "under God" in 2002. But most of all, conservatives were still heartbroken over *Roe v. Wade*, the 1973 ruling that overturned state laws against abortion.

In that landmark case, the court's liberal majority decreed that "the right of personal privacy includes the abortion decision," even while admitting that "the Constitution does not explicitly mention any right of privacy." The court solved this problem by asserting that the "right of privacy" had been established by an earlier ruling, *Griswold v. Connecticut*, which posited that Americans have rights not explicitly enumerated in the Constitution. *Griswold*'s key phrase was also its most muddled: "Specific guarantees in the Bill of Rights have penumbras, formed by emanations from those guarantees." In other words, guarantees give rise to emanations, which in turn give rise to penumbras, which themselves give rise to a right of privacy, which ultimately gives rise to legalized abortion. Such was the tortured legal logic that formed the foundation of *Roe*. Even many liberal legal scholars who supported abortion admitted that the *Roe* decision was deeply flawed. Justice Ginsburg called it "heavy-handed judicial intervention" that was "difficult to justify." In one fell swoop, the Supreme Court had imposed its abortion ruling across the nation through judicial fiat. In the process, the court silenced the voices of citizens and state legislatures in this profoundly important debate.

I asked Bush whether he considered *Roe* an example of judicial activism. After all, he described himself as a pro-life president who was opposed to activist courts. Yet Bush hesitated to connect his own dots.

"I have constantly stated my views on abortion," he told me. "And we'll leave it at that."

But I didn't want to leave it at that. So I reminded him that he once said America was not yet ready for *Roe* to be overturned.

"Will it someday, do you think, be ready?" I asked. "I mean, ever?"

"I think that as more people understand the issue of life, there will be fewer and fewer abortions," he replied. "I hope so."

Justice Scalia was blunter about *Roe*.

"It's not the job of the Constitution to change things by judicial decree," explained Scalia in January 2005. "Change is brought about by democracy."

During an appearance at American University Law School in Washington, D.C., Scalia argued that since the Constitution "says nothing about abortion," the issue should have been left to the states, many of which banned the practice prior to 1973.

"Abortion has been prohibited. You want to change that? American society thinks that's a terrible result? Fine. Persuade each other about that. Pass a law and eliminate the laws against abortion. I have no problem with change. It's just that I do not regard the Constitution as being the instrument of change."

Scalia regarded himself as an "originalist," in marked contrast to his liberal colleagues who treated the Constitution as a fungible document that could be bent to fit the whims of the day.

"You cannot adopt a theory that the Constitution is evolving and the Supreme Court will tell you what it means from age to age," he said at another Washington forum in 2005. "You cannot do that without causing the Supreme Court to become a very political institution—and when that happens, the people in a democracy will try to seize control of it. Judges have become political entities much more than they ever were."

That's because liberals, having lost control of both the executive and legislative branches of government, increasingly looked to the Supreme Court to implement their agenda.

"The Left went to the Supreme Court to achieve a range of victories it could never have managed through the political process," wrote liberal columnist Nicholas Kristof in the *New York Times*. "Barring school prayer, protecting protesters who used four-letter words, guaranteeing lawyers for criminal defendants, and securing a right to privacy that protected contraception and abortion."

As a result, liberals were terrified by the prospect of conservatives taking over the one remaining branch of government that was still willing to implement leftist policies.

"Given what this administration has done both in Congress and the presidency, the courts are now our last hope," said Congressman Jim McDermott of Washington. The Democrat, best known for standing on Baghdad soil and denouncing the president in the run-up to Operation Iraqi Freedom, told

American Prospect magazine that if Bush "guts the court, all hope is lost for everybody."

But the prospect of Bush making one or more appointments to the Supreme Court brought hope to millions of American conservatives.

"Many ordinary men and women—non-lawyers—believe our courts are in crisis. And their concerns are well-grounded," Karl Rove said in a speech to the Federalist Society, a conservative legal group. "For decades, the American people have seen decision after decision that strikes them as fundamentally out of touch with our Constitution."

Rove rattled off the cases on gay marriage and the Pledge of Allegiance before citing yet another example of judicial activism.

"Earlier this year a federal district court judge dismissed a ten-count indictment against hard-core pornographers, alleging that federal obscenity laws violated the pornographers' right to privacy—despite the fact that popularly elected representatives in Congress had passed the obscenity laws and that the pornographers distributed materials with simulations where women were raped and killed," he said.

Rove also criticized the Supreme Court's 2005 decision outlawing executions of criminals younger than eighteen.

"The majority ignored the fact that, at the time, the people's representatives in twenty states had passed laws permitting the death penalty for killers under eighteen," he said. "Just eighteen states, or less than 50 percent of the states allowing capital punishment, had laws prohibiting the execution of killers who committed their crimes as juveniles."

These and other rulings were fueling a growing public distrust of the federal court system.

"Judicial imperialism has split American society, politicized the court in ways the Founders never intended. And it has created a sense of disenfranchisement among a large segment of American society—people who believe issues not addressed by the Constitution should be decided through elections rather than by nine lawyers in robes," Rove said. "But this we know: the will of the people cannot be subverted in case after case, on issue after issue, year after year, without provoking a strong counterreaction. The public will eventually insist on reclaiming their rights as a sovereign people—and they will further insist that government return to its founding principles."

Rove laid out a stark choice for activist judges.

"We will see one of two things come to pass. The courts will, on their own, reform themselves and return to their proper role in American public life, or we will see more public support for constitutional amendments and legislation to rein them in. It will be one, or it will be the other."

He predicted that judges would eventually get the message and rein themselves in voluntarily.

"In America, conservatives are winning the battle of ideas on almost every front—and few are more important than the battle over the judiciary," Rove concluded. "The outcome of that debate will shape the course of human events."

Meanwhile, the course of human events would be shaped by liberal Supreme Court justices who felt so unconstrained by the Constitution that they cited foreign law in their opinions. In a 2002 ruling that banned executions of mentally retarded convicts, Justice Stevens clucked that the "world community... overwhelmingly disapproved" of the practice. The following year, in a ruling that overturned an anti-sodomy law, Justice Kennedy cited the European Court of Human Rights as favoring the "rights of homosexual adults to engage in intimate, consensual conduct." Justice Breyer, in an effort to bolster his argument that leaving inmates on death row for decades was cruel and unusual punishment, consulted cases from a variety of countries, including England, Jamaica, and India.

"There was one in Canada; the UN had discussions on this," Breyer mused at the American University forum with Scalia. "And then I think I may have made what I call a tactical error in citing a case from Zimbabwe—not the human rights capital of the world."

Justice Scalia responded, "What does the opinion of a wise Zimbabwe judge—or a wise member of the House of Lords law committee—what does that have to do with what Americans believe? Unless you really think it's been given to *you* to make this moral judgment—a very difficult moral judgment—and so in making it for yourself and for the whole country, you consult whatever authorities you want."

On this point, Scalia was unwavering.

"I do not use foreign law in the interpretation of the United States Constitution," he said. "We don't have the same moral and legal framework as the rest of the world, and never have. If you told the framers of the Constitution that what we're after is to, you know, do something that will be just like Europe, they would have been appalled."

This was precisely the sort of reasoning that had won Scalia high praise from Bush, who now hoped Roberts would become an ideological soul mate to not just Scalia, but also to Thomas and Rehnquist. Truth be told, Roberts seemed most like Rehnquist, who was looking forward to working alongside his old protégé after a separation of fifteen years. It would be the first time in U.S. history that a justice would be joined on the bench by his former clerk. The scenario was made possible by Rehnquist's stubborn refusal to retire, even though he was eighty years old and suffering from thyroid cancer. When media speculation about his job status reached a fever pitch just days before the president nominated Roberts, the plucky chief justice issued a statement squelching "unfounded rumors of my imminent retirement."

That allowed Bush to concentrate on getting Roberts confirmed, which he realized up front would not be easy. Liberals had been planning an attack for nearly five years, knowing that Bush would almost certainly get the opportunity to replace at least one of the court's aging justices. Fearing the overturn of *Roe v. Wade*, leftist interest groups were primed for scorched-earth political warfare, complete with well-financed TV attack ads. Senate Democrats put together their own battle plan, although they made the mistake of sharing it with the *Washington Post*.

"Democrats signaled that whoever the nominee is, their three likely lines of attack will be to assert the White House did not consult them sufficiently, then paint the nominee as ideologically extreme and finally assert that the

Senate had not received sufficient documents about the candidate," *Post* reporter Mike Allen revealed on July 3.

This valuable heads-up gave the White House plenty of time to counter the Democratic battle plan. Bush and his staff made a very public display of consulting with seventy of the one hundred senators, including many Democrats, in the weeks before announcing Roberts as the nominee. The White House also scheduled a rolling series of document dumps that would put tens of thousand of pages of Roberts's writings into the public domain, while holding back other papers that were protected under executive privilege. The public documents did not clearly indicate how Roberts would vote on the all-important issue of abortion, which deprived liberals of a rallying point. Nor could Democrats find much fodder in the forty-nine opinions Roberts had authored in his two years as a judge on the U.S. Court of Appeals for the District of Columbia. To complicate matters, the boyishly handsome judge was charming and self-deprecating. He displayed none of the prickliness that had undone Robert Bork's nomination back in 1987. In short, it was hard to dislike John Roberts.

Undaunted, the press decided to go after his family instead. The *Los Angeles Times* got the ball rolling with a breathless front-page "exposé" of the nominee's wife. Reporter Richard Serrano revealed that while Roberts's views on *Roe v. Wade* were murky, "there is no mistaking where his wife stands: Jane Sullivan Roberts, a lawyer, is ardently against abortion. A Roman Catholic like her husband, Jane Roberts has been deeply involved in the antiabortion movement."

Straining to portray John Roberts as equally pro-life, Serrano warned, "His wife's views might suggest he also embraced efforts to overturn *Roe v. Wade*."

Not to be outdone, *Washington Post* reporter Robin Givhan actually critiqued little Jack and Josie. She wrote that "the Roberts family went too far" by "costuming" their children in hopelessly "old-fashioned" clothes at the White House. Givhan said Mrs. Roberts had wreaked "aesthetic havoc" by dressing Jack in a seersucker suit and Josie in a pretty yellow dress with patent-leather shoes. Noting that Mrs. Roberts herself was wearing a pink tweed outfit, the reporter likened mother and children to "a trio of Easter eggs, a handful of Jelly Bellies, three little Necco wafers." She archly noted the mother's "controlling grip" on young Jack and mocked the entire "1950s-style tableau vivant that was John Roberts and his family." "These clothes are Old World, old money," sniped Givhan, who reserved most of her venom for Mrs. Roberts. "Please select all attire from the commonly accepted styles of this century."

Sinking even lower, the *New York Times* launched an investigation into how Mr. and Mrs. Roberts had adopted Jack and Josie from Latin America. The vaunted "paper of record" actually asked lawyers how to unseal the adoption papers, which are routinely kept secret for the protection of the children. Brit Hume of the FOX News Channel reported, "At least one lawyer turned the *Times* down flat, saying that any effort to pry into adoption case records, which are always sealed, would be reprehensible." Caught red-handed, the newspaper backpedaled furiously.

"Our reporters made initial inquiries about the adoptions, as they did about many other aspects of his background," senior editor Bill Borders told the Drudge Report, which broke the story. "They did so with great care, understanding the sensitivity of the issue."

Unconvinced, the National Council for Adoption issued a statement denouncing, "in the strongest possible terms, the shocking decision of the *New York Times* to investigate the adoption records of Justice John Roberts's two young children. The adoption community is outraged that, for obviously political reasons, the *Times* has targeted the very private circumstances, motivations, and processes by which the Roberts became parents."

Noting the newspaper's strident support for abortion, a Bush adviser shook his head and muttered to me, "Well, at least the *New York Times* has finally discovered adoption."

On August 8, the battle over Roberts intensified dramatically when NARAL Pro-Choice America began spending half a million dollars to air an incendiary TV ad. The spot opened with images of a bombed-out abortion clinic as an announcer declaimed, "Seven years ago, a bomb destroyed a women's health clinic in Birmingham, Alabama." This was followed by footage of a nurse who had been maimed by shrapnel being wheeled out of a hospital.

"When a bomb ripped through my clinic, I almost lost my life," Emily Lyons told the camera. "I'm determined to stop this violence so I'm speaking out."

Over footage of Roberts stepping to the blue goose in the State Dining Room, the announcer said, "Supreme Court nominee John Roberts filed court briefs supporting violent fringe groups and a convicted clinic bomber. Call your senators. Tell them to oppose John Roberts. America can't afford a justice whose ideology leads him to excuse violence against other Americans."

The ad was promptly exposed as a fraud by the nonpartisan Fact Check website, operated by the Annenberg Public Policy Center of the University of Pennsylvania.

"In words and images, the ad conveys the idea that Roberts took a legal position excusing bombing of abortion clinics, which is false," the organization said. "To the contrary, during the Reagan administration when he was associate counsel to the president, Roberts drafted a memo saying abortion clinic bombers 'should be prosecuted to the full extent of the law.' In the 1986 memo, Roberts called abortion bombers 'criminals' and 'misguided individuals,' indicating that they would get no special treatment regarding requests for presidential pardons."

Even most liberals found the ad shockingly false and defamatory. Frances Kissling, president of Catholics for a Free Choice, told the *New York Times* she was "deeply upset and offended" by the ad, saying it stepped "over the line into the kind of personal character attack we shouldn't be engaging in."

"As a pro-choice person, I don't like being placed on the defensive by my leaders," she added. "NARAL should pull it and move on."

Her comments were echoed by longtime NARAL supporter Walter Dellinger, a former official in the Clinton administration, who fretted that the "unfair and unwarranted" ad was creating a backlash against liberals. In a letter to fellow pro-choicer Arlen Specter, the Republican chairman of the Senate Judiciary Committee, Dellinger lamented "a downward spiral of our politics." While conceding it was "very painful for me to be critical" of NARAL, he nonetheless feared the ad would "produce public aversion to the confirmation process."

The next day, Specter called on NARAL president Nancy Keenan to pull the ad, which he called "blatantly untrue and unfair."

"The NARAL advertisement is not helpful to the pro-choice cause which I support," Specter told Keenan in a letter. "When NARAL puts on such an advertisement, in my opinion, it undercuts its credibility and injures the pro-choice cause."

Keenan quickly acquiesced under such withering public criticism. The ad was pulled that same day. But Keenan borrowed a page from the Dan Rather playbook, insisting she was right and the rest of the world was wrong.

"The ad is not 'false,'" she railed in a lengthy letter to Fact Check. "Every factual statement made in NARAL Pro-Choice America's ad is completely accurate and supported by objective documents."

But the damage had been done. Americans rallied around the unfairly attacked nominee, who was now politically inoculated against further attack ads. By overreaching, the Left had merely made it more likely that Roberts would be confirmed.

Meanwhile, conservative advocacy groups like Progress for America were in the midst of their own multi-million-dollar ad campaign, aimed at further decimating the opposition. In fact, many of the ads began running weeks before Roberts was chosen, warning Americans that Democrats would attack any nominee the president put forward. Hours after Roberts got the nod, another deluge of ads began to flood the airwaves. The most effective of these was a spot that reminded viewers that Justice Ginsburg had refused to answer hot-button questions during her confirmation hearings. The ad featured footage of Democratic senator Joseph Biden of Delaware, a member of the Senate Judiciary Committee, encouraging Ginsburg to stay mum through much of the hearings.

"You not only have a right to choose what you will answer and not answer, but in my view you should not answer," he told her.

This preemptively sensitized the public to be on the lookout for hypocrisy when it came time for Democrats like Biden, who was still on the committee, to question Roberts. Democrats glumly realized it would be almost impossible to portray Roberts as evasive now that Republicans were constantly harping about the "Ginsburg precedent."

Little by little, Democrats resigned themselves to the inevitability of Roberts being confirmed. The flawless, highly orchestrated rollout by the White House had given the nomination a powerful momentum that was becoming increasingly difficult to stop. All the while, Bush kept calling for a confirmation process that was "dignified" and "civilized." With those sorts of high-minded buzzwords being thrown around by the president, it was hard for liberals to work up much enthusiasm for a down-in-the-gutter street brawl against the nominee.

Deepening this sense of deflation among Democrats was the realization that even if they rallied the troops for an all-out assault against Roberts, they simply did not have the votes to prevail. Thanks to the president's electoral coattails, Republicans now had fifty-five Senate seats, well over the majority required for confirmation. To be sure, Democrats could always threaten a filibuster, which could only be broken by sixty votes. They had already done that many times to the president's federal court nominees. But Republicans always had the option of simply changing the Senate rules to block Democrats from employing filibusters. Democrats called this the "nuclear option," as if it were some outrageous escalation of partisan warfare. But Republicans felt that the Democrats were the ones being outrageous by filibustering judges in the first place. After all, the majority party was constitutionally entitled to write the Senate rules as it saw fit. Therefore, Republicans preferred to call their threat the "constitutional option." Whatever it was called, it drove Democrats crazy.

"If they, for whatever reason, decide to do this, it's not only wrong, they will rue the day they did it, because we will do whatever we can do to strike back," threatened Senate Minority Leader Harry Reid, a Nevada Democrat. "I know procedures around here. And I know that there will still be Senate business conducted. But I will, for lack of a better word, screw things up."

New York senator Charles E. Schumer, a Democratic member of the Senate Judiciary Committee, said any attempt to stop Democratic filibusters
"would make the Senate look like a banana republic" and "cause us to try to
shut it down in every way."

But such a shutdown had already been averted back in May, just as Republicans were about to go "nuclear" on Democrats for blocking a batch of judicial nominees from getting up-or-down votes. At the last moment, fourteen
Senators—seven from each party—struck a compromise that limited
Democrats to invoking the filibuster only under "extraordinary circumstances." If they filibustered under circumstances that were less than extraordinary, Republicans reserved the right to exercise the nuclear option. The
immediate result of this compromise was the swift confirmation of several
long-stalled nominees to the lower courts. A more far-reaching effect was the
virtual certainty that Bush's Supreme Court nomination of John Roberts
would not be filibustered.

And even if a filibuster somehow materialized, Democrats knew they
could never enforce it. The Roberts charm offensive had been so devastatingly effective that even some liberals predicted he would be confirmed with
at least seventy votes. Instead of the scorched-earth political warfare everyone had expected, there were only a few minor skirmishes.

As the summer drew to a close, Roberts's nomination appeared certain. It
seemed only a matter of time before he would be able to join his old boss on
the nation's highest court. But before this historic reunion could come to
pass, Chief Justice Rehnquist lost his battle with cancer.

Suddenly, it was time for a whole new political fight.

CHAPTER SIXTEEN

"TOTALLY DISTORTING REALITY"

Rush Limbaugh had finally gone off the deep end. The usually astute radio commentator was making a prediction so rash and far-fetched that even his fellow conservatives were taken aback. Limbaugh was insisting, without a shred of evidence, that the Left would figure out a way to blame President Bush for Hurricane Katrina, which had made landfall along the Gulf Coast just five hours earlier. With the nation still glued to television coverage of the ongoing storm, not even the most craven political opportunists were contemplating the blame game. Besides, everyone knew the monster storm was a natural disaster, an act of God— not of George W. Bush. Yet Limbaugh would not back down from his dire prophesy.

"Democrats are going to find a way to blame Bush," he insisted just after noon on Monday, August 29. "I'm just telling you that the Left politicizes everything in the country. Everything is a political issue, and this is going to end up being one—one way or the other.

"And I just want to be out in front of it, warn you of that so you're not surprised or caught short when it happens. It isn't going to be long before we're going to see headlines: 'Bush: Did He Act Too Late?'"

Bush well knew the political price of not responding immediately to natural disasters. His father had been criticized after Hurricane Andrew hammered Florida back in 1992, and Bush himself had been criticized after the Asian tsunami in December 2004.

So Bush was already involved in Katrina preparations days before Limbaugh's fanciful prediction of political blowback from the looming hurricane. On Saturday, August 27, two days before the hurricane hit New Orleans, the president declared an emergency in Louisiana and ordered "federal aid to supplement state and local response efforts." He also authorized the Federal Emergency Management Agency (FEMA) "to coordinate all disaster relief efforts." The words he used in this emergency declaration were important. After all, the role of the feds was to "supplement" state and local efforts, not commandeer those efforts. Similarly, FEMA was authorized to "coordinate" disaster relief efforts, not take charge of them. Indeed, FEMA's entire mission had always been limited to *coordinating* state, local, and charitable aid. With only 2,500 employees, the tiny agency simply was not set up to deploy armies of shock troops into disaster zones, especially one as massive as the 90,000 square miles devastated by Katrina—roughly the size of Great Britain. There was a reason that local authorities called themselves "first responders." They were in charge on the ground, with backup assistance from state officials and, if necessary, the feds. This time-honored arrangement, a manifestation of American federalism, was mandated by nothing less than the Founders' insistence on a limited national government.

Nonetheless, Bush decided to exercise more federal authority than usual, since Katrina was expected to be the most powerful hurricane to make landfall in decades. On Sunday, August 28, he declared emergencies in Mississippi and Alabama, an act that freed up federal funds to begin flowing into those states even before the storm hit. He also declared a "major disaster" in Florida, where Katrina had already come ashore as a category-one hurricane before passing into the Gulf of Mexico and growing into a category-five behemoth. Though officially on his annual August vacation, Bush devoted the entire day to Katrina. He consulted with federal and state emergency management teams. He spoke with the governors of Louisiana, Mississippi, Alabama, and Florida. He was briefed by the director of the National Hurricane Center, Max Mayfield. He huddled with FEMA director Michael Brown. He even summoned the press to his ranch in Crawford so he could broadcast an urgent warning to Americans in the path of the storm.

"We cannot stress enough the danger this hurricane poses to Gulf Coast communities," Bush emphasized. "I urge all citizens to put their own safety and the safety of their families first by moving to safe ground. Please listen carefully to instructions provided by state and local officials."

In case that wasn't enough direct involvement by the commander in chief, he sounded more alarm bells the following day, as Katrina made landfall east of New Orleans. Bush took no comfort in the fact that the storm had been downgraded to a category-four hurricane just before slamming ashore. Nor was he assuaged by the front-page headline in the *New York Times* that shrugged "New Orleans Escapes a Direct Hit."

"Don't abandon your shelters until you're given clearance by the local authorities," the president implored. "Take precautions because this is a dangerous storm. When the storm passes, the federal government has got assets and resources that we'll be deploying to help you. In the meantime, America will pray."

Bush had already taken a variety of other steps that morning to stay on top of the situation. For starters, he declared Louisiana, Mississippi, and Alabama major disaster areas, an act that made additional federal funds available just hours after Katrina slammed ashore. He twice used videoconferencing equipment aboard Air Force One to confer with Brown, who had dispatched a thousand FEMA employees to the disaster zone. The same equipment was used by White House deputy chief of staff Joe Hagin and other Bush aides to consult with federal and state emergency officials. All the while, Bush kept using his bully pulpit to focus attention on Katrina.

"This was a terrible storm. It's a storm that hit with a lot of ferocity," he told seniors in California. "The storm is moving through, and we're now able to assess damage, or beginning to assess damage. And I want the people to know in the affected areas that the federal government and the state government and the local governments will work side by side to do all we can to help get your lives back in order."

But New Orleans was already being hit by a second disaster that would prove even more devastating than the first. The storm surge sent water spilling over and crashing through several levees, causing massive flooding throughout the city, most of which had been built below sea level. The rising water forced many residents to the attics of their homes, where some chopped holes in their roofs and waited for rescue helicopters. Authorities were slow to grasp the magnitude of the flood, in part because the press remained focused on Katrina, still a powerful hurricane as it hurtled north into Mississippi on Monday afternoon.

Meanwhile, Limbaugh was quick to predict that liberals would blame Katrina on Bush's neglect of global warming.

"I just want to put you on notice," he said. "I just want you to beware that the libs are going to use this hurricane to advance all of the wacko aspects of their agenda."

This seemed unlikely. Scientists had dismissed the idea that global warming would make hurricanes fiercer and more frequent. Meteorologists pointed out that there had been no increase in the number or intensity of typhoons in the western Pacific or Indian oceans. Max Mayfield, director of the National Hurricane Center, explained that the Atlantic Ocean was in the middle of a natural cycle of increased hurricane activity that began a decade earlier and would last for at least another decade. He noted that it paralleled a similar cycle that ran from the 1940s through the '60s before giving way to a period of relative calm that lasted a generation. Global warming had nothing to do with these cycles.

And yet, incredibly, a mere three hours after Limbaugh signed off the airwaves, his prediction began to come true. With people still dying and rescue workers still struggling to cope with the magnitude of the hurricane and flooding, Democrats decided to kick off the blame game. First out of the gate was Robert F. Kennedy Jr., who blamed the hurricane on global warming, which in turn he blamed on Bush and other Republicans. He even managed to get in a shot at the war in Iraq.

"Now we are all learning what it's like to reap the whirlwind of fossil fuel dependence," he blogged on the Huffington Post website. "Our destructive addiction has given us a catastrophic war in the Middle East. And now Katrina is giving our nation a glimpse of the climate chaos we are bequeathing our children."

On Tuesday, as two more levees failed, the *Boston Globe* published a column by journalist Ross Gelbspan, who argued that Hurricane Katrina's "real name is global warming." That same day, as the floodwaters were engulfing more of the city, German environmental minister Jürgen Trittin, a member of the Green Party, denounced America as "the headquarters of climate polluters." In a screed published by the *Frankfurter Rundschau* newspaper, he railed, "The American president ignores the economic and human damage that his country, by failing to protect the climate, inflicts on the world's economy by natural catastrophes such as hurricane Katrina."

Yet these potshots were only a mild foreshadowing of the ferocious criticism that would soon be unleashed against Bush. Again, Limbaugh had been all too prescient. By the end of the week, the mainstream media and the Democratic Party would be calling the president an uncaring racist who was personally responsible for the deaths of poor black people in New Orleans. They would be accusing him of a spectacular failure of leadership in the biggest test of his presidency since September 11. A Democratic congressman would declare Bush a modern-day "Bull Connor." A Democratic senator would say on national television that she was so disgusted with the president that she would "likely have to punch him—literally."

The ferocity of these denunciations was not driven by Bush hatred alone, although that was certainly a catalyst. No, the recriminations reached a fever pitch primarily because rescue operations in New Orleans were badly botched.

Instead of rising to their jobs as "first responders," many of the city's emergency workers found themselves victims of the devastating hurricane and flood. Most of the New Orleans police department simply went AWOL. Of those who actually showed up for work, some joined in the looting of Wal-Marts and other unattended establishments. New Orleans mayor Ray Nagin could not even cajole enough bus drivers into evacuating victims. As a result, hundreds of buses sat submerged in a parking lot while tens of thousands of residents waited desperately for a way out of the drowning city. Nagin's feckless performance was a far cry from the towering leadership of New York mayor Rudy Giuliani in the wake of September 11. Utterly overwhelmed, the New Orleans mayor threw up his hands and blamed state and federal officials.

"I don't know whose problem it is. I don't know whether it's the governor's problem. I don't know whether it's the president's problem. But somebody needs to get their ass on a plane and sit down, the two of them, and figure this out right now," he wailed on WWL radio on September 1. "Get off your asses and do something, and let's fix the biggest goddamn crisis in the history of this country."

Louisiana governor Kathleen Blanco was even more feckless than Nagin. She seemed incapable of making up her mind. On August 27, President Bush asked her to order an evacuation of New Orleans. She dithered until August 28—one day before Katrina made landfall. When the flood prompted Nagin to order a second evacuation, Blanco refused to enforce the order, arguing that scientists needed more time to analyze the putrid water, even though its toxicity was painfully obvious. Corpses went uncollected for more than a week while federal officials waited for Blanco to make up her mind about what to do with them.

"Number one issue is body collection," groused Army colonel John J. Jordan, the military assistant to Brown, in an e-mail to Pentagon officials. "This issue must be addressed, and frankly, there is operations paralysis at this point."

Blanco was similarly paralyzed when it came to requesting federal troops. She neglected to ask the president on August 27 and again when she spoke with him on August 29. Even on August 31, she had still not made the request.

"I really need to call for the military," she sheepishly admitted to her press secretary that day. "And I should have started that in the first call."

Later that afternoon, she finally asked the White House for troops, which were dispatched to assist Louisiana National Guard forces. But Blanco hesitated again when Bush offered to have the federal government take over the chaotic city. Blanco said she needed twenty-four hours to think it over and ultimately rejected the federal offer. She did not want to give up her control over the National Guard. Worse yet, her state Homeland Security Department inexplicably forbade the Red Cross from bringing desperately needed food, water, and medical supplies into New Orleans.

In short, both the local and state governments proved utterly incapable of coping with the double disasters overwhelming New Orleans. With no first or second responders to save the day, the onus fell on federal officials to step up as "third responders." Instead of "supplementing" and "coordinating" relief efforts, the feds were suddenly expected to take them over. But by this time the situation in New Orleans was spiraling out of control. Thanks to the bungled evacuation efforts, more than twenty thousand people were herded into the Superdome, which was set up as an emergency shelter. But after the hurricane passed, floodwaters kept the victims trapped inside the football stadium for days. Sanitation conditions—and the evacuees' patience—rapidly degenerated. Other victims were stranded on rooftops and highway overpasses for days. Corpses floated in the fetid water or lay abandoned in the gutter. The scenes were like something out of a Third World hellhole, not the United States of America.

Into this hellhole waded the mainstream media, desperate to salvage its credibility, which had taken a major hit in August. Journalists spent that month lionizing Bush critic Cindy Sheehan, who staged a marathon antiwar demonstration near the president's ranch in Texas. Reporters wrote stories predicting that Sheehan, whose son had been killed in Iraq, would galvanize public opinion against the war, a la Vietnam. But Sheehan gradually morphed from a sympathetic mother into a raving radical. After initially meeting with Bush and finding him genuinely sorry for her loss,

Sheehan demanded a second meeting and began denouncing the president as a "terrorist." Then she veered off into Middle East politics, ranting for Israel to "get out of Palestine." In a bizarre conflation of foreign and domestic issues, she demanded that U.S. troops get out of "occupied New Orleans." Finally, Sheehan committed what the mainstream media considered a cardinal sin. She lambasted New York senator Hillary Rodham Clinton—widely regarded as the likely Democratic presidential nominee in 2008—for not being sufficiently antiwar. Fawning coverage of Cindy Sheehan declined precipitously.

Now the press viewed Katrina as a shot at redemption. CBS White House correspondent John Roberts acknowledged to *USA Today* that public approval of the media "has been at a low ebb. But the last twelve days have been a time when I've been proud to be in this profession. I think we reconfirmed our status as the voice of the people who have no voice." CNN's Christiane Amanpour summed it up even more succinctly in *National Review*. "It took a Katrina, you know, to bring us back to where we belong," she said. "In other words, real journalists, real journalism, and I think that's a good thing." But no one was more effusive than former anchorman Dan Rather.

"It's been one of the quintessential great moments in television news," he gushed to CNN's Larry King. "The coverage of Hurricane Katrina, right there with the Nixon-Kennedy debates, the Kennedy assassination, Watergate coverage, you name it. You know there's certain landmark coverages and I think this has been one."

But the only landmark the media set was a new low. As desperate as the situation in New Orleans truly was, journalists managed to grossly exaggerate it. Newspapers warned of the death toll hitting forty thousand, when the reality was closer to one thousand. Journalists hyperventilated about hundreds of bodies being stacked up inside the Superdome and scores more packed in a freezer inside the city's convention center. In reality, the two facilities contained a total of ten bodies, none of which—contrary to frenzied press accounts—had been shot. Nor had anyone slit the throat of a seven-year-old girl, another media myth. In fact, throughout the entire city of New Orleans, a grand total of four people were murdered in the week after Katrina, which is precisely the average number of homicides committed in the city every other week of the year.

"Robberies, rapes, carjackings, riots, and murder," Alan Colmes breathlessly reported on FOX News. "Violent gangs are roaming the streets at night, hidden by the cover of darkness."

The *Los Angeles Times*, in a typically overwrought passage, told readers that National Guardsmen "took positions on rooftops, scanning for snipers and armed mobs as seething crowds of refugees milled below, desperate to flee. Gunfire crackled in the distance."

Some of the worst exaggerations came from Nagin himself. He told WWL radio that New Orleans was "a place where you probably have thousands of people that have died and thousands more that are dying every day."

He added, "You have drug addicts that are now walking around this city looking for a fix, and that's the reason why they were breaking in hospitals and drugstores. They're looking for something to take the edge off of their jones, if you will. And right now, they don't have anything to take the edge off. And they've probably found guns. So what you're seeing is drug-starving crazy addicts, drug addicts that are wreaking havoc. And we don't have the manpower to adequately deal with it. We can only target certain sections of the city and form a perimeter around them and hope to God that we're not overrun."

Nagin became even more hyperbolic when Oprah Winfrey ventured into New Orleans. He told the TV talk-show host that the city's population had descended to an "almost animalistic state." He added, "They have people standing out there, have been in that frickin' Superdome for five days watching dead bodies, watching hooligans killing people, raping people."

Although not a single case of Superdome rape was ever confirmed, New Orleans police chief Eddie Compass further embellished this urban legend.

"We had little babies in there, little babies getting raped," he told Winfrey shortly before quitting his job.

Compass's departure did little to stop the proliferation of ridiculous false-hoods, most of which were aimed at politically harming George W. Bush, who was allegedly not doing enough to help the city's poor blacks.

"Black hurricane victims in New Orleans have begun eating corpses to survive," author Randall Robinson raged on the Huffington Post blog. "Thousands of blacks in New Orleans are dying like dogs."

Robinson added that he had "finally come to see my country for what it really is. A monstrous fraud." But the only fraud was his own hysterical claim of cannibalism, which he was later forced to retract.

"George Bush is our Bull Connor!" thundered Congressman Charlie Rangel of New York. "If you're black in this country, and you're poor in this country, it's not an inconvenience. It's a death sentence."

Never mind that Connor, like Rangel, was a Democrat. The important thing was to liken Bush to the infamous Birmingham police chief who had turned attack dogs and fire hoses on civil rights marchers in 1963, transforming himself into a symbol of Southern racism.

"I was disappointed in that reaction," Bush told me. "I was disappointed because I thought it was unnecessarily divisive at a time when the nation needed to be focused on how to come together to help. And yet, that's just kind of fairly typical of Washington.

"The harshness of Washington certainly didn't reflect the compassion of the rest of the country. Millions of people were taken in to different communities around America. Strangers were given food, shelter, and clothing. It was a remarkable display of the best of America. And so the politics of Washington and all that did not affect the capacity of America to love."

Yet Bush's critics were in no mood for love. Instead of repudiating Rangel's slur, other Democrats rushed to up the rhetorical ante.

"This is *worse* than Bull Connor," said Congressman Major Owens of New York, Rangel's colleague in the Congressional Black Caucus. "Bull Connor didn't even pretend that he cared about African Americans."

Owens told the *New York Sun* that Bush pretended to care about African Americans by allowing black churches to administer welfare programs previously handled by the government.

"You have to give it to George Bush for being even more diabolical," the Democrat said. "With his faith-based initiatives, he made it appear that he cared about black Americans. Katrina has exposed that as a big lie."

The Reverend Al Sharpton, one of ten Democrats who had vied for the chance to challenge Bush for the White House, also agreed that the president was a modern-day Bull Connor.

"If there is a person that is a symbol that many blacks organize around and organize against in this generation, it would be Bush—as it was with one generation and Connor," Sharpton told the *Sun*.

"Clearly Bush has become that, especially after Katrina," he added. "We've gone from fire hoses to levees."

Nation of Islam leader Louis Farrakhan went even further by complaining that "FEMA is too white" and insinuating to his followers that one of the levees had actually been sabotaged.

"I heard from a very reliable source who saw a twenty-five-foot-deep crater under the levee breach," he said. "It may have been blown up to destroy the black part of town and keep the white part dry."

Bush did his best to ignore such incendiary rhetoric, although it eventually took a toll. This became evident on the morning of September 2, when the unsmiling president emerged from a meeting in the White House Situation Room. He had just spent more than an hour with federal officials who were struggling to perform duties that had been abandoned by local and state officials.

"The results are not acceptable," he told reporters on the South Lawn. "We'll get on top of this situation."

To that end, Bush headed to the Gulf Coast for the first of many tours of the devastated region. I was the sole newspaper reporter to accompany the president on Air Force One.

First stop was Mobile, Alabama, where Bush entered a sweltering hangar beneath a "COAST GUARD" sign with paint flaking off. Inside were half a dozen orange-and-white Coast Guard helicopters and a small jet. A score of people broke into applause when the president rounded the nose of a chopper and came into view. He walked over to a large table covered with maps of hurricane damage. Flanked by various federal, state, and local officials, he listened intently to a variety of briefings, nodding his head but saying nothing while the men spoke. Then he heard from a helicopter pilot, dressed in a green jumpsuit, who told of rescuing people from rooftops at night by flying toward the telltale flashlights. When it was Bush's turn to speak, he became quite emotional, choking back tears and speaking with some difficulty.

"I want to say a few things," he managed. "I am incredibly proud of our Coast Guard. We have got courageous people risking their lives to save life. And I want to thank the commanders and I want to thank the troops over there for representing the best of America."

Regaining his composure, the president pressed on. "I'm not looking forward to this trip," he admitted. "We're in the darkest days."

He added, "The good news is—and it's hard for some to see it now—that out of this chaos is going to come a fantastic Gulf Coast, like it was before."

Turning to FEMA director Michael Brown, Bush remarked, "Brownie, you're doing a heck of a job." Everyone applauded, not realizing the statement would be thrown back in the president's face countless times as recriminations intensified in the days and weeks ahead.

The president then boarded Marine One for a flight to Biloxi, Mississippi, getting an eyeful of the hurricane damage along the way. Flying low over the shoreline, he passed entire waterfront neighborhoods that had been flattened.

"The destruction is unbelievable," he muttered. "It's destruction on the coast, and it's destruction off the coast."

But even these horrific sights did not begin to capture the devastation Bush witnessed up close after landing at Keesler Air Force Base in Biloxi. The presidential motorcade drove through the utterly obliterated city, from the beachfront casino district to the poor side streets off Martin Luther King Jr.

Blvd. At several points the motorcade had to zig-zag down narrow streets to avoid the enormous trees and debris strewn everywhere.

At length, the president got out of his car in an area that looked as though it had suffered aerial bombardment. Entire houses were ripped off their slabs and strewn across the neighborhood. Others were missing their roofs. For some houses, the roofs were the only things intact, sitting low on the ground over the wreckage of the homes themselves. Power lines were down everywhere. The landscape was littered with enormous chunks of broken trees, twisted sheets of corrugated aluminum, cinder blocks, heating ducts: the flotsam and jetsam of homes dismantled by the wind and water.

The first people Bush encountered were two weeping black women, Bronwynne Bassier and her sister, Kim. They were carrying black plastic trash bags as they scavenged for food and clothing amid the wreckage.

"I'm looking for clothes for my son," explained Bronwynne, who was twenty-three years old. "We've lost everything, and I want to take care of my baby."

Bush hugged the sisters and kissed their foreheads as they dissolved into sobs on his chest.

"It's going to be okay," he murmured. "Hang in there. We're going to take care of you."

Without disentangling, the trio began walking down the street, with Bush still trying to comfort the sisters. He slung his arms around their shoulders as they intertwined their arms around his back.

A block later, Bush came upon a man amid the rubble of a house in which he had grown up.

"Are you doing all right?" the president asked.

"I'm doing fine," the man replied. "I'm alive, and my mother is alive."

Bush was clearly overwhelmed by the magnitude of the wreckage.

"It's hard to describe the devastation that we have just walked through," he told the small group of reporters with him. "I'm telling you, it's worse than imaginable."

He added, "I don't think anybody can be prepared for the vastness of this destruction. You can look at a picture, but until you sit on that doorstep of a house that used to be, or stand by the rubble, you just can't imagine it."

Bush was then pelted with the usual questions about why it was taking so long to respond and why he had sent so many troops to Iraq when they were needed on the Gulf Coast. He pointed out that aid was finally surging into the region and insisted the United States could simultaneously fight a war and respond to a hurricane. I decided to throw him a curveball by asking about the rebuilding of New Orleans.

"Since we're going to be spending billions in tax dollars to rebuild," I said, "we might want to think about building it in such a way where it's not below sea level again."

"I'm going to delegate," Bush punted. "I'm going to call upon the best experts, starting with the people of New Orleans, and get opinions as we work with the local folks. We're going to help people rebuild, Stretch."

Bush turned and walked over to three black men who stood near a soiled and tattered American flag that was tied to a half-downed power line. After a few words of encouragement, he proceeded another couple of blocks to a Salvation Army trailer, where he greeted people with hugs, kisses, and words of comfort.

"These are tough times. This is a storm the likes of which I pray I never see again," he said. "There's a lot of sadness, of course. But there's also a spirit here in Mississippi that is uplifting."

He added, "It's going to take a monumental effort to continue moving forward, but we will. And this is a nation that has done a lot of big things before, and this is going to be one of the biggest, which is to recover from one of the worst storms, if not the worst storm."

Next the president choppered to New Orleans, getting a bird's-eye view of yet more devastation.

"It's as if the entire Gulf Coast were obliterated by the worst kind of weapon you can imagine," Bush said.

After landing at the New Orleans airport, Bush went into the conference room of Air Force One and listened to the complaints of a variety of officials, including a trio of Democrats—Nagin, Blanco, and Louisiana senator Mary Landrieu. Before long, Landrieu was sobbing, Nagin was shouting, and Blanco was demanding a private audience with the president. Nagin wanted Bush to federalize the entire relief effort, meaning that the feds would take control of the Louisiana National Guard away from Blanco. When Bush asked the governor for her opinion, she said she would answer him only in private. So the two had their own separate meeting, during which Blanco could not bring herself to relinquish control. The president, for his part, could not seize control without violating the Posse Comitatus Act of 1878, which forbade federal troops from performing civilian law enforcement functions. The only way around that ban was to invoke the Insurrection Act, although Bush could foresee the political fallout that would result from a conservative Republican president declaring an insurrection in a city of black Democrats.

After a final chopper ride to tour the wreckage of New Orleans, Bush landed at a Coast Guard station where workers were loading tons of sand into enormous white bags. The bags were then picked up by Black Hawk helicopters and dropped into a 300-foot breach of the 17th Street Levee. The president walked toward the levee, stopping along the way to greet hardhats clogging the roadway with all manner of trucks and heavy construction equipment. The back of the president's pale blue shirt was plastered with sweat. At length he reached a giant dragline crane that was scooping up lumber and other debris from the water while a huge backhoe raked the muck away from the shore. Bush jawboned with the workers in a scene that was reminiscent of his visit to the hardhats at Ground Zero on September 14, 2001. Only this time around, the press complained that Bush did not have a "bullhorn moment," as if he were supposed to vow revenge against Mother Nature.

The president stood on a bridge and watched as a steady stream of Black Hawks dropped their enormous sandbags into the water. At first the bags disappeared beneath the murky water, but after a while some of them came to rest above the surface. The breach was finally beginning to close. It was one of several encouraging signs that the relief effort, after stumbling for days, was finally beginning to hit its stride. Indeed, earlier that day, National Guardsmen had arrived in force and fanned out across the city, securing the Superdome and passing out food and water.

It had been a very long day, but before boarding Air Force One for the return trip to Washington, Bush wanted to offer some final words of encouragement to the battered region. Rather than criticize the ineptitude of Nagin and Blanco, Bush heaped praise on the Democrats as they stood with him on the tarmac.

"You know, I'm going to fly out of here in a minute, but I want you to know that I'm not going to forget what I've seen. I understand the devastation requires more than one day's attention," the president said. "The great city of New Orleans will rise again and be a greater city of New Orleans. I believe the town where I used to come from Houston, Texas, to enjoy myself—occasionally too much—will be that very same town, that it will be a better place to come to. That's what I believe."

Bush cut a good-natured glance at Nagin when he made this self-deprecating reference to his drinking days. It was the president's way of showing the mayor there were no hard feelings. Yet the press seized on this innocuous remark as more proof of Bush's heartless disregard for black hurricane victims.

"W. finally landed in Hell yesterday and chuckled about his wild boozing days in 'the great city' of N'Awlins," *New York Times* columnist Maureen Dowd seethed. Her column, headlined "United States of Shame," went on. "He was clearly moved. 'You know, I'm going to fly out of here in a minute,' he said on the runway."

Dowd savaged "our tone-deaf president" for telling the "blithering idiot" FEMA director, "Brownie, you're doing a heck of a job." Refraining from criticism of local and state authorities, Dowd reserved all her vitriol for Bush officials, whom she denounced as "deaf for so long to the horrific misery and cries for help of the victims in New Orleans—most of them poor and black."

Finally, Dowd did her part to perpetuate media exaggerations of mayhem in New Orleans. She described the city as "a snake pit of anarchy, death, looting, raping, marauding thugs, suffering innocents, a shattered infrastructure, a gutted police force, insufficient troop levels and criminally negligent government planning."

Such ad hominem attacks were echoed by the entertainment industry. During a benefit for hurricane victims on NBC, rapper Kanye West wailed, "George Bush doesn't care about black people!" At a similar fund-raiser, singer Bette Midler called the president a cocaine addict and admonished the Republican Party, "Go f— yourself!"

On September 15, Bush gave a prime-time speech to the nation from the empty, flooded city of New Orleans.

"It was not a normal hurricane—and the normal disaster relief system was not equal to it," he acknowledged. "The system, at every level of government, was not well-coordinated, and was overwhelmed in the first few days. It is now clear that a challenge on this scale requires greater federal authority and a broader role for the armed forces—the institution of our government most capable of massive logistical operations on a moment's notice."

Bush was essentially telling his critics, "You want to blame me? Fine. I'll take the hit. But now I'm going to increase the powers of the presidency and the Pentagon to make sure this never happens again." The move recalled Bush's implementation of the Patriot Act in the wake of September 11, giving greater powers to federal law enforcement authorities.

Sensing they had overplayed their hand, Democrats belatedly tried to tone down the savagery of their attacks. They realized the spectacle of so many critics piling on Bush was unseemly to the public. Democrat Donna Brazile, who had run Al Gore's 2000 campaign against Bush, even praised the president's New Orleans speech.

"After watching him speak from the heart, I could not have been prouder of the president and the plan he outlined to empower those who lost everything and to rebuild the Gulf Coast," wrote Brazile in the *Washington Post*.

"Mr. President, I am ready for duty," added the black New Orleans native. "Let's roll up our sleeves and get to work."

But Bush was already working full-time on disaster relief. He signed $10.5 billion in emergency aid, the largest such package in history, and promised tens of billions more. He dispatched thousands of federal troops to assist the National Guardsmen. He steadfastly refused to engage in the blame game. But the same could not be said of officials from Louisiana.

"I intend to find out why the federal—particularly the response of FEMA—was so incompetent and insulting to the people of our states," Landrieu said. "I am not going to level criticism at the local level."

Landrieu then accused Bush of blaming local and state officials for the botched evacuation—something he had not done.

"If one person criticizes them or says one more thing—including the president of the United States—he will hear from me," she told ABC during a helicopter tour of New Orleans on September 4. "One more word about it after this show airs and I might likely have to punch him—literally."

Having just committed a federal crime by threatening bodily injury to the president, Landrieu once again burst into sobs as she looked down at workers repairing the 17th Street Levee.

"The president could have funded it," she said. "He cut it out of the budget. Is that the most pitiful sight you have ever seen in your life? One little crane."

Landrieu would later admit on the FOX News Channel that Bush had allocated more funding for New Orleans levees than had President Clinton. But first she felt compelled to take a potshot at Bush for daring to visit the city in the first place.

"Our infrastructure is devastated, lives have been shattered," Landrieu said. "Would the president please stop taking photo-ops?"

Such criticism stunned Ken Mehlman, who had managed the president's reelection campaign and was now chairman of the Republican National Committee.

"It's outrageous and unprecedented," he told me. "There's never been a time in American history before where leaders of a national party would use a natural disaster to point fingers instead of lending a hand. It's absolutely unprecedented. And the response of the mainstream media is unbelievable in the amount of things they got wrong.

"What it indicates is the extent to which politics has become bloodsport for those on the other side. Were there people in the '90s who did it for us? Yes, and they were wrong. Does that mean I think it was wrong to impeach Clinton? No. Clinton lied under oath. But there were people on our side, clearly, who took sport at personally attacking people as opposed to attacking their ideas. I'm never for that. And we never do that here."

The Left placed all the blame for the Katrina debacle on Bush and none on the local and state officials. Yet a Gallup poll revealed that only 13 percent of Americans blamed Bush, while nearly twice as many—25 percent—blamed local and state officials.

Bush made it clear that he was willing to accept his share of the blame.

"Katrina exposed serious problems in our response capability at all levels of government," he told reporters at the White House. "To the extent the federal government didn't fully do its job right, I take responsibility."

He manifested that responsibility by relieving "Brownie" of his duties on the Gulf Coast and summoning him back to Washington, where the FEMA director resigned. The mainstream media was triumphant. "How Bush Blew It," blared the headline in *Newsweek*. *Time* magazine suggested the out-of-touch president had been "living too much in the bubble." Both newsweeklies clucked that Bush did not grasp the magnitude of the disaster that was clear to the rest of America until a staffer gave him a DVD of TV coverage highlights.

Chris Matthews of MSNBC's *Hardball* was downright gleeful about Bush's "slowness to act."

"The president admitted that he hadn't given enough attention to this appointment, to who he put at FEMA," the Democrat crowed inaccurately. "He didn't give enough attention initially to Katrina."

Such gloating was too much for Matthews's guest, Republican congressman Peter King of New York.

"Chris, there is sort of a frenzy here by the media," King said. "Let's not forget the incompetence of the mayor of New Orleans, the governor of New Orleans. They were the ones in the first instance who were required to do the job, and they didn't.

"As far as President Bush, it's wrong for you to say he wasn't caring. He certainly was caring. What he was not equipped for was to explain for the incompetency of the local officials or to explain the hysteria, anticipate the hysteria created by people like you in the media who go off the deep end. Let's treat this with a little bit of rationality and a little bit of decency."

Matthews felt compelled to defend the press.

"The fact is that most people trust the media on this story, because the pictures of what was happening down there in New Orleans apparently got to them before they heard of any federal action," he protested.

King was unimpressed.

"Chris, you are totally distorting reality. And that's the problem with you. You are distorting reality. You are on the story. You and MSNBC have [become] carried away with this. You should all be ashamed of yourselves. You have disgraced yourself and the media."

Matthews appeared shell-shocked. He was being dressed down on national television by someone who could actually talk faster than he could.

"I'm talking about distorting President Bush's role," King continued. "Somehow, this was almost entirely blamed on him. That was a certain impression given by the media from the very first moment, when the levees broke. And you had Andrea Mitchell on, talking about how that was because President Bush didn't put enough money into the water projects in Louisiana, or the levee control projects, when it turns out that he put more money in, in his first five years, than Bill Clinton did in his last five years.

"There was much more focus put on what President Bush was supposedly not doing, when the fact is it was the mayor who didn't provide the trucks, the buses to evacuate the people, sent the people to the Superdome without adequate food or water. And then also, there's the governor."

King launched into a discussion of how Blanco had predicted that a storm of this magnitude would kill twenty thousand people.

"The fact is, so far there's less than eight hundred," he said. "Every death is tragic, but why isn't your story: 'Less than 4 percent of those who were supposed to have been killed were . . . because of the efforts of the federal government'? The Coast Guard, remember, is part of Homeland Security. They were in the very first day rescuing thousands and thousands of people. That's just an example of the distortion. It's continuing today."

Matthews was incredulous.

"Do you believe that the president was on top of this matter from the time after the hurricane hit, Hurricane Katrina hit?" the host said. "Do you think it's fair to give the guy good ratings for the way he responded?"

"I think it's good to give him at least adequate ratings, because he was relying on what everyone, including page one of the *New York Times*, said, which was that New Orleans had ducked the storm," King said. "It wasn't until Tuesday that we realized how bad the situation was. And by then, the president had no way of knowing that the New Orleans police and fire departments were going to disappear, that the governor wasn't going to adequately use the National Guard, and that the mayor had not put sufficient water and food into the Superdome. It takes a good thirty-six to forty-eight hours to move troops, the amount that were necessary, to provide relief in the Superdome."

Matthews then expressed outrage that "the president had to be shown a DVD" of hurricane television coverage.

"Weren't you dismayed," he said, "that the president of the United States didn't watch television for all those forty-eight hours? That he had to be shown a picture of what we'd all been watching?"

Before King could answer, Matthews began patting himself on the back.

"I'm very proud of the media this last couple of weeks," he said. "We're not always perfect, but I've got to tell you something. The latest polling shows almost 80 percent of the American people say the media has done a fabulous job in handling this hurricane. Because it's the pictures that people have seen on television, in their homes, that have alerted them to this tragedy. And maybe to a large extent, push the politicians to move a little faster."

"The fact is, Chris, you guys are giving yourselves too much credit," King said. "You guys dwell in self-congratulation. The fact is, the media's shots were distortive—"

"No," Matthews interrupted. "It's rare that we have anything to congratulate. Most of the time, people give us—"

"Chris, you won't give me a chance to answer the questions," King said. "Just because the president doesn't watch you on television, it doesn't mean he's not doing his job. You know, Franklin Roosevelt wasn't hired to listen to radio accounts of D-Day. You're hired to do the job, and the president can do his job without having to listen to Chris Matthews or Andrea Mitchell or Tim Russert, or any of the others. He is doing his job.

"Now I agree the military should have been brought in sooner," King conceded. "But that was primarily the fault of the local government not being more responsive. And then the president did the best he could. Could he have been there a few hours earlier? Perhaps. But nowhere near the criticism he's getting from you people."

Incredibly, every aspect of Rush Limbaugh's dire prophecy had come true. The Left *had* figured out a way to blame President Bush for a natural disaster. Democrats had started with global warming, just as Limbaugh predicted, and then worked themselves into hysterical rants about Bull Connor in the White House. Even the mainstream media's apocalyptic exaggerations had been foreshadowed by the talk-show oracle.

"I predicted this, folks," Limbaugh reminded his vast audience. "It's exactly what I told you was going to happen."

Less than a month after Katrina brutalized the Gulf Coast, residents braced for the arrival of another powerful storm—this one named Rita. At that precise moment, Nagin was determined to bring upwards of 180,000 people— a third of the city's population—back to their waterlogged homes. Experts said it was premature, and Bush urged the mayor to reconsider.

"There is deep concern about this storm causing more flooding in New Orleans," the president said of Rita. "The mayor has got this dream about having a city up and running. And we share that dream. But we also want to be realistic about some of the hurdles and obstacles that we all confront in repopulating New Orleans."

Nagin resisted the president's advice, even when the warning was repeated by Coast Guard vice admiral Thad Allen, the president's replacement for Michael Brown as onsite relief director.

"Maybe he's the new crowned federal mayor of New Orleans," Nagin complained bitterly on FOX News.

But by the end of the day, the mayor reversed course and halted the repopulation of New Orleans. Sure enough, Rita brought torrential rains that broke through the levees, reflooding poor black neighborhoods that had just been pumped dry.

Naturally, the Left refused to give the president any credit. In fact, after accusing Bush of responding too slowly to Katrina, the press now accused him of responding too quickly to Rita. *Newsweek* critiqued his performance with an article headlined "First, a slow-footed response. Then: hyperactivity." *Time* complained the president's frequent trips to the Gulf Coast were "making him look too cloying and calculating." NBC News said he risked looking like a "political opportunist" by returning to the disaster zone so often.

"I mean, what can you actually do?" NBC's David Gregory sniped to the president. "I mean, isn't there a risk of you and your entourage getting in the way?"

Undaunted, Bush made his seventh trip to the region on September 27. That was the final straw for Democratic political analyst Bob Beckel.

"The guy's been there enough times that he could register to vote," Beckel groused. "I mean, enough is enough, okay?"

CHAPTER SEVENTEEN

ALITO A-GO-GO

This time, young Jack Roberts sat obediently in his chair. Oh, he was still lighting up the White House with that million-dollar smile of his. But now his every move was being carefully monitored by his sister, Josie, who sat next to him in the front row of the East Room with an expression of mild trepidation. In the ten weeks since Jack first appeared on the State Dining Room floor, the towheaded toddler had become something of a celebrity in official Washington. His break-dancing performance had been featured on Comedy Central's *Daily Show*. His crawl through the State Dining Room had been replayed on FOX News and CNN. When he accompanied Daddy into the Senate Judiciary hearings, he got to shake hands with a big, red-faced, white-haired senator named Teddy. Even at home in Chevy Chase, whenever Jack pressed his nose against the front window, someone outside the house would take his picture. And now he was back in the White House, nattily dressed in a black suit, complete with short pants—as if to tweak the *Washington Post*. Josie was resplendent in a pale blue dress and matching bow in her blonde hair. This time around, there were a lot more people in the room, including Jack's grandparents and aunts and other relatives. Also on hand were the First Lady, vice president, attorney general, assorted senators, and seven Supreme Court justices. There were two grandmotherly ladies whom everyone referred to as Mrs. Thurgood Marshall and Mrs. Potter Stewart. And of course there were Mommy and Daddy who, as usual, were over by the blue goose with the president and some really old guy in a bow tie.

"This is a proud day for John Roberts's family," Bush was saying. "We extend a special welcome to his wife, Jane, their daughter, Josie, and son, Jack."

The president shot the boy a playful look, as if to say, "I'm well aware that you're a shameless ham." Knowing laughter filled the room as Bush added, "A fellow who is comfortable with the cameras." More appreciative laughter before the mood turned serious.

"It was nineteen years ago, almost to the day, that Chief Justice William Rehnquist took the oath of office in this very room with President Ronald Reagan as a witness," Bush said. "In a few moments, John Roberts will take his place in a distinguished line that began in 1789, when President Washington appointed Chief Justice John Jay."

Although Roberts had originally been chosen to replace Sandra Day O'Connor, his nomination was upgraded to chief justice in the wake of Rehnquist's death. That put an end to talk of Bush promoting Scalia or Thomas, a move that would have required another round of potentially rancorous hearings before the Senate Judiciary Committee. That was fine with Bush, who figured two rounds were plenty anyway. The first round had gone extremely well; Roberts had deftly charmed senators while telling them nothing controversial. Whenever someone reminded Roberts that he had argued against abortion while working as a young lawyer in the Reagan administration, the nominee would explain that he had merely been advocating a position on behalf of a client. As for his personal views on abortion, Roberts shrewdly invoked the "Ginsburg precedent" and kept his mouth shut. As a result, the Senate confirmed him 78–22, with all Republicans and half the Democrats voting for him. The second round of hearings had not yet been scheduled, of course, because Bush had not yet selected another nominee. And he was not about to take that step until after Roberts was safely sworn in. Meanwhile, O'Connor agreed to remain on the bench until a replacement could be found. After all, it was already September 29, and the court would begin its session on the first Monday in October.

"The incoming chief justice will carry on in the tradition of his mentor and friend, the late William H. Rehnquist," Bush said. "I know that Chief Justice Rehnquist had hoped to welcome his former law clerk as a colleague. Although that was not meant to be, we are thinking of William Rehnquist today."

The president then stepped from behind the blue goose to watch Roberts take the oath of office from eighty-five-year-old Justice John Paul Stevens, who had been on the court nearly thirty years. In fact, as the oldest and longest-serving member of the court, Stevens would have become acting chief justice if Bush had not elevated Roberts to the job. Given Stevens's status as the most liberal member of the court, however, even a temporary elevation to chief justice was never seriously contemplated by the president.

After taking the oath, Roberts stepped to the blue goose and thanked those in attendance, including members of the Senate Judiciary Committee.

"With this nomination, the committee faced a very special challenge," Roberts said. "And yet, working together, we met that challenge. We found a way to get Jack into the committee room, introduced to the committee, and back out again—without any serious crisis."

Bush laughed along with everyone else, although the true source of his mirth was the fact that he had managed to get Roberts confirmed without any serious crisis of his own. It was an amazing accomplishment, when you got right down to it. George W. Bush had just presided over the flawless installation of only the seventeenth chief justice in the nation's history. With any luck, the youthful and vigorous fifty-year-old would help shape American society for the next quarter century—perhaps longer. Even more amazing was the fact that the scorched-earth political warfare that everyone had predicted never materialized. Senators on both sides of the aisle had actually heeded the president's calls for a "dignified" and "civilized" confirmation process. In fact, some Senate Democrats were now giving Bush friendly advice on his next nomination. They were urging him to look "outside the judicial monastery." The president liked the sound of that phrase. It appealed to his sense of rugged individualism—something he acquired while growing up in Texas. Maybe the Democrats were on to something. Maybe they were finally hearing his calls for change in the partisan tone in Washington. From the beginning Bush had wanted to drain Washington of partisan rancor and make the nation's capital more like Austin, where, when he was governor, debate had been friendlier and more constructive. And to think Bush had nearly given up on his quest to elevate the discourse in Washington, only to stumble on the magic formula this late in the game.

Such self-confidence—perhaps even hubris—contributed to the president's decision for his next Supreme Court pick. Discarding the list of the usual constitutional brainiacs, Bush decided to try something really unexpected. Instead of choosing another federal judge like Roberts, he would select someone who had never served on a bench. Someone who hadn't attended the usual Ivy League schools, studied the usual constitutional cases, or clerked for the usual Supreme Court justices. Someone who would bring a different sort of life experience to the job. Someone from the great state of Texas, which—come to think of it—had no representation on the high court.

And so, on the first Monday in October, even before Roberts took his center seat on the Supreme Court, the president walked into the Oval Office to announce his much-anticipated nomination.

"I considered a wide variety of distinguished Americans from different walks of life," he said. "We consulted with Democrats and Republicans in the United States Senate. We received good advice from more than eighty senators. And once again, one person stood out as exceptionally well suited to sit on the highest court of our nation.

"This morning, I'm proud to announce that I am nominating Harriet Ellan Miers to serve as associate justice of the Supreme Court."

Huh?

Miers was the White House counsel, also known as the president's lawyer. Her name had been suggested to Bush by Senate Minority Leader Harry Reid, of all people. The Nevada Democrat had gotten to know Miers when she helped shepherd Bush's judicial nominees, including Roberts, through the Senate confirmation process. Along the way, Reid and other Senate Democrats built up a good rapport with the sixty-year-old, soft-spoken Miers, who had a law degree from Southern Methodist University. Bush figured those Democrats would now find it hard to oppose her. On this point, he was correct.

What Bush failed to anticipate, however, was the possibility that his own party would be less than thrilled with his selection. Conservatives had been fiercely loyal to the president for nearly five years, even when he crossed them on immigration and disappointed them by expanding the size of the federal government. But the Supreme Court was the institution that would likely decide the nation's most divisive and important issue—abortion. And Miers, while she sounded like a nice lady and was certainly an accomplished lawyer, did not exactly strike conservatives as another Antonin Scalia.

"Disappointed, depressed, and demoralized" was the way *Weekly Standard* editor Bill Kristol described himself on the conservative magazine's website that morning.

"There is no evidence that she is among the leading lights of American jurisprudence, or that she possesses talents commensurate with the Supreme Court's tasks," wrote conservative columnist George Will.

Republican senators were similarly nonplussed.

"There are a lot more people—men, women, and minorities—that are more qualified, in my opinion, by their experience than she is," said Republican senator Trent Lott of Mississippi on MSNBC. "Right now, I'm not satisfied with what I know. I'm not comfortable with the nomination."

In an effort to counter such doubts, Miers spent long hours in "murder boards," or practice sessions designed to prepare her for the grueling confirmation hearings before the Senate Judiciary Committee. Bush administration officials peppered her with questions about constitutional law in a room at the

Justice Department. But it quickly became apparent that she was no John Roberts.

"She needs more than murder boards," Senate Judiciary Committee chairman Arlen Specter told the *New York Times*. "She needs a crash course in constitutional law."

Bush bristled at such complaints.

"She is plenty bright," he insisted to reporters in the Rose Garden. "People are going to be amazed at her strength of character and her intellect."

But even the press wasn't buying it.

"Of all the people in the United States you had to choose from, is Harriet Miers the most qualified to serve on the Supreme Court?" a reporter asked with obvious incredulity.

"Yes," the president snapped. "Otherwise I wouldn't have put her on."

Bush regarded Miers's lack of a judicial record as an asset. After all, there was no paper trail of rulings that might give ammunition to hostile senators.

"It's important to bring somebody from outside the system, the judicial system, somebody that hasn't been on the bench and, therefore, there's not a lot of opinions for people to look at," the president reasoned.

At the same time, he was beseeching conservatives to trust him on Miers because he had known her for more than a decade and was confident she was a solid conservative.

"I know her, I know her heart. I know what she believes," he said. "Because of our closeness, I know the character of the person. It's one thing to say a person can read the law, and that's important—and understand the law. But what also matters [are] the intangibles. To me, a person's strength of character counts a lot. And as a result of my friendship with Harriet, I know her strength of character."

In case conservatives still didn't get the hint, he added, "She knows the kind of judge I'm looking for—after all, she was a part of the process that selected John Roberts. I don't want somebody to go on the bench to try to supplant the legislative process. I'm interested in people that will be strict constructionists."

But conservatives had been burned too many times by Republican presidents whose inscrutable Supreme Court appointees turned out to be liberals. Particularly leery were Republican senators who were planning their own bids for the White House in 2008. These men were reluctant to blindly trust Bush on an issue that was being closely watched by presidential primary voters.

"I want to be assured that she is not going to be another Souter," Republican senator George Allen of Virginia told the *New York Times.* "I understand the president knows her well, but I don't."

His doubts were echoed by Republican senator Sam Brownback of Kansas, another presidential hopeful.

"We've seen a past pattern where people without a set judicial philosophy go on the bench and veer left over time," he told National Public Radio.

"There is so much that rides on the line," he said. "This could possibly— probably will be—the swing vote on any number of key cases."

Chief among those, of course, was *Roe.*

"We don't know her viewpoint on that issue or a number of others— marriage, God in the public square, private property rights," Brownback said. "And yet those are such critical, core issues."

Since Miers refused to discuss how she might rule on these issues, she did little to inspire confidence during courtesy calls to senators on Capitol Hill. After a private, one-hour meeting with Brownback, the senator emerged to say he might vote against her.

White House officials tried to reassure conservatives by pointing out that Miers was a born-again Christian who belonged to a strongly pro-life church. They even resorted to a trick usually employed by Democrats—labeling the nominee's detractors sexist. But that only further inflamed conservatives, who were amassing a growing body of evidence against the nominee. In 1988, Miers gave $1,000 to the presidential campaign of Democrat Al Gore. In 1993, she gave a speech that seemed to explain abortion as a manifestation of women's "self-determination."

Democrats were delighted by the rift among Republicans. They decided to sit back and let conservatives slug it out. It was a rare and impressive display of discipline from a party that had overplayed its hand on so many other issues, ranging from Cindy Sheehan to Memogate to Vietnam nostalgia.

The situation degenerated even further on October 19, when the Senate Judiciary Committee told Miers to redo her answers to parts of a questionnaire because her initial responses were incomplete and in some cases even "insulting." Two days later, conservatives told the *Washington Times* that the White House had begun making contingency plans for Miers's withdrawal. Although Bush officials denied the report, the handwriting was on the wall.

On the morning of October 27, Bush was quietly informed by Senate Majority Leader Bill Frist that the Miers nomination was in trouble. Even the handful of religious conservative leaders who had initially supported her were starting to turn. Frist, who was mulling a run for president in 2008, reiterated his concerns in a call to White House chief of staff Andy Card at 9:30 p.m. But by then it was already over.

Miers had withdrawn her nomination an hour earlier during a phone call to the president. In a transparent effort to save face, the administration blamed the debacle on the Senate's demands for White House documents that were protected by executive privilege. But the truth was all too obvious. After the flawless rollout of John Roberts, the president had stumbled badly in trying to install his old friend on the highest court in the land.

Bush told me the setback was particularly painful because he was so close to Miers.

"I was sad," he confided. "I thought Harriet didn't get a fair shake, that people jumped to conclusions about Harriet before she had a chance to make her case."

The president said his sentiments were shared by many in the White House.

"A lot of people were very disappointed that she withdrew," he told me. "A lot of people didn't like the treatment she was receiving. And the reason why they were disappointed and didn't like the treatment is because they love Harriet as a person. She is a remarkable person."

Instead of hanging her head and awkwardly waiting for sympathy from her colleagues in the West Wing, Miers smiled and tried to buck up *their* spirits. Still, that didn't change the fact that Bush had just suffered through the first open rebellion of conservatives since he had taken office.

"Did you misjudge their loyalty?" I asked.

"People should stand on principle based upon what they believe, not based upon they should be loyal to me," he said. "I was just disappointed for her, as much as anything else. But I understand people who believe strongly about something will speak out about it. And that's just part of the process."

The president told me he remained confident that if Miers had made it to the hearings, she would have been confirmed. He called her "a class act," adding, "Thank goodness my lawyer is back."

But less than forty-eight hours after getting his lawyer back, Bush suffered a second major setback. A federal grand jury indicted Vice President Dick Cheney's chief of staff, Lewis "Scooter" Libby, who immediately resigned from the White House to fight the charges. Libby was accused of lying to investigators who were looking into whether the White House had leaked the identity of CIA employee Valerie Plame.

It was a convoluted case. Back in February 2002, Plame learned that Vice President Cheney's office had asked the CIA to investigate reports that Iraq tried to purchase uranium from Niger. She persuaded her bosses at the CIA to assign the mission to her husband, retired diplomat Joseph Wilson. Wilson was dispatched to Niger, although he didn't exactly crack the case. In fact, by his own admission, he barely cracked a sweat.

"I spent the next eight days drinking sweet mint tea and meeting with dozens of people," he mused in a *New York Times* column on July 6, 2003. "Niger formally denied the charges."

Thus satisfied by his own due diligence, Wilson proceeded to publicly excoriate the Bush administration for invading Iraq.

"The intelligence related to Iraq's nuclear weapons program was twisted to exaggerate the Iraqi threat," he wrote in the *Times*.

Wilson was far from an objective fact-finder. Although he had served in the administration of former president George H. W. Bush, he went on to work for President Clinton and later became an outspoken critic of the younger Bush. He publicly opposed the invasion of Iraq and denounced the president's "imperial ambitions" in the left-wing magazine *The Nation*. In his *New York Times* column, he conveniently omitted the fact that his junket to Niger had been arranged by his own wife. Indeed, he insinuated that he had been sent on this vital mission by no less than Cheney himself.

"The vice president's office asked a serious question. I was asked to help formulate the answer. I did so," Wilson huffed in one of three references to Cheney.

Although Cheney was accustomed to taking heat over the Iraq war, he did not appreciate Wilson implying he had been personally dispatched by the vice president. Sure, Cheney had asked the CIA to look into the Niger case, but he didn't know the CIA would end up sending the Bush-hating husband of an agency employee. Worse yet, Wilson was portraying himself as an antiwar hero, giving countless interviews to the media and bashing the administration at every opportunity.

Journalists were obliged to seek a rebuttal, so they called Libby. The vice presidential aide tried to set the record straight by explaining to reporters such as Judith Miller of the *New York Times* and Matt Cooper of *Time* that Wilson had been sent to Niger not by the vice president, but by his own wife. This revelation was first published by conservative Robert Novak in his syndicated column on July 14, 2003, although it was not clear whether his source was Libby or someone else.

"Wilson never worked for the CIA, but his wife, Valerie Plame, is an agency operative," Novak wrote. "Two senior administration officials told me Wilson's wife suggested sending him to Niger to investigate."

Wilson complained that the column blew his wife's cover at the CIA, even though she was not considered a covert operative. In fact, he and Plame cashed in on the publicity by posing for a photo spread in *Vanity Fair* magazine. Wilson saw nothing hypocritical about appearing with his supposedly undercover wife in a national magazine while publicly blaming the disclosure of her identity on Karl Rove.

"It's of keen interest to me to see whether or not we can get Karl Rove frog-marched out of the White House in handcuffs," Wilson told an audience in Seattle. "And trust me, when I use that name, I measure my words."

But it turned out Wilson had not measured his words, because he soon backpedaled from this accusation. He explained that he had mentioned Rove as "kind of a metaphor for the White House." Still, he added, "I have every confidence that Karl Rove condoned it and did nothing to shut this off."

Wilson's complaints prompted an investigation by the Justice Department, which assigned the case to Patrick Fitzgerald, a hard-charging prosecutor from Chicago. Fitzgerald was named special counsel and spent more than two years asking journalists and administration officials to reveal their conversations with each other. At one point he jailed Miller for eighty-five days for refusing to testify about her conversations with Libby. He also threatened to jail Cooper, although this was averted at the last moment when *Time* editor in chief Norman Pearlstine agreed to turn over Cooper's notes against the reporter's will. This allowed the *New York Times* to seize the moral high ground, from which publisher Arthur Sulzberger Jr. sniffed that he was "deeply disappointed" by *Time*'s capitulation. He added sanctimoniously, "Our focus is now on our own reporter, Judith Miller, and in supporting her during this difficult time."

In October 2005, Fitzgerald appeared to be finally wrapping up his investigation. The federal grand jury hearing his case was scheduled to be dismissed at the end of the month. This prompted a frenzy of media speculation that Fitzgerald was about to indict not only Libby, but also Rove—who had appeared before the grand jury four times—and perhaps even Cheney. Some commentators actually predicted the scandal would reach into the very Oval Office and bring down the president. MSNBC's Chris Matthews kept hyperventilating about the CIA leak case being another Watergate. The press preemptively lionized Fitzgerald. The *New York Times* gushed that he was "Eliot Ness with a Harvard degree." *People* magazine ranked him among the "sexiest men alive."

But on October 28, Fitzgerald disclosed that after more than two years of investigating, he was not charging anyone with leaking Valerie Plame's identity.

In fact, he was not charging Bush, Cheney, or Rove with any crime at all—or even suggesting they had done anything wrong. Instead, Fitzgerald was reduced to going after the most obscure figure in the scandal, a vice presidential aide named "Scooter" who had been virtually unknown to anyone outside the Beltway until now. Unable to come up with sufficient evidence to charge Libby with actually outing a CIA agent, Fitzgerald contented himself with accusing the vice presidential aide of lying to investigators.

Not that Libby had denied disclosing the Plame connection to reporters. To the contrary, he freely admitted making such disclosures and Fitzgerald freely admitted he could find nothing illegal about it. Hence, the prosecutor resorted to charging Libby with lying about how he first learned this information. Libby said he learned it from other reporters, while Fitzgerald said he learned it from other government officials. In other words, Fitzgerald was splitting hairs.

"Mr. Libby's story that he was at the *tail end* of a chain of phone calls— passing on to one reporter what he heard from another—was not true. It was false," Fitzgerald thundered at a triumphant news conference. "He was at the *beginning* of the chain of phone calls, the *first official* to disclose this information outside the government *to a reporter*."

This disclosure, according to Fitzgerald, took place on June 23, 2003.

"Libby was the first official known to have told a reporter when he talked to Judith Miller. And then he lied about it afterwards, under oath and repeatedly!"

Fitzgerald's accusation, however, quickly unraveled. Within days, a senior government official contacted the special counsel and claimed to have divulged the Plame connection to another reporter *before Libby disclosed it to Miller*. And it wasn't just any other reporter. It was the most famous reporter in America—Bob Woodward of the *Washington Post*. "Eliot Ness" Fitzgerald's supposedly exhaustive two-year investigation had missed a bombshell. He now sheepishly went through the motions of calling in Woodward for questioning. Sure enough, Woodward confirmed that he had been told about the Plame connection by another government official at least a week before Libby told Miller. After being questioned by Fitzgerald for more than two hours,

Woodward went public, blowing a very large hole through the prosecutor's case against Libby.

"The person told me Wilson's wife worked for the CIA," Woodward said of his source, whom he declined to identify, in a lengthy statement published in the *Post*. "I testified that the reference seemed to me to be casual and off-hand, and that it did not appear to me to be either classified or sensitive. I testified that according to my understanding an analyst in the CIA is not normally an undercover position."

As if to add insult to Fitzgerald's injury, Woodward further testified that after learning of the Plame connection from his source, he had several conversations with Libby, who never saw fit to mention the subject. And yet these conversations took place at precisely the time when Libby, according to Fitzgerald, was supposedly smearing Wilson by telling every reporter within earshot he had been sent to Niger by his wife, a CIA analyst.

Ironically, the probe that was supposed to discredit Bush was now discrediting the president's very detractors. Fitzgerald had humiliated himself by falsely accusing Libby of being "the first official to disclose this information outside the government to a reporter." Now the whole world knew that some other official had disclosed this information earlier to the vaunted Bob Woodward.

Not that Woodward came out of this smelling like a rose. It turned out he neglected to tell his own editors for more than two years that he had been informed by the Bush administration of the Plame connection, and evidently before anyone else. Woodward sat silently as his colleagues at the *Post*—not to mention every other mainstream media news outlet—relentlessly pursued the Plame story for twenty-eight long months. He didn't utter a peep until after Libby was falsely accused of being the first government official to tell a reporter about the Plame connection. Only then did Woodward contact his source, who in turn alerted Fitzgerald.

"What did Bob Woodward know, and when did he know it?" asked Jack Shafer of *Slate*, a liberal online magazine.

Incredibly, liberal reporters were now attacking Woodward with the very battle cry he had invoked while bringing down Richard Nixon in the Watergate scandal. Three decades later, Woodward was getting a taste of his own medicine. And his reaction was downright Nixonian.

"I hunkered down," Woodward muttered to fellow *Post* reporter Howard Kurtz. "I'm in the habit of keeping secrets. I didn't want anything out there that was going to get me subpoenaed."

His boss was unimpressed.

"Those are not sufficient reasons for not bringing me into his confidence," complained *Post* executive editor Leonard Downie, Jr. on MSNBC. "He should have told me about it."

He added that Woodward had "always kept me informed about the important things he's discovered in his reporting. This is the first time that I can recall in the thirty years of this relationship that he's failed to tell us something that he should have told us."

Sufficiently chastened, Woodward slunk into Downie's office and apologized.

"I should have told him about this much sooner," he later told Kurtz.

But his failure to disclose his involvement in the case was not the only blunder by Woodward. It turned out that he had also been publicly trashing Fitzgerald on television and radio without informing the audience of his own involvement in the CIA leak case. Woodward had called Fitzgerald "a junkyard dog" whose behavior was "disgraceful" and whose investigation was a joke. Media critics who had spent decades fawning over Woodward now pounced.

"Since he knew he had information that was relevant and he chose not to disclose that information for reasons he said had to do with confidentiality, it's odd that he would rip into the prosecutor so publicly and so persistently," scolded Marvin Kalb of Harvard University's Kennedy School of Government to Reuters.

Jane Kirtley, director of the Silha Center for the Study of Media Ethics and Law, told the wire service that Woodward was guilty of "a genuine ethical breach."

This gave Downie a second reason to take Woodward to the woodshed.

"I've also told him that when he appears on television, he's not supposed to state his personal opinion," Downie told Chris Matthews on *Hardball*. "That's a policy of the *Post*."

The newspaper's ombudsman, Deborah Howell, said Woodward was guilty of "deeply serious" journalistic sins that "put the paper in the terrible light."

"The *Post* took a hit to its credibility," she wrote in the paper on November 20. "Many readers think Woodward ought to be fired or disciplined." She added, "Disappointment was rife in the *Post*'s newsroom."

So was resentment.

"While Woodward is listed as an assistant managing editor, he has no management duties. He comes and goes as he pleases, mostly writing his best-selling books," Howell groused. "He has to operate under the rules that govern the rest of us—even if he's rich and famous."

Such slaps on the wrist did not satisfy Joseph Wilson, who demanded the *Post* launch a full-blown investigation into why its most famous reporter publicly criticized the Fitzgerald probe without disclosing his involvement.

"It certainly gives the appearance of a conflict of interest," Wilson told Reuters. "He was taking an advocacy position when he was a party to it."

It wasn't long before journalists were comparing Woodward to Miller, who had just been forced out of her job at the *New York Times* over the scandal. Her colleagues at the *Times*, who initially lauded her willingness to go to prison rather than reveal Libby as her source, soon turned on Miller for having been too close to the Bush administration and for having written too many prewar stories about how Iraq was teeming with weapons of mass destruction. *Times* columnist Maureen Dowd went so far as to publicly label her colleague a "woman of mass destruction" whose jail stint was an attempt at "career rehabilitation." When *New York Times* executive editor Bill Keller sent the *Times* staff an e-mail saying Miller had "misled" her editor about her involvement in the Plame case, the reporter's fate was sealed. Her twenty-eight-year career at the *Times* was terminated less than four months after Sulzberger, the paper's publisher, had piously boasted of "supporting her during this difficult time."

Such was the carnage of the vaunted Fitzgerald investigation. Instead of bringing down the Bush administration with a scandal of Watergate proportions, the prosecutor had managed to smear one obscure aide with a demonstrably untrue accusation. In the process, he had severely damaged his own credibility. The only other victims of the debacle were journalists, the very people who had openly wished for heads to roll—and in the process revealed the intra-staff jealousies and hatreds at the *Washington Post* and the *New York Times*.

Three days after the Libby indictment, Bush steered the national conversation back to the Supreme Court. On the last Monday in October, he nominated a new replacement for Justice Sandra Day O'Connor: federal appeals court judge Samuel A. Alito Jr. The announcement did not please CBS News, which kicked off the debate with a particularly low blow.

"The president said repeatedly that Harriet Miers was the best person for the job," CBS reporter John Roberts reminded press secretary Scott McClellan at the White House. "So does that mean that Alito is sloppy seconds?"

The Drudge Report immediately posted this unfortunate sexual reference, forcing Roberts to apologize to McClellan.

Meanwhile, conservatives were overjoyed that the chastened president had chosen a candidate with impeccable credentials. Alito came armed with degrees from Princeton and Yale, experience as a Reagan administration lawyer arguing a dozen cases before the Supreme Court, and a strong judicial record since his appointment to the federal bench in 1989 by President George H. W. Bush.

Democrats who had taken delight in the GOP civil war over Miers now realized that the fifty-five-year-old Alito posed a much greater threat to liberal orthodoxy. To complicate matters, it was difficult for Democrats to attack Alito on the all-important issue of abortion. After all, he had sided with abortion proponents in three of four rulings during his fifteen years as a judge on the Third U.S. Circuit Court of Appeals in Philadelphia. Granted, those rul-

ings were based not on the central question of whether the Constitution provided the right to abortion, but rather on technical issues and existing legal
precedent. Moreover, federal appeals court judges routinely deferred to precedent, while Supreme Court justices *made* precedent. Yet Alito's supporters
tried to confound critics by citing his abortion rulings as evidence that he had
no intention of overturning *Roe v. Wade*.

I decided to help clarify the issue. Two weeks after the president selected
Alito, I published a document that significantly escalated the debate over the
nominee's fitness for the Supreme Court. It was nothing less than the personal political manifesto of Alito himself, issued twenty years earlier, when
the young career lawyer was seeking his first political appointment in the Reagan White House. Eager to demonstrate his conservative bona fides, Alito
wrote in clear, unambiguous language that "the Constitution does not protect a right to an abortion."

"I personally believe very strongly" in this legal position, Alito wrote on
his application to become deputy assistant to Attorney General Edwin I.
Meese III.

Disclosure of this document meant that Alito would not be able to tell the
Senate Judiciary Committee, as Roberts had done, that he was merely advocating for his client, the Reagan administration. Alito had gone much further
with this document, which I obtained the day before it was to be publicly
released by the Ronald Reagan Presidential Library. When I splashed the document across the front page of the *Washington Times*, liberals expressed grave
alarm, while conservatives were torn. On the one hand, conservatives were
relieved to have evidence that Alito was one of them. But on the other, they
feared that his cover was now blown.

Alito tried to assuage jittery senators during his courtesy calls to Capitol
Hill by emphasizing that he had written the document years before he
became a judge. He assured them that during his fifteen years on the federal
bench, he had never let his political beliefs creep into his jurisprudence. White
House officials insisted that the document did not necessarily mean Alito
would overturn *Roe*. But liberals pointed out that Alito, in the document, had

also questioned the constitutionality of another hot-button initiative—
affirmative action. Worse yet, Alito made many other declarations that scared
the Left to death.

"I am and always have been a conservative," he wrote. "I am a lifelong registered Republican."

Well, at least the Senate Judiciary Committee would know where Alito
stood when he showed up for his confirmation hearings, which were to begin
in January.

"I believe very strongly in limited government, federalism, free enterprise,
the supremacy of the elected branches of government, the need for a strong
defense and effective law enforcement, and the legitimacy of a government
role in protecting traditional values," he wrote in the application. "In the field
of law, I disagree strenuously with the usurpation by the judiciary of decision-
making authority that should be exercised by the branches of government
responsible to the electorate."

The document also provided the clearest picture of Alito's intellectual
development as a conservative.

"When I first became interested in government and politics during the
1960s, the greatest influences on my views were the writings of William F.
Buckley Jr., the *National Review*, and Barry Goldwater's 1964 campaign," he
wrote. "In college, I developed a deep interest in constitutional law, motivated
in large part by disagreement with Warren Court decisions, particularly in the
areas of criminal procedure, the Establishment Clause, and reapportionment."

That was music to the ears of Republicans, who had long hungered for a
more conservative Supreme Court. Truth be told, Roberts's succession of
Rehnquist had not made the court any more conservative. In fact, as far as
conservatives were concerned, it was no better than an ideological wash. But
Alito's succession of O'Connor was another matter altogether. By replacing a
moderate swing justice with a staunch conservative, the Right would finally
achieve parity with the Left on the nation's highest court.

There would be four conservatives (Roberts, Scalia, Thomas, and, if confirmed, Alito), four liberals (Stevens, Ginsburg, Breyer, and Souter), and one

moderate (Kennedy). This would be a significant step in the right direction, as far as Bush was concerned.

In fact, two days after nominating Alito, the president confided to me that he had inherited a court that was too liberal, too activist, and too reliant on foreign law. But he vowed the situation would be improved by the time he left office.

"I will have named at least two judges who will be highly competent, highly qualified people who will not legislate from the bench, not have a particular end in mind and then conform the law to meet that end," Bush said. "They will be judges, pure and simple. They will represent the third branch of government, whose purpose is to adjudge whether or not laws passed by another branch and signed by another branch meet the guideline which is prescribed in the Constitution. And they will be the same judges twenty years from now that they are today.

"And they will use the Constitution—not the Constitution plus other constitutions overseas—as the guide," he concluded with satisfaction. "They will use *our* Constitution. I'm certain of that."

CHAPTER EIGHTEEN

"CHANGE THE FACE OF THE PLANET"

One year after winning reelection, President Bush discovered that he missed John Kerry. Oh, he didn't miss the constant threat of losing his job to a determined rival. But he did miss having a foil who conveniently epitomized everything the president opposed. John Kerry was the personification of what Bush regarded as the Democratic Party's wrongheaded vision for America. By battling Kerry, day in and day out, for those eight long months of the general election campaign, Bush had been able to remind Americans not only of his own merits, but also of the Democrats' deficiencies. That kept conservatives constantly energized and forced moderates to at least consider that Bush's policies might be superior to those of the Democrats.

But after he won the election, the president figured he could take the high road. He no longer considered it necessary to constantly argue with Democrats over how to move the country forward. And since the biggest argument of the election had been over Iraq, Bush concluded that he had essentially won that round and could move on to other issues. "There's no need to rehash my case," he had said of Iraq at his post-election press conference. "I've got the will of the people at my back." Granted, he never stopped talking about his hopes and aspirations for Iraq's fledgling democracy throughout the following year. But it became a secondary consideration to the president's new hobbyhorse—staving off the bankruptcy of the doomed Social Security system. Day after day, week after week, month after month, Bush crisscrossed the country in a stubborn effort to cajole Congress into finally tackling the long-neglected issue. But Democrats were too bitter about their ongoing loss of political power to grant the president a legislative victory of this magnitude. And Republicans were skittish about tinkering with a retirement system considered sacrosanct by many senior citizens. It eventually became clear that Bush was headed for a rare defeat on a major initiative.

Meanwhile, Democrats never stopped complaining about Iraq. After all, it was easy to highlight problems with the ongoing war while downplaying Iraq's political, economic, and military accomplishments. Indeed, the mainstream media did it every day, with devastating consequences to the president's job approval ratings. By late 2005, the ratings had begun to slip below 40 percent, a level that would have doomed his reelection bid a mere year earlier. More than two-thirds of all Americans now disapproved of his handling of Iraq, according to Gallup. It was a precipitous decline in support from just twenty-nine months earlier, when more than three-quarters of Americans approved of his Iraq policies. Clearly, Bush was losing the nation's moderates.

Not that conservatives were exactly pleased with the president. Their enthusiasm had been waning ever since Bush decided to take the post-election high road, from which he stubbornly refused to answer Democratic attacks on his handling of Iraq. While conservatives remained supportive of the president on this issue, they couldn't help but notice how much political hay the Democrats made when the number of U.S. fatalities in Iraq passed the two thousand mark. On other issues, especially illegal immigration and runaway government spending, conservatives were becoming increasingly restless. They were still smarting over the attempt to install Harriet Miers on the

Supreme Court. They remained unsettled by the indictment of Scooter Libby and the possibility that Rove might also be ensnared in the ongoing CIA leak probe. And they hadn't quite recovered from the savagery of the Left's attacks on the president's response to Hurricane Katrina. Again, it didn't help matters that Bush refused to fire back at his critics.

Thus, by late 2005, Bush found himself every bit as beleaguered as he had been at the outset of the general election campaign, when Abu Ghraib and the ongoing carnage in Iraq seemed to threaten his very presidency. The mainstream media was only too eager to reprise its stories about a snakebitten president failing on every front.

Dan Balz's ostensibly objective front-page news stories for the *Washington Post* were typical. "Bush's administration has become a textbook example of what can go wrong in a second term," Balz wrote on October 29. "Ineffectiveness, overreaching, intra-party rebellion, plunging public confidence, and plain bad luck."

The next day, Balz wrote of "a White House in crisis" and warned that "the route back to genuine recovery is likely to be slow and difficult—and without a clear blueprint for success."

This was followed by a Balz piece asserting that "several pillars of Bush's presidency have begun to crumble under the combined weight of events and White House mistakes."

Emboldened by such gloom-and-doom coverage and deteriorating public support for Bush, Democrats stepped up their rhetoric on Iraq, which they regarded as their best issue for destroying his presidency. The beauty of their position, from a political perspective, was that they could pillory the president's Iraq policy while never offering a clear alternative of their own, since that might be subject to equal criticism. "At the right time, we will have a position," mumbled Representative Rahm Emanuel of Illinois, a former Clinton aide who now chaired the Democratic Congressional Campaign Committee. In the meantime, Democrats contented themselves with relentlessly savaging the president's position. They seized on the indictment of Scooter Libby as vindication of their argument that the White House had taken the country to war on false pretenses. Never mind that the prosecutor himself explicitly rejected any such connection.

"This indictment is not about the war," Patrick Fitzgerald emphasized during his high-profile press conference. "People who believe fervently in the war effort, people who oppose it, people who have mixed feelings about it should not look to this indictment for any resolution of how they feel or any vindication of how they feel."

He added, "The indictment will not seek to prove that the war was justified or unjustified. This is stripped of that debate, and this is focused on a narrow transaction. And I think anyone who's concerned about the war and has feelings for or against shouldn't look to this criminal process for any answers or resolution of that. They will be frustrated and, frankly, it wouldn't be good for the process and the fairness of a trial."

This admonition was summarily ignored by Senate Minority Leader Harry Reid.

"The Libby indictment provides a window into what this is really all about, how this administration manufactured and manipulated intelligence in order to sell the war in Iraq and attempted to destroy those who dared to challenge its actions," the Nevada Democrat said.

On November 1, Reid shocked Republicans by forcing a rare closed session of the Senate. He did so for a secret discussion of what Massachusetts senator Edward Kennedy called "clear manipulation of intelligence in the run-up to the Iraq war." In short, Democrats were giving credence to the Left's mantra "Bush lied, people died."

This was the final straw for the president, who now recognized the folly of his yearlong attempt to take the high road on Iraq. Looking back on that failed experiment, he explained to Brit Hume of FOX News Channel that he had been trying to avoid "dragging the presidency into the name-calling and the finger-pointing and the blaming."

"I just came off an election, and we're trying to elevate the debate and put politics behind and see if that couldn't happen. It didn't happen," he acknowledged. "And we took a blasting."

Even after belatedly recognizing his blunder, the president did not immediately make a correction.

"I was ready to make the case for Iraq coming out of the summer," he explained. "The problem was that that strategy was derailed by Katrina. During Katrina, it made it very difficult to talk about anything other than Katrina."

Then, after Katrina, Bush was obliged to make several overseas journeys that had been planned months in advance.

"And so the decision was made after my foreign trips," he told Hume, "to come back here and to start laying out the case as clearly as possible, not only in a series of speeches, but punching back when we're being treated unfairly."

The counterattack began, appropriately enough, on Veterans' Day. The forum was Tobyhanna Army Depot in Pennsylvania, where Bush decided to remind soldiers and veterans why they had given him a second term.

"While it's perfectly legitimate to criticize my decision or the conduct of the war, it is deeply irresponsible to rewrite the history of how that war began," he said. "These baseless attacks send the wrong signal to our troops and to an enemy that is questioning America's will."

The president even took the unusual step of criticizing the opposition party by name in a foreign policy speech.

"Some Democrats and antiwar critics are now claiming we manipulated the intelligence and misled the American people about why we went to war," he said. "These critics are fully aware that a bipartisan Senate investigation found no evidence of political pressure to change the intelligence community's judgments related to Iraq's weapons programs. They also know that intelligence agencies from around the world agreed with our assessment of Saddam Hussein. They know the United Nations passed more than a dozen resolutions citing his development and possession of weapons of mass destruction."

For the first time in a year, the president actually criticized Kerry, pointing out that he was one of more than one hundred Democrats in the Senate and House who had voted to authorize the war. Bush even quoted his old foe's words from the floor of the Senate.

"When I vote to give the president of the United States the authority to use force, if necessary, to disarm Saddam Hussein," Kerry said at the time, "it is because I believe that a deadly arsenal of weapons of mass destruction in his hands is a threat, and a grave threat, to our security."

As soon as the president finished his speech, Kerry made clear he did not appreciate his words being resurrected.

"This administration misled a nation into war by cherry-picking intelligence and stretching the truth beyond recognition," he thundered.

Bush was relieved to have Kerry back, if only as a foil. Republicans were thrilled to see their president in combat mode again after his yearlong hiatus. Democrats were furious and upped the rhetorical ante by demanding a timetable for withdrawal from Iraq. The measure was defeated in the Senate by Republicans, who said it amounted to cutting and running. Still, Republicans were rattled enough to pass a weaker measure stating that 2006 "should be a period of significant transition to full Iraqi sovereignty."

Unfazed, the White House kept up its counteroffensive.

"The suggestion that's been made by some U.S. senators that the president of the United States or any member of this administration purposely misled the American people on prewar intelligence is one of the most dishonest and reprehensible charges ever aired in this city," said Vice President Cheney.

This prompted a savage attack the next day from an obscure House Democrat, John Murtha of Pennsylvania, who had won a Bronze Star and two Purple Hearts in Vietnam. Borrowing a page from Kerry's campaign playbook, Murtha sarcastically denounced the vice president for failing to serve in Vietnam.

"I like guys who've never been there that criticize us who've been there," the congressman said. "I like that. I like guys who got five deferments and never been there and send people to war, and then don't like to hear suggestions about what needs to be done."

So Murtha made a suggestion of his own. He called on the administration to immediately begin withdrawing America's 160,000 troops from Iraq and complete the pullout within six months. At long last, a Democrat had taken a clear alternative position on Iraq instead of just slamming the president's.

"The U.S. cannot accomplish anything further in Iraq militarily," Murtha shrugged. "It is time to bring them home."

Incredibly, he asserted that American troops "have become the enemy" in Iraq, which he said deserved to be "free from United States occupation."

Although fellow Democrats showered Murtha with accolades, virtually none of them endorsed his radical proposal. Sensing an opportunity, House Republicans decided to call Murtha's bluff by scheduling a surprise vote on the question of withdrawal.

"It is the sense of the House of Representatives that the deployment of United States forces in Iraq be terminated immediately," read the one-sentence resolution.

Outmaneuvered Democrats howled in protest, especially when Republican congresswoman Jean Schmidt relayed the sentiments of a Marine colonel from Ohio.

"He asked me to send Congress a message—stay the course," said Schmidt, the most junior member of Congress. "He also asked me to send Congressman Murtha a message—that cowards cut and run, Marines never do."

Schmidt was shouted down by angry Democrats on the House floor, including Congressman Harold Ford of Tennessee, who charged across the aisle as if ready for blows.

"You guys are pathetic!" bellowed Congressman Martin Meehan, a Massachusetts Democrat. "Pathetic!"

Schmidt later retracted her statement, but that did not satisfy John Kerry over in the Senate.

"I won't stand for the Swift-Boating of Jack Murtha," he railed, just like old times.

In the end, however, House Democrats joined Republicans to defeat the pullout proposal by an overwhelming margin, 403–3. It was a victory for Bush, who was still worried about Ayman al-Zawahiri's malevolent message.

"The first stage: expel the Americans from Iraq," the terrorist had written to his underling Abu Musab al-Zarqawi. "The aftermath of the collapse of

American power in Vietnam—and how they ran and left their agents—is noteworthy."

Bush recited this passage while addressing U.S. troops at a military base in South Korea on November 19, two days after the House rejected Murtha's call for a pullout. The president drew parallels to other episodes in which the U.S. had cut and run, only to embolden enemies.

"The terrorists witnessed our response after the attacks on American troops in Beirut in 1983, and Mogadishu in 1993," he said. "They concluded that America can be made to run again, only this time on a larger scale, with greater consequences. The terrorists are mistaken. America will never run. We will stand and fight, and we will win the War on Terror. We will never back down, and we will never give in, and we'll never accept anything less than complete victory."

The troops roared their approval. They understood the stakes of this epic clash between good and evil. So did Cheney, who accused Democrats of "corrupt and shameless" revisionism on the Iraq war and called their demands for a pullout "self-defeating pessimism." He even felt compelled to remind some of his fellow citizens which side they were on.

"The United States of America is a good country, a decent country," he said in a speech. "And we are making the world a better place by defending the innocent, confronting the violent, and bringing freedom to the oppressed."

The Bush-Cheney team's new combativeness went a long way toward assuaging disaffected conservatives. The president decided to press his advantage by traveling to the Mexican border and calling for a crackdown on illegal immigration. It was a major shift in emphasis for Bush, who had spent his first term advocating a guest-worker program that conservatives derided as amnesty. His tough new rhetoric on immigration was not the only reason for conservatives to cheer. As November gave way to December. Bush also started to claim credit for the booming economy. As December gave way to January, his Supreme Court nominee, Samuel Alito, emerged unscathed from hearings before the Senate Judiciary Committee, although Democrats managed to reduce his wife to tears with their bullying questions. All the while, Bush kept turning up the heat on Democrats by proclaiming that it was more important to win in Iraq than to withdraw. He refused to put a timetable on any drawdown and warned that a precipitous pullout would dishonor the American troops who had died in Iraq.

"To all who wear the uniform, I make you this pledge: America will not run in the face of car bombers and assassins so long as I am your commander in chief," Bush told cadets at the Naval Academy in Annapolis. "We will stay as long as necessary to complete the mission."

But that same day, House Minority Leader Nancy Pelosi shocked Washington by announcing that she supported an immediate pullout.

"I'm endorsing what Mr. Murtha is saying," the California Democrat said. "I believe that a majority of our caucus clearly supports Mr. Murtha."

In reality, not even Pelosi's second in command, House minority whip Steny H. Hoyer of Maryland, supported Murtha.

"I believe that a precipitous withdrawal of American forces in Iraq could lead to disaster, spawning a civil war, fostering a haven for terrorists, and damaging our nation's security and credibility," Hoyer said.

By sharpening the debate on Iraq, the White House had opened a major rift among Democrats, who were finally taking clear positions instead of just sitting back and criticizing the president's position. Bush could now contrast his strategy for victory against what he called the "cut-and-run" Democrats. And he could position Republicans as united, while Democrats were all over the map. In one camp were Murtha and Pelosi, who wanted an immediate pullout. In another camp were Hoyer and senators like Joseph Lieberman of Connecticut, who warned that a pullout would be disastrous. And in a third camp were the nervous middle-of-the-roaders who were planning to run for president in 2008 or faced competitive congressional reelection campaigns in 2006. This latter group included Senator Hillary Rodham Clinton of New York, who was widely regarded as the leading Democratic candidate for president in 2008. Under pressure from the White House to take a stand, Hillary declared that a pullout would be a "big mistake," which angered her party's liberal base.

I asked Bush in an Oval Office interview what advice he might give to a Republican presidential candidate going up against Hillary.

"Well, I think Hillary Clinton will be a formidable candidate," he warned.

Perhaps realizing he was already treating Hillary's nomination as a fait accompli, Bush quickly backpedaled.

"It's just too early," he said. "She will be a formidable candidate in the Democratic primary, is what I meant."

He added, "And I don't know the inner workings of the Democratic primary that much."

Still, the president cautioned that it would be foolish for any candidate, Democrat or Republican, to underestimate Hillary's political prowess.

"She is a smart person, and obviously has got a lot of experience," he said. "It is helpful, to a certain extent, to have seen the presidency and presidential campaigns firsthand."

Rove, the architect of two successful presidential campaigns, agreed.

"She has seen what the job requires," he told me in his West Wing office. "And she has been through six gubernatorial campaigns, two presidential campaigns, and then two senatorial campaigns in a big, industrial state. So she will be a formidable campaigner. She'll be sure-footed.

"For somebody who is philosophically very liberal, she'll be a very cautious candidate at times," he added. "That cautiousness will serve her well a lot of times. Not always, but a lot of times. For example, her cautiousness had her vote for the Iraq war. Her cautiousness has led her to do things to try to position herself as a centrist."

But as Bush had demonstrated, a president sometimes needed to be bold, not cautious. And Hillary had other weaknesses, according to Rove, not least among them "her personal philosophy." For try as she might to posture as a centrist, everyone knew that deep down, Hillary was a liberal with radical roots. Even former Clinton aide George Stephanopoulos once described Hillary as "the most powerful liberal in the White House." Moreover, she lacked her husband's charisma. As Rove told me, there was a "brittleness about her" that could prove a weakness in the general election. As for the primaries, he said the "hard-driving" Hillary would easily overtake Democratic rivals like New Mexico governor Bill Richardson or Virginia governor Mark Warner, both of whom were testing the presidential waters.

"She is the dominant player on their side of the slate," Rove told me. "Anybody who thinks that she's not going to be the candidate is kidding themselves. I mean, all this stuff about, you know, Warner or Richardson—all these guys are preening for the vice presidential slot."

Rove hinted that while Hillary would easily win the Democratic nomination, closing the sale in the general election would be far more difficult.

"The question people will ask is: do we want to have her as president?" he said. "And the answer to that will be determined in part by how she conducts herself. But it will also be settled in part by who the Republican nominee is and how he or she conducts themselves."

Bush vowed to refrain from anointing a GOP successor. "I won't be involved in picking," he assured me. Still, he had praise for two Republicans whom I mentioned, even though both claimed not to be interested in running for president.

The first was his younger brother, Jeb Bush, the governor of Florida. When the Bush brothers were young, most observers speculated that Jeb, not George, would become president one day. After all, he was considered more articulate and less polarizing than his older brother. And Jeb's wife, Columba, had been born and raised in Mexico, which might help with the burgeoning Hispanic vote. Democrats were already bad-mouthing the idea of a Bush "dynasty," even though they had once openly fantasized about a Kennedy dynasty. Mindful of the dynasty debate, Jeb opted to sit out the 2008 race, although he left the door open for a future White House bid.

"He's a wonderful person who has got a great record as governor. And most of the presidents have come from the governor's ranks because they have shown the capacity to set agendas and get results and administer," the president told me. "Should he say that 'I'm interested,' I think he would be a formidable candidate. But he has said he's not interested, and I think he means that."

The other Republican candidate Bush praised was Secretary of State Condoleezza Rice. Although Rice had already told me in an interview that she had no plans to run, a top aide kept encouraging reporters to ask her "the president question." Instead, I asked her the abortion question. Her answer—that she considered herself "mildly pro-choice"—was anathema to Christian conservatives who would vote in the Republican primaries. Still, the president said Rice had a lot of potential.

"She's a remarkable woman," he told me. "But, again, I think you've got to take her for her word."

The president pointed out that Dick Cheney's plan to retire after finishing his term as vice president would leave the 2008 presidential election "wide open" to candidates from both parties. Bush noted that for the first time in fifty-two years, the field of hopefuls would not include an incumbent president or vice president.

"Isn't that interesting?" he marveled. "I don't know what that means. It may mean all bets are off."

Although Bush insisted he did not have a dog in the 2008 fight, he obviously wanted Republicans to continue winning elections.

"We should be the party in power because we've got ideas," he told me. "As opposed to a party that's against everything, we're for things."

Truth be told, Bush was more concerned about the 2006 congressional elections because they might impact his ability to enact a second-term agenda. The mainstream media was already filled with dire predictions for the president's party.

"One year before the 2006 midterm elections, Republicans are facing the most adverse political conditions of the eleven years since they vaulted to power in Congress in 1994," wrote Dan Balz in yet another story on the front page of the *Washington Post*. "Powerful currents of voter unrest—including unhappiness over the war in Iraq and dissatisfaction with the leadership of President Bush—have undermined confidence in government and are stirring fears among GOP candidates of a backlash."

Balz concluded, "If the public mood further darkens, Republican majorities in the House and Senate could be at risk."

The *New York Times* agreed.

"Suddenly, Democrats see a possibility in 2006 they have long dreamed of," gushed *Times* reporter Robin Toner in a front-page article. "A sweeping midterm election framed around what they describe as the simple choice of change with the Democrats, or more of an unpopular status quo with the Republican majority."

Never mind that Senate Minority Leader Harry Reid had admitted fewer than six months earlier that it would take a "miracle" for his fellow Democrats to win back the Senate in 2006. Never mind that the Left had wrongly predicted Republican losses in the congressional elections of 2002 and 2004. These inconvenient realities never seemed to get in the way of the mainstream media's wishful thinking.

"Republicans will keep the House; Republicans will keep the Senate," Rove flatly predicted to me. "The question is: What will be the margin? Will we gain a couple of seats? Will we lose a couple of seats? Will we lose more than a couple seats? I'm, frankly, very optimistic."

Bush agreed to campaign for his fellow Republicans, although it remained unclear how much energy he would expend. After all, the first year after his own reelection had taken a toll on the fifty-nine-year-old president. He had spent a great deal of political capital on Social Security only to come up empty-handed. He had suffered through a failed Supreme Court nomination and a full-blown conservative insurrection. He had been called a heartless racist in the Hurricane Katrina debacle. And his administration had been tainted, at least peripherally, by the CIA leak case.

On the other hand, he *had* won reelection, hadn't he? Any other president would have waited until his second term to liberate Iraq, but Bush had rolled the dice in his first—and lived to tell about it. Counting Afghanistan, Bush had liberated *fifty million people*, which is not something every president could say. In the first year of his second term alone, he oversaw the creation of a democratic Iraq, complete with a constitution and successful elections. Domestically, he had already installed one conservative on the Supreme Court and was on the verge of seating a second. Sure, Bush may have accumulated some political scar tissue along the way. But he was still president of the United States, with enough ambition to choke a mule.

Furthermore, many of his detractors in the press, the Democratic Party, and abroad were in far worse shape than the president.

The mainstream media had driven down Bush's job approval ratings, but its five years of open warfare against the president had been self-defeating as well. A Pew Research Center poll of American voters found "a notable rise over the past two years in the percentage who say the press is too critical of the Bush administration." The biased coverage was constantly backfiring on the mainstream media. Even CBS News president Andrew Heyward, the only participant in the Memogate fiasco who had initially managed to cling to his job, was eventually forced out. "It was just time," explained CBS chairman Leslie Moonves to the *New York Times*. "This has been a very difficult year for CBS News, for Andrew, for other people in CBS News." In an effort to minimize yet another round of embarrassing fallout, Moonves made his announcement just days before Mary Mapes published her CBS-bashing memoir that argued the documents were authentic after all. Her delusion was still shared by Dan Rather, the disgraced former anchor who now dwelt in the "magical, mystical kingdom of journalistic knights." Of course, CBS officials Betsy West, Josh Howard, and Mary Murphy had also done battle with Bush and lost. The vessel for their attacks, the Wednesday edition of *60 Minutes*, was a mere memory. Even the CBS *Evening News*, anchored by aging liberal Bob Schieffer (after John Roberts was passed over for the job), remained dead last in network ratings, its audience shrinking by the day.

Of course, CBS was not the only news outlet on the ropes. *Newsweek* had been forced to apologize and retract its bogus accusation that U.S. authorities had flushed a Koran down a toilet. *Time* magazine had surrendered the confidential notes of one of its own reporters, the *Washington Post* had criticized its own star reporter Bob Woodward for ethical violations, and the *New York Times* had turned against its own journalistic martyr, firing reporter Judith Miller.

As part of the Bush administration's belated counteroffensive against its critics, Secretary of Defense Donald Rumsfeld excoriated the media.

"We've arrived at a strange time in this country where the worst about America and our military seems to so quickly be taken as truth by the press and reported and spread around the world, often with little context and little scrutiny, let alone correction or accountability after the fact," Rumsfeld said in a speech. "Recently there were claims by two Iraqis on a speaking tour that U.S. soldiers attacked them with lions. It was widely reported around the United States. It is still without substantiation. And yet that story was spread across the globe.

"Not too long ago, there was a false and terribly damaging story about a Koran that was supposedly flushed down a toilet in Guantanamo, and in the riots that followed in several countries, some people were killed. And a recent *New York Times* editorial implied that America's armed forces—your armed forces—our armed forces—use tactics reminiscent of Saddam Hussein."

Rumsfeld had no compunction about implicitly questioning the media's patriotism.

"We are all Americans. We are all in this together," he scolded. "I suggest that we ask: how will history judge, if it does, the reporting some decades from now, when Iraq's path is settled?"

As for the Democrats, John Kerry and John Edwards—the best and brightest that the Democratic Party had to offer—had lost the presidential election by more than three million votes. Kerry's top campaign strategist, Bob Shrum, who had prematurely addressed his client as "Mr. President" on Election Night, gave up trying to get Democrats elected president now that all eight of his candidates had failed. Also gone were the two congressional leaders who had led the Democratic opposition during Bush's first term—Senate Minority Leader Tom Daschle and House Minority Leader Richard Gephardt. In addition, fifteen lesser Democrats lost their jobs in the congressional elections of 2002 and 2004, expanding the GOP majorities in both the House and Senate.

Even Democrat Sandy Berger, the former senior adviser to Kerry, finally pleaded guilty to destroying highly classified documents from the National Archives during the presidential campaign. He admitted spiriting the papers to his office and cutting them up with scissors! So much for his initial explanation that he "made an honest mistake" by "inadvertently" taking the documents because of his "sloppiness." So much for Bill Clinton's laughing dismissal of this "non-story" about his former national security adviser, who was always "buried beneath papers." So much for *Time* magazine's forgiving portrayal of the "absent-minded professor" or the *Washington Post*'s apologetic story about Berger's tendency to "constantly lose track of papers." *He stuffed them in his pants and cut them up with scissors!* Berger would have been sent to prison if he hadn't copped a plea. He was fined $50,000, sentenced to one hundred hours of community service, placed on probation for two years, and stripped of his security clearance for three years. The press, reserving all its moral outrage for Scooter Libby, yawned.

The Democrats fell into further disarray now that they were split over the question of a pullout from Iraq. Seeking to exploit this advantage, Bush ratcheted up the pressure by giving a series of high-profile speeches touting the military, political, and economic accomplishments in Iraq. This rattled Democratic National Committee chairman Howard Dean, who caused an enormous controversy by telling a San Antonio radio station: "The idea that we're going to win this war is an idea that, unfortunately, it's just plain wrong." He went on to compare the Iraq war to Vietnam and the prewar intelligence flap to Watergate, proving once again that the Left never tired of its two favorite story templates. Meanwhile, John Kerry essentially called U.S. troops terrorists during an interview with Bob Schieffer of CBS. "There's no reason, Bob, that young American soldiers need to be going into the homes of Iraqis in the dead of night, terrorizing kids and children, you know, women," he said. Such incendiary rhetoric allowed the GOP to brand Democrats the party of "retreat and defeat." The Republican National Committee even produced an Internet ad showing the white flag of surrender waving over images of Dean and Kerry as they made their defeatist remarks. Suddenly the Democrats, not Bush, were on the defensive about Iraq. Just one month after the *Washington Post* published a front-page story by Dan Balz warning that "Republican majorities in the House and Senate could be at risk" in the 2006 midterms, the newspaper published a front-page story by Jim VandeHei headlined "Democrats Fear Backlash at Polls for Antiwar Remarks." That same day, the *New York Times* published its own front-page story on a five-point jump in the president's job approval rating—a sure sign that the aggressive new strategy was already paying dividends.

On the international scene, Bush had used his bully pulpit against Syria, helping topple its puppet government in Lebanon and forcing the withdrawal of Syrian troops. The president's initial suspicions that Damascus was behind the Valentine's Day assassination of Rafik Hariri were borne out by a UN report that implicated top officials in the government of Syrian president Bashar al-Assad. Bush seized on the report as grounds for new UN sanctions against Syria. As for the broader Middle East, Bush's ongoing push for democratization was having profound ramifications, prompting Lebanese socialist Walid Jumblatt to marvel, "The Berlin Wall has fallen."

Meanwhile, despite ongoing difficulties in Iraq, Saddam Hussein was being tried for war crimes as the nation pulled off a second round of successful elections in October. This time, Sunnis participated in much greater numbers than they had in January, signaling that they were finally beginning to join Kurds and Shi'a in Iraq's daring democratic experiment. When the votes were counted, Iraqis had passed a new constitution. This paved the way for a third and even more successful round of elections in December, which established a permanent, democratic government fewer than a thousand days after the U.S. liberated the longtime dictatorship.

"That's just another sign of a political track that is making very good progress," Bush told me. "On the security side, this is a very difficult battle because Zawahiri—in corresponding with his man Zarqawi—has made it clear that they must succeed in Iraq, or it will be a serious blow to their ambition. And that's why you're seeing such a titanic struggle there."

Al-Zarqawi was already expanding his al Qaeda franchise beyond the borders of Iraq. He sent suicide bombers into three hotels in Amman, Jordan, where they killed fifty-nine people, including innocent revelers at a wedding reception. The shocking attacks triggered massive street protests against al Qaeda in Jordan. Clearly, al-Zarqawi was not carrying out al-Zawahiri's orders to win over the hearts and minds of the Muslim masses. His ongoing use of suicide bombers and improvised explosive devices (IEDs) was a sign of "desperation," according to Bush.

"They cannot defeat us militarily," he told me. "They can kill by the IED, or the suicide bomber, but they'll never defeat America and our Iraqi friends militarily. The only thing that can defeat us is because we have lost our nerve and our will and our vision about what is at stake."

During his speech in Annapolis, the president became visibly emotional in telling the story of Marine corporal Jeff Starr, who was killed while fighting terrorists in Ramadi months earlier. The commander in chief recited a letter that was found on the dead Marine's laptop computer.

"If you're reading this, then I've died in Iraq," Starr wrote. "I don't regret going. Everybody dies, but few get to do it for something as important as freedom. It may seem confusing why we are in Iraq. It's not to me. I'm here helping these people, so they can live the way we live—not to have to worry about tyrants or vicious dictators.

"Others have died for my freedom," he concluded. "Now this is my mark."

After struggling through this passage, Bush said, "There is only one way to honor the sacrifice of Corporal Starr and his fallen comrades—and that is to take up their mantle, carry on their fight, and complete their mission."

Despite the daily drumbeat of gloom and doom from the mainstream media, there were plenty of Americans who agreed with Bush that the mission must be completed. In fact, for every Cindy Sheehan, whose hatred of Bush attracted wall-to-wall media coverage, there were countless other families of fallen soldiers who quietly stood by the president.

"I know people are pushing you, but please don't pull the guys out of Iraq too soon," implored war widow Crystal Owen in a private meeting with Bush in North Carolina. She begged the president not to let the deaths of soldiers, including her husband, "be in vain."

"They were over there, fighting for a democratic nation," cried Owen, clutching the president's hands. "I hope you'll keep our service members over there until the mission can be accomplished."

Owen gave the president a stainless steel bracelet engraved with the name of her husband, Staff Sergeant Mike Owen. Bush kissed her on the cheek, slipped the bracelet on his left wrist, and wore it during a prime-time address to the nation.

"We have lost good men and women who left our shores to defend freedom and did not live to make the journey home," he said as his eyes turned glassy. "I've met with families grieving the loss of loved ones who were taken from us too soon."

Through it all, Democrats sought new ways of impaling the president on the sword of Iraq. They seemed determined to repeat their mistake of 2004, when they kept steering the national conversation back to the war against terrorism. They seemed to forget that Americans trusted Republicans more than Democrats on issues of national security. Democrats even went after Bush for authorizing the National Security Agency to eavesdrop on international phone calls between al Qaeda suspects and Americans. Yet the public overwhelmingly favored the program as a way of preventing terrorist attacks. Bush was defiantly unapologetic, which further flummoxed Democrats still reeling from the president's decision to fight back after his year on the high road.

"It's almost like what I had to do in the campaign—you know, stay on message," he told me. "It's just constantly speaking to the people."

He added, "I look forward to it. I like campaigning; I like ideas; I like the battle for ideas."

Besides, that first year after his reelection had taught him that no other issue of his presidency, not even Social Security, would ever be as important as Iraq. It reminded him that as long as the United States had an army fighting for freedom on foreign soil, the commander in chief had no higher priority than his unrelenting advocacy for those brave men and women. That advocacy included constantly engaging the political opposition in robust debate, even though Bush would never again run for reelection. In short, the president remembered that it was his solemn duty to continue arguing over Iraq, the central front in the War on Terror.

"With the rise of a deadly enemy, and the unfolding of a global ideological struggle, our time in history will be remembered for new challenges and unprecedented dangers," he told troops in South Korea. "We don't know the course our own struggle will take, or the sacrifices that might lie ahead.

"We do know, however, that the defense of freedom is worth our sacrifice. We know that the love of freedom is the mightiest force in history. And we do know the cause of freedom will once again prevail."

Mort Kondracke, the journalist who had accused Bush of "hubris" for his "scary" second inaugural address, now admitted that the president might be right after all. The admission came during Kondracke's nightly appearance on FOX News Channel's *Special Report with Brit Hume.*

"Of all the things that the president confronts," Hume said, "which one is the one that's going to say the most about how he finishes his presidency?"

"Oh, Iraq," Kondracke replied. "I mean, if Iraq succeeds, he's going to go down as a world historical figure. I mean, it's going to change the face of the planet, and he'll deserve all the credit in the world."

"Will it?" Hume asked. "In the end?"

Kondracke answered with a single word: "Yes."

Not surprisingly, Vice President Cheney shared Kondracke's view of Bush as a historic figure.

"Part of that has to do with the times in which you govern," the vice president told me. "September 11 really was a seminal event, a fundamental change. The fact that we could lose so many people in an hour to a handful of terrorists led the president to embark upon a strategy to fundamentally change the political structure in an important part of the world. I think it will be one of the most consequential presidencies in modern times."

Mehlman said the Republican president he helped elect was destined for historical comparisons to a Democratic predecessor.

"I think President Bush will be remembered in many ways like President Truman is remembered for his leadership in the Cold War," he told me. "President Truman faced a new threat and set up a paradigm which, over a long period, produced a victory in the Cold War. And it was not going to be resolved in four years.

"The fact that we stopped the Reds from coming into Berlin and stopped them from going any further than they went in Europe—and that we had the Marshall Plan, and set up democracies in Western Europe, and helped them with their economic plans—ultimately saved civilization, I would argue.

"And I think that President Bush will be remembered as similarly devising a new strategy for a new challenge," he predicted. "And he will be judged by the long-term success of that strategy."

In the short term, Bush was unlikely to be evaluated in such a sweeping context by the mainstream media, which was more interested in obsessing over whatever happened ten minutes ago than pondering whether the president would save civilization.

"Right now, all over Washington, people are talking about the fact that Karl Rove testified before a grand jury," Mehlman marveled. "And yet no one's talking about the fact that people who three years ago were being tortured and killed in soccer stadiums are voting on the Iraqi constitution.

"What does that *say* about people? It's unbelievable! It's like people are looking at the *Mona Lisa* and saying, 'Why is that frame that color?' It's just crazy."

Bush, for his part, insisted, "I don't spend a lot of time analyzing myself." Besides, he was too busy trying to implement his audaciously idealistic second-term agenda, the centerpiece of which was nothing less than "ending tyranny in our world."

"There are things changing," he told me. "And what's important about the change is that history has shown that democracies will yield peace. Europe no longer wars, and yet a hundred years ago—oh my goodness, the cauldron of conflict! Japan doesn't war. And so this is what's happening in the Middle East. And it's difficult work."

An impatient man, Bush was acutely aware of the clock ticking away his precious time in office. Even on the day Kerry conceded the election, thereby giving Bush four more years in office, the president could already foresee the moment that he would leave the world stage. He knew it would be difficult, especially if his work remained unfinished. And yet there would also be a sense of relief after eight years of ceaseless toil. In a way, Bush was already looking forward to the peace and quiet of Prairie Chapel Ranch in the tiny town of Crawford, Texas. In fact, he made a point of mentioning it in his speech at the Ronald Reagan building after he stayed up most of Election Night, waiting for that final victory of his political career.

"Let me close with a word to the people of the state of Texas," said the president, weary but gratified. "We have known each other the longest, and you started me on this journey. On the open plains of Texas, I first learned the character of our country—sturdy and honest, and as hopeful as the break of day. I will always be grateful to the good people of my state.

"And whatever the road that lies ahead," concluded George W. Bush, "that road will take me home."

ACKNOWLEDGMENTS

"Today I finished my book—again!" That became a running joke in my household, where completion of this manuscript took weeks longer than expected because of ongoing developments at the White House. Although the joke must have worn thin after awhile, it always prompted a good-natured chuckle from my wonderful wife, Becky, and spectacular children, Brittany, Brooke, Ben, Billy, and Blair. I thank them for their patience and understanding. Equally helpful were my colleagues at the *Washington Times*, especially publisher Douglas Joo, editor in chief Wes Pruden, managing editor Fran Coombs, national editor Ken Hanner, and fellow White House correspondent Joe Curl. A special thanks to my many friends at FOX News Channel, especially Roger Ailes, Brit Hume, and Kim Hume. I'm also indebted to Regnery publishers Jeff Carneal and Marji Ross for encouraging this project, which was improved immeasurably by editors Harry Crocker and Paula Decker. Finally, I would like to thank President Bush, Vice President Cheney, Karl Rove, Andy Card, and countless other White House officials, high and low, for indulging my endless questions about this important period in American history.

INDEX